THE AMERICAN

SYSTEM OF GOVERNMENT.

ITS CHARACTER AND WORKINGS, ITS DEFECTS, OUTSIDE PARTY MACHINERY AND INFLUENCES, AND THE PROSPERITY OF THE PEOPLE UNDER ITS PROTECTION.

BY EZRA C. SEAMAN,

COUNSELLOR AT LAW,

AND AUTHOR OF ESSAYS ON THE PROGRESS OF NATIONS.

NEW YORK:

CHARLES SCRIBNER & CO., 654 BROADWAY.

LONDON: SAMPSON LOW, SON AND MARSTON.

1870.

THE NEW YORK PRINTING COMPANY,
81, 83, *and* 85 *Centre Street,*
NEW YORK.

To the

MEMBERS OF THE BAR

AND OF

THE PRESS OF THE UNITED STATES.

The defects in the representative and elective branches of the American system of government, which have led to party organizations, party committees, caucuses, and nominating conventions, increased the intensity and violence of party spirit, fostered intrigue, corruption, and a despicable scramble for office and power, tending to demoralize the people as well as politicians, and threaten the stability of our government if the evil be not arrested, have suggested the ideas and remedies contained in the following pages; and the work is respectfully inscribed to you, *without distinction of party*, as the most effective classes of persons to aid in enlightening and forming public opinion upon the subject, and preparing the public mind for such reforms as the exigencies of the country imperatively demand, to arrest the downward course of our political system.

PREFACE.

It is more than forty years since I commenced the study of the law. All the great changes in the State constitutions, and in the modes of electing State, County, City, and other local officers, as well as in the election of presidential electors, have been made since my recollection. The first partisan State nominating-convention was held in the year 1824, in the State of New York; and the first partisan national convention was held in the year 1832.

For more than forty years I have been an attentive observer of the current of events; of the workings of our system of government—of our political, religious, educational, industrial, and philanthropic institutions, and of our great corporations and partisan organizations. I have participated sufficiently in the practice of courts, in official life, in practical business of various kinds, and in partisan politics, party committees, party meetings and conventions, and witnessed enough of such matters, to enable me to judge pretty accurately of the current reports of events which I did not witness. My mind has been much exercised with such matters, and in forming opinions in relation to them; and more particularly when I was editing a newspaper, and preparing information and comments for my readers—both during the great rebellion and since its close. I have, to a large extent, witnessed the facts and current of events which form the judicial, legal, constitutional, political, industrial, commercial, railroad, and banking history of our country, or learned them contemporaneously, for about forty years past; and have witnessed the political agitations, the mutations of public opinion, the growth and development in our country of party organizations, from a very weak and imperfect state, to their present form, extent, and power.

Having studied the institutions and history of our country, observed and inquired carefully into the workings of our complicated dual system of government, and the outside party machinery now in use to carry it on, *I have discovered, or think I have discovered, great defects in our representative and elective systems, and have sought to point them out to my readers, and to suggest suitable remedies.* It is obvious to me, as well as to many other candid observers, that, however prosperous our people and country may be in most respects, our politics and politicians have been growing more and more corrupt; that for nearly half a century party spirit has been undermining and taking the place of patriotism; that party organizations have dictated more and more the policies and leading measures of the government; and that our political system has been deteriorating, and gradually sinking into corruption and party despotism. These evil tendencies I have endeavored to trace to their causes, and to point them out; and I find many, and I may say the most of them, originate in the defects of our representative and elective systems of government, and admit of a remedy.

The views presented upon woman and her rights and proper sphere, upon the increase of territory and population, industry and power, and upon taxation, debt, and finance, currency and banking, are intended to show the agitating questions of the day, and the difficulties and dangers which beset and threaten us as a nation, as well as the prosperity which the people have enjoyed under our system of government.

The results of my observations and inquiries into the operations of the American system of government, and the deductions of my reasoning upon the subject, are presented to my readers in the following pages. I have endeavored to present, in this little work, correct and philosophical views of the character and workings, tendencies and defects, of our dual system of government, and to suggest proper remedies; and if it should aid in calling public attention to the evil tendencies and bad workings of our political system, and to the defects in the representative and elective branches of our system of government, and induce an examination of the subject, and inquiries for proper remedies, good will grow out of it, and I shall feel well compensated for my labor.

Something should be done to correct the corrupting influences of an intense partisanship and party machinery, which have been produced, to a large extent, by defects in the representative and elective branches of our system of government. The necessity of reform is indicated by the tone of some of our most influential newspapers. The New York *Observer* of February 10th, 1870, says:—

"A community is on the brink of a crisis, when public confidence in the stern and impartial exercise of justice is shaken. When the judge, whose solemnly imposed duty it is to interpret and apply the law, is regarded as the *accomplice of speculators or political partisans,—when he allows himself to ignore all responsibility, except to those by whom he has been elected or by whom he hopes to be re-elected,—the very foundations of social order are undermined. Criminality is sheltered by partisanship. Wickedness exults in assured impunity.* All through the community the countlessly varied *elements of avarice and intrigue are let loose without check*, to prey upon the *vitals of society, and mock at all threats* of restraint. The very air is thick with moral pestilence. From the highest to the lowest sphere there is a *new impulse given to the development of corruption.* * * *

"We regard *legislative corruption and judicial faithlessness*—in the extent to which they now prevail—*as the exuberant fountains of mischief.* Law cannot be enforced so as to repress the outbreaking violence. *The daily record of crime is appalling. Taxation becomes—to the extent to which it is carried—organized and legalized robbery. The safeguards and barriers of justice are overthrown*, and *office itself becomes the reward and premium of successful invasion of the rights of the people. When chicanery and fraud pay better than honest labor, honest labor will be despised;* and when *bounties instead of infamy and penalty are set on crime*, the *vilest haunts of gamblers and desperadoes will name our legislators and appoint our judges.*

"How far we are from this state of things, every intelligent observer must judge for himself. Christianity has powerful influences at its command, but it is unjust to expect it with oars, to retard the progress to ruin of the ship of State, when this is floated on by *the powerful currents of legislative and judicial abuse.* We need an awakened public conscience. We need a bold exposure of the shameless iniquity of *political partisans and the 'rings' that distribute patronage and dictate legislation.* There is danger lest, if legal restraints prove vain, the crisis may come when popular indignation will break over all organized barriers, and carry desolation along its track, involving precious interests in the common fate.

"The charges of public dishonesty or political corruption have become so common, that *the criminated parties are sheltered to some extent by their very number.* The individual offender is lost in the crowd. The *echo of accusation is drowned in the voice of some new accuser.* * * *

"If there is a *radical defect in our method of judicial selection, let it be remedied. If it has come to this, that rogues by management contrive to elect those that will befriend them from the bench,* let us see if some way cannot be devised for placing men in that responsible position, who shall be known as fearing God and hating covetousness."

Referring to the city of New York, the *Observer* says:—

"We are living in the midst of an ungoverned race of thieves, robbers, and murderers. Police officers are regarded by the public as little better than the criminal classes. They take bribes. They commit violence on unoffending citizens. They wait for rewards before they seize criminals. They suffer rogues to escape when they have them in charge. The police is about as bad as it can be, and not have anarchy. * * *

"Ruled as this city is, by selfish, corrupt, and greedy politicians, we believe a fair majority of the legal voters desire an enlightened, honest, faithful government."

The New York *Times* says:

"The strength of the criminal classes is constantly increasing, while no corresponding efforts are made to keep them under restraint. The present police force is not adequate to deal with the desperadoes who have taken up their permanent quarters in New York, and, moreover, the policemen generally are demoralized. They perform a service of great danger, and rarely derive proper support from magistrates or judges. After an officer has been half killed in the attempt to arrest some well-known jail-bird, he has the *mortification of seeing his prisoner set free by a judge with whom he happens to have influence.* How could any police force be expected to do its duty properly, under these circumstances? The men lose all heart and confidence. They know that it is useless to risk their lives. *A corrupt judiciary will be sure to neutralize their most earnest efforts,* and probably rebuke them for exhibiting too much zeal in the service of the public."

E. C. S.

ANN ARBOR, Mich., February, 1870.

TABLE OF CONTENTS.

CHAPTER I.

CHAPTER II.

CHAPTER V.

CHAPTER VI.

CHAPTER I.

CHARACTER AND FORM OF THE GOVERNMENTS OF THE UNITED STATES OF AMERICA—THEIR THEORY, DEFECTS, AND THE PRACTICE UNDER THEM.

SEC. 1.—*Character of our System of Government.*

THE government of the United States is an elective, representative, federal Republic. The State governments were originally continuations of, or substitutes for, the Colonial governments, with slight changes in some of their features—which were rendered necessary by the revolution. The federal Union grew up in a measure spontaneously—being suggested and produced by common dangers, common interests, a common origin and language, and nearly uniform laws and institutions.

The State constitutions, adopted after the declaration of independence, and the Constitution of the United States also, were formed and adopted by the freemen of the several States; and all officers are elected, directly or indirectly, by the freemen, or appointed by those that are so elected, or appointed. The theory is, that all political power emanates from the freemen, who are voters, and is delegated by them to the several officers and departments of the federal and State governments, in accordance with the constitution and laws of the country. The sovereignty of our country is divided into many parts. Our system of government is dual—the people of each State being subject to two distinct governments, and two codes of law,—each supreme and sovereign within its legitimate and proper sphere,—the one federal, national, and mostly external in its jurisdiction and powers, and the other internal and municipal, or State,—to each of which the people owe obedience and allegiance, in accordance with their respective powers and jurisdiction. A divided and double allegiance results from a divided sovereignty.

The union, constitution, and government of the United States, having been formed by the freemen of the original States, was based upon their State governments, laws, and institutions; the organization and action thereof, in various ways, being based upon the laws and action of the State governments. The theory is, that the regulation of the elective franchise belongs exclusively to the States, or to the freemen or people thereof—and that members of Congress to represent the people of each State, should be elected by the same voters that elect members of the most numerous branch of the State legislature. The Constitution of the United States was framed in accordance with that theory—allowing each State to determine for itself, who should vote for its members of Congress—leaving the election of United States Senators to State legislatures,—and allowing each State to elect, and to regulate by law, the mode of electing, its own Presidential electors,—and to appoint officers for their own militia—when called into the service of the United States. Such was the theory and the organization of our dual system of government; and such was the uniform practice under it, until the passage of the acts of Congress in 1867, generally known as the Reconstruction Acts.

SEC. 2.—*Corner Stones and Principles of the American Governments.*

The leading principles upon which the American governments are founded, are stated in their constitutions, and in the declarations or bills of rights—forming a part of nearly all the State constitutions, and prescribing the limits of power. The following are the corner stones upon which our governments, both State and national, are established.

1st. *Popular Sovereignty*—recognizing the liberty and rights of the people, and that the exercise of political power should be regulated by the freemen, who are capable of using the elective franchise properly.

2d. The *religious liberty* of every individual, and the entire freedom, independence, and equality of each and every religious sect. Each sect being independent of all others, and independent also of the State and national governments.

3d. *State Sovereignty* upon all subjects of a local, domestic, interior, police, and municipal character—over persons and property, personal rights and contracts, education and morals, interior commerce and navigation.

4th. *Federal Union*, and *National Sovereignty* over all matters of a national, international, and inter-State character.

Full and complete religious liberty was firmly established in all the States (except Massachusetts and Connecticut) prior to the formation of the constitution of the United States. It was finally established in Connecticut by the adoption of their first constitution in 1818; and in Massachusetts by an amendment to their State constitution in 1834. It is the very essence of American Protestantism.

But so far as churches hold property, they must hold it under State laws. They cannot hold property, without being incorporated under the laws of the State. So far, and no farther, they are dependent upon State legislation and State laws; but never upon the national government, except in the District of Columbia, and in the Territories of the United States.

From these principles result the *co-ordinate supremacy and sovereignty of the national and State governments*, over the *same country and people—each being supreme and sovereign within its proper sphere;* and the acts of each being mere usurpations of power, and theoretically void, when it travels beyond its legitimate sphere of action. From this results also, the double allegiance of our citizens. The powers to tax property for the legitimate purposes of government, to organize, call out, and govern the militia, and some other matters, are in their nature concurrent powers—to be exercised by each government over the same persons and property. In all cases of concurrent power and jurisdiction, the national government, in accordance with the sixth article of the federal constitution, takes priority, and precedence, nothing more. That is, its demands must be satisfied first. Its supremacy consists in its right to priority, which gives it no right to overrule, annul, change or interfere with the operation of the State laws, any farther than is necessary to satisfy its legitimate claims for legitimate and constitutional purposes, and to confine the State governments to their proper sphere of action. It cannot protect property from State taxation, nor protect persons from military duty under State laws; nor can it exercise its powers of taxation and over the militia, except for legitimate national purposes and objects according to the true intent and meaning of the constitution.

SEC. 3. *State independence, and the doctrines of non-intervention.*

The union of the States under one national government, is a *federal union—not a consolidated union. It is a union for exterior, inter-State, and national purposes; and not for interior, domestic, and municipal purposes.* With the exception of a few cases and purposes (mostly of concurrent jurisdiction), the powers of the several States are absolute and exclusive, in matters over which they have jurisdiction; and in all such matters (except the rights of national citizenship) the States and the people thereof are as independent of each other, and of the federal government and laws, as they are of the king, parliament and laws of Great Britain. Neither the Congress of the United States, nor the people or government of any State, have any more right to intermeddle with the proper municipal and local laws, customs, or domestic institutions of another State, than with those of Turkey or Russia. They may think Mahometanism, the despotic governments and the arbitrary and cruel punishments inflicted in Turkey and Russia, all wrong; *but it is none of their business.* They cannot interfere to reform them, without violating the laws, and disturbing the harmony of nations. The principle of non-intervention forms the corner stone of international law, and the only rule that will secure the peace and harmony of nations.

One individual cannot intermeddle with the domestic concerns or business of another, without assuming a right to dictate to him, and to direct his conduct; which would be inconsistent with his equality of right, freedom, and independence. All such intermeddlings of one person in the affairs of another (except that of parents with their children), is generally regarded as officious, impertinent, and insolent,—as meriting rebuke; and it very generally stirs up and excites ill-feeling and violent resentments, and often leads to bitter quarrels and bloodshed. Nor can the government or people of one State intermeddle with the laws, customs, or institutions of another, with any propriety,—except so far as may be necessary to protect their own rights, under the constitution of the United States, and particularly under the second section of the fourth article thereof. Ill-feeling and bad consequences will necessarily follow any other interference.

The second section of article four of the constitution of the United States, declares that "the citizens of each State shall be entitled to all privileges and immunities of citizens in the several States." That provision gives to citizens of each and every State, the right to go into, and to travel in any other State, as often as they please,—to remove to or from it, their personal property, without molestation,—to make contracts and attend to any industrial pursuit or business therein—and to purchase, hold, enjoy and sell property therein, either personal or real, in the same manner as if they were citizens of such State, and under the protection of the laws thereof. They may also remove to, and become citizens of any other State. But the citizens of one State have no other rights in States where they do not actually reside. They have no right to participate in the government of any State, except the one in which they reside; and when they do business in any other State, they must do so under, and submit to its laws; and have no right to complain of them, so far as they are equal, nor to interfere to change them.

SEC. 4.—*What are, and what are not, the proper objects and purposes, and within the legitimate sphere of governments.*

Governments are instituted to maintain order, secure peace, administer justice, and protect the rights of all the people—*to protect rights, not to create them*—not to destroy or diminish them—not to enlarge the rights of some by contracting the rights of others, in order to equalize them—and not to make men equal, either in property, social position, or political power. To enlarge the natural rights of some by law, involves in the process the infringement and the contraction of the rights of others. Pope says

> "Order is Heaven's first law, and this confess'd,
> Some are, and must be, greater than the rest,
> More rich, more wise; but who infers from hence,
> That such are happier, shocks all common sense."

The Providences of God have made very great inequalities in the intellectual and physical strength and activities, and in the faculties and capacities, as well as in the wisdom of men—whereby the industry of some is from two to ten times as productive as that of others; and hence some accumulate wealth, while others remain poor. It is not within the proper sphere of governments to equalize the fortunes and conditions of men, by taking from one class and giving to another—but to secure every person in the proper exercise of his faculties, and in the enjoyment of all his rights—including rights fairly acquired, as the results of the proper exercise of his natural rights and faculties.

It is not the business of governments to take from the strong and wealthy, to give to the weak and poor—

except so far as humanity may require proper provision to be made for paupers, at the public expense—and so far as the public welfare and justice may require provision to be made for the support of schools, by taxation, for the education of children.

Governments should enact just, equal, and good laws—to protect the rights and promote the welfare of all; should devise a wise and just system of taxation—to defray its expenses; and should administer laws and justice to all alike—without favor, partiality, or prejudice; but it is no part of the business of a government, to act as a special guardian over any class of adult well persons, who are able to labor, and to provide for their own wants by their own industry. For a government to act as the special guardian over such classes of persons, would necessarily infringe their freedom; take from them the rights and privileges of self-government, and of thinking and judging for themselves; make them intellectually weaker, by accustoming them to depend upon the government; and be productive of vastly more evil than good. All the federal government can properly do for the negro, is, to protect him from unjust State laws; and let him learn to live and thrive, by his own industry and economy.

Republican governments like ours, are not instituted for the purpose of giving to each and every man an equal voice and influence therein,—but for the purpose of securing the rights of all.

Our system of government is not based upon popular elections, to secure to each and every man an equal voice, and equal influence, as an important end to be attained; but it is based upon such elections as *the best means* to obtain enlightened legislators, good officers, and faithful representatives of the rights, interests, and wishes of the whole people—to the end that enlightened legislation, wise laws, and a fair and good administration of the laws and government, may be secured. Hence no one should participate in the government, by the exercise of the elective franchise, who has not sufficient intelligence and independence of mind and thought, to do so properly, consistently with the general good, and with the ends to be attained. Persons so ignorant and weak-minded, that they are easily misled, and made the tools of designing politicians, induced to sell their votes, or influenced by a clannish feeling to support unfit men for office, because they belong to the same race, are unsafe voters, and exert a pernicious and dangerous influence upon popular elections; and therefore, they are not entitled to the elective franchise. If allowed to them, it is as a favor, not as a right. The exercise of the franchise by such men, is not consistent with law and order, and even their own welfare is not promoted by it.

By extending the franchise to men too ignorant and weak-minded to exercise it properly, many bad and unfit men are elected to office; and the tendency of it is, to throw the government into the hands of cunning and intriguing politicians, and to subject the better classes to the rule of the most unprincipled and selfish. By giving political power to an ignorant and inferior class, the helm of power is practically taken from the superior class, and the government becomes corrupted, by means of the degradation of the suffrage.

If there were two classes of electors,—one having a small amount of property subject to taxation, as a qualification for the election of State senators, governor, and some other officers—to exercise a conservative influence; the other class might, with more safety, embrace nearly all the adult males of the country. In such case, each branch of the legislature would exercise a more effective and salutary check upon the other.

SEC. 5.—*Political parties exist under every free and popular government.*

Political parties exist under every free and popular government. They necessarily arise from differences of opinion as to systems of government, measures, and policies; and also as to the relative merits of men who are supported for the highest elective offices. Candidates for the chief offices change, and measures and policies of government should change with changing circumstances; and differences of opinion in relation to subjects constantly changing, cannot form distinct and permanent dividing lines between two great political parties. On the contrary, as such differences of opinion are constantly changing, parties should change with them, and be re-formed whenever new candidates for President and Vice President of the United States are presented for the support of the people, or new issues and questions arise for their consideration. Measures and policies must, or should change with the changing condition and circumstances of a country; and yet differences of opinion upon such subjects, and in relation to candidates for office, constitute the only proper ground of division between parties. As it must depend mostly upon the President and Heads of Departments, and a few leading members of Congress, to determine such questions, so far as they relate to our national government, the division of parties should depend more upon a choice of men for all the higher offices, and less upon party creeds and platforms. The cry for *principles, not men*, is a miserable delusion. It is idle to talk about principles, without proper men, and men of principle, to carry them into effect. It is very unwise and dangerous, to elect selfish and corrupt men, to carry into effect good principles, and wise policies. The conclusion is obvious—that there is no good reason for maintaining permanent party organizations in our country, or in any country; and that there is no propriety in doing so. All political parties should be temporary and changeable—based upon the questions and issues of the day, and upon the opinions of voters of the relative merits of the candidates for President of the United States, for Governors of States, and other high offices.

So far as political parties and the lines of division between them are produced by differences of opinion in relation to the principles, policies, and measures of government, they will be as permanent as the causes and issues upon which they are based; and they should be no more so, and should pass away with the causes which produced them. Parties should not be based upon mere abstract principles, which have no direct practical bearing; nor upon dead issues which have passed by, and are of no practical importance; nor should they be sustained and made permanent by organization, party machinery, and party creeds, to promote the election and aggrandizement of party leaders,—regardless of the public good.

Political parties spring up spontaneously, in every free country having a government with popular elements in it. They are the natural offspring of honest differences of opinion among a free and intelligent people. They existed in Ancient Greece; in Ancient Republican Rome; and have existed in England since the early part of the reign of Charles I.; and political clubs, which are the germs of more extensive organizations, were formed in revolutionary France; but no such party organizations and machinery, as have been developed and now exist in the United States, ever existed in Europe, or in any country of the old world. Such organizations have sprung up in this country as incidents to our elective system, and to supply its defects.

SEC. 6.—*Defects in our mode of representation and system of elections.*

The mode of representation and the system of elections in the United States, are both very imperfect and defective. The former is defective, in giving the entire representation and power to majorities, and practically disfranchising minorities,—by allowing them no representation, and no voice in the government: and the latter is defective in omitting to provide any mode of selecting candidates for office, to be voted for by the electors at popular elections; and in furnishing at the polls no ballots for the electors.

SEC. 7.—*Development of party organizations, and uses of nominating conventions.*

No attempt has been made to furnish a remedy for the defect in representation; but to supply the other defects, resort has been had to outside party influences, to make nominations, and furnish tickets or ballots for voters at elections; which has caused the gradual development and growth of the party organizations and machinery of the present day—consisting of National, State, County, City, ward, Township, and village committees for each party—to call and provide for the holding of National, State, County, City, village, ward and township meetings, caucuses and conventions, for the purpose of making nominations, party creeds and platforms; and also to distribute political documents and other information among the people procure speakers at political meetings, furnish ballots for voters at elections,—to rally the voters of their respective parties out to the polls, and to resort to any other means, which the consciences of politicians will permit—to carry an election.

The law should provide means and methods of carrying on all the operations of the government—including the selection of its officers—without the necessity of aid from outside party influences; but such is not the case. The laws of all the States and of the United States also, are defective, in not providing any mode or method by which the voters, irrespective of party, can participate in nominating candidates to be supported at popular elections; and hence party organizations, and nominating conventions or caucuses, are indispensably necessary to supply the defects. Until such defects are supplied, the government cannot be carried on, independent of outside aid, and combinations of men to make nominations, and to procure and distribute tickets at the polls.

The defects in our electoral system can be very easily supplied, and the machinery of partisan organizations and nominating conventions, with all their pernicious influences, can be dispensed with—by holding two elections following each other with a short interval—the results of the first to be used as the designation of candidates to be supported at the second.

For more than thirty years after the organization of our national government, Presidential electors were elected by the State legislatures; candidates for President and Vice President of the United States were nominated by Congressional caucuses; and candidates for Governors of States were nominated by legislative caucuses. Since the system of electing Presidential electors by the people, by general ticket, was adopted by nearly all the States, nominating State conventions have become more necessary than they were previously;—though national conventions are by no means necessary, but mere party expedients—to concentrate their votes.

The first State convention of the kind, I think was held in the State of New York in 1824—when De Witt Clinton was nominated for Governor, and triumphantly elected. The first national conventions for nominating candidates for President and Vice President of the United States, were held in 1832. Since that time, national nominating conventions have been held every four years, by two political parties, sometimes by three, and in 1860 by four; and State, County, City and township nominating conventions have been held pretty regularly, in nearly all the States; and in most of them party conventions have been held in each Congressional district, to nominate candidates for Congress.

SEC. 8.—*Theory of our government, and the practice under it, contrasted.*

In theory, we have a popular government, in which the masses of the people select their own rulers; but owing to the defects of its organization, system of representation and mode of electing officers, the practice is very different from the theory.

Officers to be elected by the people are not selected by any considerable number of the voters, but by the dominant faction or clique of the dominant party—by whom and their associates in nominating conventions, they are presented to the people, to be by them confirmed by formal vote—the masses of the voters having no choice, except between two sets of nominees, presented for their suffrages, by partisan conventions. In nine cases out of ten, a mere choice of evils is presented to a large portion of the voters,—the candidates of neither party being such as they would have preferred.

Though nominally a popular government, controlled by the voice of the people, practically our government has degenerated into an oligarchy of the leaders of the dominant clique or coterie, of the dominant party of the day; and the people act a very subordinate part, even in the election of their own representatives—a majority of them merely ratifying and confirming the nominations made, and supporting the measures and policies prepared by the party oligarchy—while the minority look on and have no substantial voice or participation in the government. Party organizations and the party character of our government, have been in the process of development gradually, during a period of nearly fifty years—ever since the inauguration of State and national, as well as local nominating conventions, the adoption of party creeds and platforms, and the election of Presidential electors by the people—by general ticket.

The theory of the government is, that it is a representative government—in which all the adult male citizens, (with few exceptions) are equally and fairly represented, by men of their own choice, and through their representatives have a voice in legislation, and in the government of the country—making it in some measure a self-government; a government of the whole people, by the people themselves. But in practice, under our defective electoral system, the majority of the voters in each electoral district elect all the representatives, and the minority none—whereby the minority are unrepresented, and practically disfranchised, have no voice in the government, and no one to represent, advocate or defend, their special interests and rights.

The theory of the government is, that each State is sovereign within its own limits, as to all matters of a domestic and police character, and has full and sovereign power to regulate the elective franchise therein; but the war and the dissensions and discords growing out of it and its causes, the struggles of one party to keep the negro in a condition of subordination and semi-serfdom, and of the other to make the negro an element of party power, and to force negro suffrage upon the country as a means of perpetuating their own ascendency, have seriously impaired the powers and local sovereignty of the States, as established by our forefathers; and concentrated nearly all the supreme and sovereign power of the country in Congress. This partisan object is to be effected, through *a cry for equality between races, which have been made unequal, by the Providence of God;* and by efforts to elevate an inferior race of people, to an equality with the superior races of our country, who are the only races which have ever shown themselves capable of an elective representative system of government. The efforts are, to place the balance of power between parties in the hands of the inferior race, and to subject the superior race to their domination and government, wherever they constitute a majority. If the scheme be entirely successful, the effect must be to place the helm of power in several of the States in the hands of a race, which has never, in any country, shown any capacity for improvement and progress, for business, for the proper management of their own concerns, or for any branch of self-government.

The theory of the national government is, that its powers are limited, and divided between Congress, the President of the United States, and the Supreme Court—and that each is supreme within certain spheres of action, prescribed by the Constitution. But the tendencies now are to undermine and destroy many of the powers of the President, and of the Supreme Court also, as well as those reserved to the States—to degrade the President from his rightful position as the head of an independent and concurrent department of the government, to the subordinate position of a mere agent and instrument to execute the decrees and orders of Congress; and to concentrate more and more sovereign power in the Congress of the United States. The power of party organizations and party spirit, is increasing, and the power of Congress is increasing also; and both are becoming more and more absolute and irresistible; while all other powers of the government, and the legitimate powers of the people and of the State governments, are gradually dwindling away and perishing.

The theory of our government is, that it is a government of checks and balances—its sovereign powers being divided between distinct governments over the same people, and between distinct departments of the same government—so balanced and regulated that each may act as a check upon the others—to check popular passion as well as party passion and ambition—to prevent class and improper sectional legislation, and the adoption of violent party measures; and to save the country from being plunged into war, without due consideration, to gratify the President, or the dominant party in Congress.

The theory of the Constitution is, that each House of Congress should act as a check upon the other—by deliberately passing upon all its legislative acts, with power to amend, approve, or reject them; that the President shall act as a check upon the two houses—by approving or disapproving and vetoing their acts; that in the *dernier ressort*, the Supreme Court may pass upon acts of Congress, and determine without appeal, whether they are, or are not consistent with the constitution; that Congress, by legislation and the power of impeachment, may act as a check upon any violent or improper measures of the President; and that the State governments, by their organization and action, remonstrances and protests, as well as by withholding moral and military support, may in some measure check the course of the federal government—when impelled by party passion, and induce more consideration and moderation. But when the same political party elect the President, a majority of each house of Congress, and the Governors and major part of the legislatures of a majority of the States, and have the entire control of all branches of the national government, and of the governments of a majority of the States also, and all are animated by the same opinions, passions, and ambition for power, all the checks provided by the constitution are neutralized and become unavailing—and there is really no effective check to the adoption of any measures, however violent and revolutionary. Under such circumstances the minority have very little security for their rights. Popular passions, delusions, and fanaticism, often make governments as well as people, terribly reckless. Unfortunately for our country, both of the great political parties which have ruled the country for more than sixteen years past, have been afflicted with strange delusions.

When the convention met in 1787, to form our federal constitution, there were but three banks in the United States—the bank of North America at Philadelphia, incorporated by Congress in 1781, and the charter ratified and confirmed by the Legislature of Pennsylvania, in 1782; the bank of Massachusetts incorporated in 1784—and the bank of New York, established as a joint-stock company in 1784, but not incorporated until 1791. These were the only institutions in the United States which issued notes intended to circulate as money. The people had suffered so severely from continental money, and from the issues of Provincial paper money or bills of credit, by several of the colonies, previous to the revolutionary war, that they seemed generally resolved on having in the future, a specie currency only. To accomplish that end, which then seemed so desirable, the government of the United States was authorized to coin money and regulate the value thereof, and the provision was inserted in the constitution, prohibiting the several States from issuing bills of credit.

The theory of the constitution and government then was, to have a specie currency only; but the bank of North America, like the bank of England, proved to be so useful to the government as a fiscal agent, that under the influence of Alexander Hamilton and his reports as Secretary of the Treasury, Congress passed an act in 1791, to incorporate the first Bank of the United States, with a capital of ten millions of dollars. The provisions of the constitution to secure a specie currency were found to be defective and entirely insufficient. Though the States were prohibited from issuing bills of credit, individuals and joint-stock companies were not inhibited from so doing; nor were the States prohibited from incorporating banks, and authorizing them to issue notes—to circulate as money. The advantages of banks and paper money to stockholders, and business men, were so great, that the State legislatures could not resist the temptation to incorporate numerous banks; and before the close of the year 1800, there were in the State of New York four incorporated banks; in Massachusetts 4; in Maine 1; in New Hampshire 1; in Rhode Island 4; in Connecticut 5; in Pennsylvania 2; in Delaware 1; in Maryland 2; in Virginia 1; in South Carolina 1; and in the District of Columbia 1; making in all 27 banks, with an aggregate authorized capital of over eighteen millions of dollars—besides the United States Bank. Instead of having an exclusively specie currency, the country was again supplied with paper money.

The enemies of the first Bank of the United States claimed that it was unconstitutional, and the question was brought before the Supreme Court of the United States, and settled by that Court, in favor of the power of Congress to charter such an institution, as a fiscal agent of the government. An act was passed by Congress in 1832, to charter a third Bank of the United States; but President Jackson vetoed it, as unconstitutional, and dangerous to our republican institutions.

We had a national bank and State banks during periods in all of about forty years. From the expiration of the charter of the second Bank of the United States, in 1835, to the time of the inauguration of the system of national banks in 1863, we had State banks only; which had increased in 1859, to over 1,500—including branches.

It was claimed by the Secretary of the Treasury, in 1863, that the framers of the constitution—by vesting in Congress power to coin money and regulate the value thereof, and to regulate foreign commerce and commerce among the States, and also prohibiting the States from issuing bills of credit—intended to, and did grant to Congress, full power over paper money, as well as coin, as an instrument and medium of commerce; and thereupon Congress passed the general banking law, under which nearly 1,700 national banks have been organized, with an aggregate capital of over $425,000,000; and Congress also passed laws to drive the State banks out of existence, by imposing excessive taxes upon their issues.

Such have been the mutations and changes of the predominant opinions and practices, under our system of government. *The federal constitution has been found sufficiently flexible, for any purpose of the dominant party* —whether of war or peace; to put up or put down a national bank, State banks, or any system of banking or currency; to acquire territory by purchase, by filibustering and annexation, or by conquest; to extend without limit, to limit, or put down and abolish—slavery. By fiction of law, and without reference to the fact, or to principles of law previously established, States have been regarded as in or out of the Union, according to party exigencies; and treated as in the Union for some purposes, and out of it for others. Anything can be done by the dominant party, under the forms of law; about as well as the Emperor Augustus Cæsar, preserved the republican forms of the Roman government, during nearly forty years of his reign.

The national banks and banking systems have performed their functions the best, and given the most general satisfaction of any system of banks ever established in the United States; and if the currency can be properly equalized and the amount reduced, until its value is nearly equal to gold, and the amount be kept down by Congress so as to be worth within one or two per cent. as much as gold, we shall have the best banking system in the world. If the national banks continue to be popular, and commend themselves to nearly universal favor, *the general banking law will be recognized as constitutional, by all parties;* but if the leaders of one of the great political parties, should hereafter think that the strength and power of the party can be increased, by attacking the national banks and banking system, an outcry will be raised against the banks as odious monopolies, and the banking law will be denounced, in the party creed and platform, as unconstitutional, inconsistent with State rights, and dangerous to public liberty and to our system of government.

The theory of our government is, that our country should enjoy peace, and the fruits of peaceful industry —have a small army, a small navy, and be burdened with very light taxes—the people enjoying local self-government, and a federal Union and organization, merely to give greater security, and sufficient strength to repel invasions and suppress insurrections—but not to wage foreign wars, for purposes of conquest. Under that theory and a practice in accordance with it, our country prospered, improved rapidly, and increased, with wonderful rapidity, in population, wealth and power, for more than fifty years; when a restless filibustering spirit arose in relation to Texas, and we annexed it in 1845, by statute.

The expansion of the culture of cotton, the increasing demand for it, and the greatly increased importance of the cotton crop; the increased and increasing value of slave labor; and the annexation of Texas, all contributed to stimulate the ambition of the then dominant party, for party glorification—by means of the acquisition of new territory. Our government picked a quarrel with Mexico; invaded her territory, under pretences in some respects false; stormed the forts around her capital, and took the city; forcibly entered the halls of the Montezumas, seized California, dictated terms of peace, and acquired title to California and New Mexico honorably by treaty, and the payment of a fair price; explored the Sierra Nevada and Rocky chains of Mountains, and the intermediate plains and valleys; discovered and developed the rich gold and silver mines of those regions; swelled with pride over our achievements, our conquests, and our prospective wealth and power; and then came our domestic trials and difficulties—to divide our acquisitions between a pro-slavery and ambitious South, and an anti-slavery, and an anti-extension of slavery North.

So long as our settlements were confined to the country between the Atlantic Ocean and the Mississippi river, and to the tier of States lying west of, but bounded by that river, and before we entered upon a career of conquest, our country enjoyed peace and prosperity, and was reasonably harmonious in support of nearly all the measures of the government; but when we acquired Texas, murmurs began to burst forth from the Northern people, on account of the extension of slavery and the increase of the slave power; and the settlement of Kansas induced a deadly strife between the pro-slavery propagandists of the South, and the anti-slavery and anti-extension of slavery parties of the North, which soon kindled into civil war. Many persons were assassinated, numerous skirmishes were fought with fire-arms, between small bodies of men—and great numbers of lives and a large amount of property were sacrificed, in 1855 and 1856; which prepared the public mind on both sides, for the great secession movement and revolution of 1861, and the gigantic civil war which raged for more than four years.

The extension of territory, the war, the debt created by the war, and a redundant paper currency, have increased the taxation and expenses of the federal government about fourfold; changed the practice of the government, from great economy, and made it one of the most extravagant and prodigal governments upon the face of the earth. Previous to 1855, members of Congress were paid for their services $8 per day, during their attendance; which generally amounted to less than $2,500 per term of two years—exclusive of mileage. The ideas of the members having expanded in relation to the value of their services, they fixed their own salaries in 1856 ? at $3,000 per year, over and above mileage; and growing more and more liberal to themselves, they raised their own salaries, in 1866, to $5,000 per year, or $10,000 per term; which is more than four times as much as their former per-diem compensation. Extravagance and prodigality have become common in every branch of the public service.

Subtle interpretations of the Constitution and violent party measures, have been so numerous and various under different parties, as to form plausible precedents for almost any change of the government which the leaders of an ambitious and triumphant party may hereafter desire. If they cannot interpret, to the satisfaction of their party, the constitution as it may happen to be, so as to warrant the change desired, they can propose an amendment, and by party tactics and power, eventually force it upon the country. There will therefore be no occasion for *coups d'état*, and the violent modes adopted by Sylla and Cæsar, Cromwell and Napoleon, Santa Anna and Louis Napoleon—to attain their less violent ends. There is, however, no danger of an imperial government and an aristocracy (as some have supposed); for they are not in accordance with the spirit of our people, and the tendencies of the age. But there is great danger of such reckless conduct by party majorities—such corruption and prodigality, and such grievous taxation and oppression of many classes of people, as to lead to mobs and riots, occasional resistance, and a chronic state of anarchy and civil war—as in Mexico and Hayti. There is also danger of the country being frequently involved in foreign wars, to concentrate the attention of the people upon a foreign enemy, and divert their minds from a consideration of the corruptions and abuses of power, of the dominant party at home.

We are a great people, have a great country, and a wonderful destiny; but unfortunately statesmanship is dying out, for want of aliment to develop and sustain it—and partisanship has taken its place. Party spirit will no longer tolerate the degree of independence of thought and action, necessary to develop sound statesmanship; and we have fallen under the dominion of party politicians, many of whom, of each party, are sharp and adroit managers of party conventions and elections, and the distribution of party patronage—but have no clear conceptions of the true principles of political economy, finance, currency, or social or political science of any kind. The degradation of the elective suffrage, party spirit and party domination, with negro domination at the South, and the centralization of supreme power in Congress, will tend to produce extravagance, oppressive taxation and despotism, by the national government—anarchy, mobs and riots in the States, and particularly in the Southern States and large cities—and prodigality and corruption everywhere.

SEC. 9.—*Powers and jurisdiction of the federal and State governments—Law and jurisprudence.*

Within the several States, the federal government has power to levy taxes for national purposes; to establish post offices and post roads, receive, transport and distribute mail matter; to regulate foreign commerce and commerce and navigation between States; to exercise certain enumerated military powers; to borrow money; to establish a uniform rule of naturalization, and uniform laws upon the subject of bankruptcies; to secure copyrights to authors and patents to inventors; to coin money, regulate the value thereof, and of foreign coin, and to regulate the currency as is now claimed, and fix the standard of weights and measures; to punish certain enumerated crimes, and all violations of its own laws; and to hold courts to administer its own laws, and to administer justice between citizens of different States, and in a few other cases. Here its powers and jurisdiction, within the limits of the States, end. All other legitimate powers of government within the States, belong to the State governments. With the exceptions enumerated, the federal government has no power in a State over persons or property, contracts or rights, schools or education, marriage or the domestic relations, matters of internal government or police, vice or crime, morals or religion.

It belongs exclusively to the State governments, to protect, within their respective limits, both persons and property; to regulate contracts, and the mode of acquiring and using, selling and conveying property, or transmitting it to heirs and next of kin; to regulate wills and testaments, marriages and the domestic relations; to provide roads* and bridges for the people; to provide for education and for the poor; to preserve order, and regulate all matters of police; to provide for the punishment of vice and crime; and to levy and collect taxes for all purposes of local and interior government. These subjects embrace nearly the whole domain of jurisprudence, municipal law, and what we include in the terms common law—though not the whole of the code of commercial law, and not any of the code of maritime law. The United States as a unity, as a country, and as a government, have no civil code, no municipal law, and no common law, in the ordinary sense in which those words are used. They have no civil jurisprudence, except in admiralty matters. The federal courts, while sitting in civil cases, other than those of a maritime character, administer not only the local common law, but also the statute laws of the States in which they sit. The United States have no law upon such subjects, either statute or common; no power to enact laws

* The United States may make post roads and military roads, and perhaps roads to promote commerce among the several States—but no others.

upon such subjects, to operate within the States; and no power to enact or administer laws within the States, to punish crimes or offences against either persons or property —unless the offence be against the property or rights of the United States, or against the person of one of its officers, while in the actual discharge of his duties. They have no power even to protect the character of their own officers, from slanders and libels, uttered and published within a State. For such wrongs, federal officers must rely upon State laws for their remedies; and they must generally resort to State courts for redress.

Each State having exclusive and supreme power to legislate upon all domestic and municipal subjects within its limits, the result is, that each State has not only its own code of statute law, but also its peculiar customs, usages, and judicial decisions—forming a common law, varying in some particulars from that of every other State. Each State has borrowed more or less from the laws of other States, and also from the laws of England and from the Code Napoleon of France—so that the laws of the several States have been constantly expanding, in a state of development, and generally improving and assimilating more and more to the principles of universal law. Our complex system has, therefore, worked well in practice, as a general rule; the State and federal courts have moved on in harmony; the latter in civil matters, administering the same law as the former—the principal evils resulting from a general tendency to too great laxity in the laws, as well as in their administration, for the collection of debts, the punishment of fraud, vice and crime, and in matters of police. The principal defects, however, are more in a want of energy in the execution of the laws, than in the laws themselves.

The defects and inefficiency in the administration of

justice, is greatly owing to the modern system of electing nearly all judicial as well as executive officers by the people—or rather by the dominant political party of the county or district; but it results, partly, from the extremes to which the principles of freedom and philanthropy have been carried; whereby sentiments of tenderness, and in some cases of sympathy, have been excited for criminals as well as for defaulters and debtors, as unfortunate persons. We need a remedy for these evils. The fact stands out in bold relief, that there is less security for life, person and property in this country, than there is in either France or England. This is owing to the state of public opinion, the inefficiency of the police, and too much laxity in the administration of justice. It is undeniable that our national character has suffered in Europe from these causes.

Sec. 10.—*Character and slow development of federal law.*

The most of the politicians and people of this generation live in ease and luxury, when compared with the condition of our revolutionary fathers. They are divided into political parties and cliques; nearly all independence of thought upon political subjects is worked out of them by party organizations and party discipline; and party creeds and doctrines supply the place of individual thought. Our revolutionary ancestors were very differently situated. They were not much divided into parties and factions struggling for the ascendency; but were united and nearly unanimous, in declaring their independence and right to self-government; and in defending their rights from British domination. They had experiences which tried men's souls, tested their patriotism, and formed many distinguished men. They were schooled in adversity and severe trials, in war and devastation, in severe taxation and poverty, and in industrial and commercial depression, which developed their energies and power of thought. It may well be doubted, if any body of men ever assembled on this earth, equal as a whole, in high mental endowments and wisdom, in independence of thought, and in political science and patriotism, to either the convention which formed the constitution of the United States, or the first Congress which assembled under it.

The Articles of Confederation were framed and agreed upon by Congress, in November, 1777; but did not take effect until March, 1781, after they had been signed by the delegates of all the States. Many of their features were suggested by the Articles of Alliance and Confederation of the United Provinces of the Netherlands (or Holland), and by those of Switzerland. The Confederacy of the United Provinces, formed in 1579, had been in practical and successful operation about two centuries, and formed an efficient commonwealth; under which that country prospered, and increased in industry and commerce, wealth and power. Their confederate system of government, so far as regards the legislative department thereof, and so far as it was applicable, was adopted by the American Congress, as the basis of the Articles of Confederation of the United States; but the executive department of that government, which constituted its strong features, were not adopted.

Our government, under the Articles of Confederation, was more nearly assimilated to the government then existing in Switzerland, than to that of Holland; and experience soon showed that it was not adapted to a large country, with various interests, consisting of many States —having republican representative governments, with frequent elections, numerous rival commercial cities upon the seaboard, very trifling commercial intercourse between distant States, to bind them together, and no aristocracy nor ecclesiastical organization, to strengthen the bond of union. When put into practice and tested by experience, it was found to have several very grave defects.

1st. In not giving Congress power to levy and collect taxes and excises, and duties on foreign imports, to enable the government to raise its own revenues; and in making the federal government entirely dependent upon the several States for its revenues, and for raising and supporting its armies.

2d. In not giving Congress power to regulate foreign commerce and navigation, and commerce among the States—as a means of raising revenue, and of establishing a uniform system of commercial intercourse with foreign nations, and superseding the conflicting commercial laws, and injurious commercial rivalships of the several States.

3d. In not providing for the establishment of an efficient executive branch of the government, distinct from mere committees of Congress.

4th. In not providing for the establishment of a Supreme and Inferior Courts, to expound the constitution and laws, and aid in executing them—and in determining the boundary lines of power between the federal and State governments.

The experience and wisdom of the members of the convention which formed the constitution of the United States, enabled them to supply those defects, and to produce the most perfect constitution ever framed for the government of a nation. The government established under the federal constitution, being grafted upon the State governments, and in many respects depending upon them for its proper action, and in others acting independently, formed a very complicated system, in many respects entirely new. Some of the leading features of the new system originated with the distinguished statesmen who framed the constitution. They were suggested by experience and wisdom, and matured by the Convention, and may be claimed as American law.

It required also great legal acquirements and experience, and much wisdom and originality of thought, to frame laws to organize the executive and judicial departments of the government, to put it into operation; for there were no precedents for many provisions of those laws, and it was necessary to originate them, and to adapt them to our peculiar federal and dual system of government. This was done by the first Congress which met under the constitution. The judiciary act of 1789, which provided for the organization of the Supreme, Circuit and District Courts of the United States, and prescribed their jurisdiction, powers, and modes of procedure, is a model of excellence. The 25th section of that act, gives the Supreme Court appellate jurisdiction from any final judgment or decree of the highest court of a State, in any case where the validity of a treaty or statute of the United States, or an authority exercised under the United States, is drawn in question, and the decision is against their validity; or where is drawn in question the validity of a statute of, or an authority exercised under any State, on the ground of their being repugnant to the constitution, treaties, or laws of the United States, and the decision is in favor of their validity; or where is drawn in question the construction of any clause of the constitution, treaty, statute, or commission held under the United States, and the decision is against the title, right, or privilege claimed under such clause of the constitution, treaty, statute, or commission; and authorizes the Supreme Court to re-examine and revise or affirm such judgment or decree, upon a writ of error, and to proceed in certain cases, to a final decision of the same, and to award execution to carry their judgments into effect.

The most of our judicial system, both State and national, as well as our jurisprudence, was borrowed from the laws and judicial system of England; but the 25th section of the judiciary act was entirely new. It gave to the Supreme Court of the United States a jurisdiction and powers previously unknown, and not exercised to this day, by the highest judicial tribunal of any other country. That section of the judiciary act made the Supreme Court of the United States the *ultimate expounder*, *not only of the laws and treaties of the United States*, *but of the constitution also; and clothed it with authority to sit in judgment upon the validity of any treaty of the United States, any statute of Congress, or any law, statute, or act of a State government, or under its authority, and to decide and finally determine whether such treaty, statute, or act, be or be not consistent with the supreme law of the land,—the Constitution of the United States.*

That section of the judiciary act is in accord and harmony with the Constitution of the United States, and was and is necessary to carry the constitution into full effect; and yet it made the Supreme Court the *balance wheel* of our complicated system of government—*the umpire* between the federal and State governments; and clothed it with authority to determine the *boundaries of power between the federal and State governments, and the limits to the powers of each.* Under that section, a large number of the acts and laws of the States have been overruled, declared void, and virtually annulled, as repugnant to the constitution, laws, or treaties of the United States; and all conflicts of jurisdiction, power and authority between the federal and State governments, have been thereby avoided.

Very few acts or parts of acts of Congress have been declared by the Supreme Court inconsistent with the constitution; and the opinion of Judge Taney, in the Dred Scott case, in which the court were divided, and a majority of the judges declared the Missouri Compromise act repugnant to the constitution, was the first decision of that distinguished tribunal, in which a majority of the people of the United States refused to concur, and which they denounced as unsound. That opinion has been repudiated by at least two-thirds of the people of the United States, as a sectional and partisan effort to extend slavery into the Territories, and make it a national institution. Such a decision would never have been made, if Southern men had not used the powers of Congress improperly, and obtained for the then slave States, five of the nine judges, and the control of the court upon questions affecting the institution of slavery; when the population and business of those States scarcely entitled them to four judges. That tribunal has been reformed since 1860—so as to secure to the North and West their proper influence in its decisions, and prevent the operation in future, of sectional interests and prejudices.

The extraordinary powers conferred upon the Supreme Court of the United States, give it an importance which no other judicial tribunal ever had. As the umpire and final judge between the powers of the federal and States governments, that Court has had a very salutary influence in deciding questions of jurisdiction and power; in preventing conflicts between the two governments, which exercise power over the same territory, and over the same people, in each of the States; and in harmonizing the various elements, in our federal and dual system of government.

It has had a benign influence in perfecting our federal system of government, and promoting the cause of civil liberty, and constitutional law. It has gradually built up a code or system of constitutional law, which serves to enlighten and guide legislators and statesmen, as well as courts, jurists, and lawyers, throughout the civilized world.

Acts were passed by the first Congress to organize the State, Treasury, War, and Post-Office departments, and the then necessary bureaux thereof; to regulate processes and proceedings in the courts of the United States; to provide for registering and clearing vessels, and for regulating the coasting trade; to impose duties on tonnage, and on goods, wares, and merchandise imported into the United States; to establish and support light-houses, beacons, buoys, and public piers; to establish a uniform rule of naturalization; to promote the useful arts by patent rights; to encourage learning by copyrights; to regulate trade and intercourse with the Indian tribes; to provide for the payment of the debts of the United States; for the government of the Territories; for the punishment of certain crimes and offences against the United States; and for various other purposes, to put the government into operation, and provide for carrying it on.

The Criminal Laws of the United States.

The act for the punishment of certain crimes against the United States, approved April 30th, 1790, defines the crimes of treason, misprision of treason, and various other crimes and offences against the United States, and prescribes the punishment, and modes of trial thereof—including the crime of forging or counterfeiting any certificate or security of the United States; stealing, taking away, or altering any record, writ, or proceeding of the United States; committing perjury in any suit or cause depending in any court of the United States, or in any deposition taken pursuant to any law of the United States; bribing or attempting to bribe any judge of the United States; obstructing or opposing any officer of the United States, in serving, or attempting to serve, judicial process; rescuing any person convicted or charged with the commission of any crime or offence against the United States; assaulting, striking, wounding, or imprisoning an ambassador or other public minister, or sueing out or executing process against him.

Any of the foregoing crimes and offences could be committed anywhere in the United States, or in any territory thereof—either within or without the territorial jurisdiction of a State—the powers of the State governments not extending to crimes and offences against the United States.

The same act of the first Congress, provided for the punishment of piracy, murder, or robbery, committed on the high seas, or in any river, haven, basin or bay, out of the jurisdiction of any particular State; for the punishment of any person guilty of wilful murder or manslaughter, committed within any fort, arsenal, dockyard, or magazine of the United States, or in any other place or district of country, under the sole and exclusive jurisdiction of the United States; of maiming any person within any of the places upon land, under the sole and exclusive jurisdiction of the United States, or upon the high seas, in any vessel of the United States, or belonging to any citizen or citizens thereof; or of stealing and purloining the goods or property of another, or of the United States, within any of the places under the sole and exclusive jurisdiction of the United States, or upon the high seas.

The class of crimes lastly enumerated, are such as can be committed only where the State courts and governments have no territorial jurisdiction; while the class of crimes firstly enumerated, may be committed where a State has territorial jurisdiction, but no jurisdiction over such offences—because they are not committed against the government of any State, but against the majesty and laws of the national government.

The federal government has the exclusive police of the high seas, of the District of Columbia, and of the territories, forts, arsenals, and dockyards of the United States. With those exceptions, each State has the exclusive police of all places within its limits. The lines of distinction between federal and State power, to punish crime, as well as to levy and collect taxes, regulate commerce, and for other matters, depends generally upon subject-matter, object, and purpose, and seldom upon locality. Hence the lines of distinction, between federal and State powers, are often nice, and not easily determined, until defined by statute, or by a decision of the Supreme Court. It required such master minds as those of Alexander Hamilton, James Madison, John Jay, and John Marshall, and their compeers, to determine and define the powers of the federal government, and the boundaries of power between it and the State governments; and the process is still going on—for the federal government never exercised many of its powers, until the great rebellion revealed the necessity of extraordinary powers to put down the Confederate government, and maintain the supremacy of the constitution and laws of the United States; and suggested new laws, and developed powers never before exercised by the government of the United States.

The criminal laws of the United States were altered, amended, and enlarged, and new provisions enacted in many instances, between the years 1790 and 1860; and laws were made to punish mail robberies, obstructions to, and violations of the United States mails, purloining moneys, letters, and other things therefrom; counterfeiting or forging coin, or notes of the United States bank; uttering and passing false and counterfeit coin or notes of the United States bank; extortion by an officer of the United States; carrying on the slave trade; committing murder, rape, striking, stabbing, poisoning or shooting at any person under certain circumstances within the admiralty jurisdiction of the United States; attacking a vessel with intent to plunder; breaking into a vessel with intent to commit a felony; plundering, stealing, or destroying the effects of a wrecked vessel; setting fire to, burning or otherwise destroying a United States vessel of war, or any vessel of which the person doing such act is not the owner; inciting a mutiny or revolt on board a vessel; maltreating the crew by the master of a vessel; committing arson in any place within the sole and exclusive jurisdiction of the United States; conspiring, combining and confederating to cast away, burn, or otherwise destroy any vessel, with intent to injure and defraud the insurers thereof; committing a fraud upon the customs, or violating the revenue laws of the United States; or cutting timber upon the lands of the United States.

The subjects enumerated embrace, in general terms, all the most important criminal laws of the United States, enacted prior to the year 1861. Many defects in the criminal code were supplied; the laws extended from time to time to new subjects; and acts not previously made criminal, were declared by Congress to be crimes and offences, as the exigencies of the country, and the commission of such offences, developed the necessity of prohibiting them, and punishing them as crimes.

Much was done, during the first seventy years after the adoption of the federal Constitution, to mature and perfect a criminal code for the United States; but there was one glaring defect in that code. Although the law to punish treason against the government of the United States was well matured and complete, there was *no law to punish conspiracies against the federal government.* In December, 1860, and January, 1861, a conspiracy against the government of the United States, was concocted in the Capitol at Washington, by Senators and Representatives in Congress, who communicated by both letter and telegraph, with their friends and co-conspirators at the South, and thus aided in forming and directing conspiracies and combinations to overthrow the federal government in the Southern States; and *there was no law to punish such inceptive acts of treason*, until the Confederate government was organized, commenced making preparations for rebellion, and *actually committed overt acts of treason, in levying war against the United States.*

That great defect in the criminal laws was known to the conspirators, and served to embolden them in their acts and movements. Some of them remained in their seats in Congress for several weeks, conspiring, from day to day, to defeat any measures to strengthen the executive branch of the government and prepare to meet the coming rebellion—voting against all such measures, and communicating frequently with their friends in the Southern States. If we had had an efficient law to punish conspiracies, such things could not have been done without exposing the conspirators to arrest, imprisonment, trial, and punishment, if convicted; which would have held them in check, induced more caution, and less activity in organizing combinations, and preparing for rebellion, and deterred many from joining the conspirators.

That great defect in the law was cured by an act of Congress, to define and punish certain conspiracies, approved July 31st, 1861. That act provides that if two or more persons within any State or Territory of the United States, shall conspire together to overthrow, or to put down, or to destroy by force, the government of the United States, or to levy war against the United States, or to oppose by force the authority of the government of the United States; or by force to prevent, hinder, or delay the execution of any law of the United States; or by force to seize, take or possess any property of the United States, against the will, or contrary to the authority of the United States; or by force, or intimidation, or threat, to prevent any person from accepting or holding any office or trust, or place, under the United States, each and every person so offending, shall be guilty of a high crime, and, upon conviction thereof, in any Circuit or District Court of the United States having jurisdiction thereof, or District or Supreme Court of a Territory, shall be punished by fine not less than five hundred nor more than five thousand dollars; or by imprisonment with or without hard labor, not less than six months, nor more than six years, or by both such fine and imprisonment.

Under such a law, with an efficient and vigilant administration, with the aid of the electric telegraph, and the facilities of railroads and steam navigation, every future conspiracy against the government can be nipped in the bud, before a confederate rebel government can be organized, or much preparation made to wage war against the United States. Threats of a dissolution of the Union were occasionally thrown out in Congress and elsewhere for more than thirty years prior to the great rebellion of 1861; but in future, such threats will subject the party making them to suspicion, and surveillance.

Congress passed an act approved August 6th, 1861, to confiscate property used for insurrectionary purposes: an act approved June 2d, 1862, to prevent and punish fraud on the part of officers intrusted with making contracts for the government; and an act, approved July 1st, 1862, to punish bigamy, and prevent the practice of polygamy in the Territories of the United States. The last act referred to has been disregarded by the Mormons, and never executed.

An act was passed and approved July 17th, 1862, to suppress insurrections, punish treason and rebellion, and to seize and confiscate the property of rebels. The 24th section of the act for enrolling and calling out the national forces, approved March 3d, 1863, provides, that every person, not subject to the rules and articles of war, who shall procure or entice, or attempt to procure or entice, a soldier in the service of the United States, to desert; or who shall harbor or conceal, or give employment to a deserter, or carry him away, or aid in carrying him away, knowing him to be such; or who shall purchase from a soldier his arms, equipments, ammunition, clothing, or any part thereof, shall upon conviction thereof, be fined not exceeding five hundred dollars, and imprisoned not more than two years, nor less than six months. Section 25 provides that if any person shall resist any draft of men enrolled under that act, or aid any person to resist any such draft; or shall assault or obstruct an officer in making such draft; or shall counsel any person to assault or obstruct any such officer, or shall counsel any drafted man not to appear at the place of rendezvous, or wilfully dissuade them from the performance of military duty as required by law, such person shall be subject to summary arrest, and upon conviction of such offence shall be punished by fine not exceeding five hundred dollars, or by imprisonment not exceeding two years, or by both of said punishments. Section 30 provides that in time of war, insurrection or rebellion, persons in the military service of the United States, who shall be guilty of murder, assault with intent to kill, mayhem, wounding by shooting or stabbing, robbery, arson, burglary, rape, or an assault and battery with intent to commit rape, shall be tried and punished by a court-martial or military commission. Section 38 provides that spies may be tried by general court-martial or military commission; and upon conviction shall suffer death.

Congress passed an act, approved March 3d, 1863, to prevent and punish frauds upon the revenue; an act, approved June 27th, 1864, to prevent and punish smuggling; and an act, approved July 1st, 1864, prescribing the punishment for enticing or aiding seamen to desert the naval service of the United States. Penalties have been imposed by other acts of Congress, and the criminal laws have been amended, improved, and added to, from time to time, and defects supplied, until the United States have now an efficient criminal code for periods of war, and insurrection, as well as peace—to punish and prevent conspiracies against the government, and many acts of sedition, as well as other crimes. But it has required wisdom, time, and experience, in war and rebellion as well as in peace, to develop and mature our national criminal code. While the most of our criminal laws have been suggested by circumstances and the exigencies of the country, they have been constructed by the wisdom of American statesmen. A good, complete, and efficient criminal code adds largely to the efficiency, security, and stability of a government.

The State of New York inaugurated at Auburn, about the year 1820, a penitentiary system of punishment, with solitary confinement in separate cells at night, and hard labor in silence, in workshops by day; which unites the purposes of punishment, with the reform of the criminal, so far as is practical, and the acquisition of a useful trade with habits of industry—that will enable him to earn an honest living when discharged. That system has been adopted by all, or nearly all the States, and has been well matured, during a period of about fifty years, and brought to a high state of perfection. It is a great improvement upon the modes of punishment for most crimes, previously in use, in America as well as in Europe. Such prisons afford an efficient means of punishment, with a view to the acquisition of habits of industry and skill in some useful trade—and to reform blended with punishment. Our system has been adopted by many countries of Europe, and will have a salutary and benign influence upon the civilized world. One of the greatest defects of all the governments of ancient times, as well as of Europe, until a recent period, was the want of good criminal codes, of an efficient police, and of good prisons and penitentiaries, with workshops, for the confinement of criminals at hard labor.

The punishment of crime, both against person and property, committed within the territorial jurisdiction of a State, together with the police power, belongs exclusively to the State government—excepting only offences against the government and laws, or property of the United States. Hence there are two distinct codes of criminal law, in operation in each State. The criminal laws of most of the States, including the State of New York, are very defective, in not providing properly for the punishment of directors and other officers of corporations, for the embezzlement or other misapplication of their funds, for fraudulent issues of stocks, and other abuses of power, and frauds practised upon stockholders. A law to punish such offences, with a proper degree of severity, might have prevented many of the frauds and swindling operations practised by the controlling spirits of the Erie Railroad.

The United States are allowed the use of the State prisons and penitentiaries, for the confinement and punishment of their convicts, and the use of the local jails, for the confinement of persons charged with crime against the United States; which adds greatly to the economy, as well as to the facility, of executing the criminal laws of the federal government.

The civil, revenue, land, postal, pension, and military laws of the United States.

The federal government has no municipal common law, either civil or criminal; and no law which is usually termed municipal law, either statute or common. Nor has Congress any power to legislate upon municipal subjects, except for the Territories, and the District of Columbia. While sitting in the several States in civil suits, other than admiralty cases, the courts of the United States administer the local municipal law. The 34th section of the judiciary act of the United States of 1789, provides that the laws of the several States, except where the constitution, treaties, or statutes of the United States shall otherwise require or provide, shall be regarded as *rules of decision in trials at common law, in the courts of the United States*, in cases where they apply.

The act of Congress for the establishment of a Freedman's bureau for the Southern States, can be justified and maintained as constitutional, only on the ground that the States in which those laws operated, were *practically and de facto out of the Union, and subject to the laws of the United States as conquered territories.* That is the practical interpretation which Congress has given to the constitution of the United States; and a majority of the

American people have acquiesced in that interpretation. The constitutionality and validity of the acts of Congress known as the reconstruction laws, can be defended upon that ground, and by that interpretation of the constitution, and no other. The interests of the country can never be promoted by disturbing that practical interpretation, which will teach men caution, and the great danger of rebelling against the federal government hereafter. That interpretation of the constitution will tend to increase the security and stability of the government; and may save the country from future efforts to dissolve or divide the Union.

The evils of secession and a division of the Union, were recently portrayed in a clear light by the *London Examiner*.

Speaking of the prosperity of this country, the *Examiner* said: "Had secession succeeded, the Border line would now be bristling with bayonets; and men's thoughts, instead of being fixed on works of peaceful development and progress, would have been concentrated upon systems of strategy, works of fortification, and schemes of vengeance and destruction."

Revenue Laws.—The federal government has been supported by duties on imports and tonnage, the sale of public lands, internal duties, stamps, licenses, and income taxes, and to a very limited extent, at different periods, by direct taxation; but its revenues have been mostly derived until recently, from duties on imports.

Since the system of direct taxation of lands and other property was abandoned by Congress in 1862, and a high tariff, income tax, heavy internal duties, and taxes for licenses and stamps, were imposed, the government has been eminently successful in raising larger revenues and loans than were ever raised before, by any government, in any country, from the same number of people. And yet the loyal States were in a high state of prosperity even during the war, and more so since its close—notwithstanding the heavy burthens of taxation; and the prosperity of the seceding States is rapidly reviving. The errors and blunders of our revenue systems, both internal and commercial, are so overbalanced in their influences by virtues, that on the whole they have been very salutary in their effects. They both need revision, and the number of articles upon which taxes are levied, should be greatly reduced. The character and policy of the revenue laws, will be discussed in a subsequent chapter.

The federal government has frequently changed its revenue laws, and particularly its duties on imports. It has also made many changes in internal taxes. It has experimented extensively, and tested the effects of taxes at various rates, upon great numbers of articles, and learned the amount of revenue that can be derived from each—and thereby created as well as collected, a large amount of materials to guide statesmen and legislators in framing a better and wiser system of revenue laws, than this or any other nation, ever had. The information collected with the national census each ten years, serves also as a guide to legislation.

PUBLIC LAND SYSTEM.—Our system of surveying, selling, and disposing of the public lands, was originated by American statesmen, and is very different from that of every other country. The British, French, Spanish, and Dutch governments, have been in the habit of making large grants of land, of thousands of acres, sometimes of a whole province, and often of a tract as large as a county, to a single prominent and influential man; generally as a matter of favoritism, or to encourage him to introduce emigrants to settle and improve the country. The colonies of New York, New Jersey, Pennsylvania, Maryland, Virginia, North and South Carolina, and Georgia, were originally under proprietary governments, each of them having been granted to one or a few great proprietors. Nearly all Spanish America was settled under large grants and concessions of the King of Spain, made in most cases to favorites, without any pecuniary consideration paid to the government. The grants and concessions of the French government in America, were smaller in extent, but generally of the same character—having been made without any consideration paid for them. The tendency of such a system was and is, to build up and maintain an aristocracy; to make a few wealthy proprietors, and a poor, humble, and dependent peasantry—of very little energy of character or public spirit—having few schools, roads, or other public improvements, and but little commercial intercourse.

Our land system is very different in its effects, as well as in its character and operation. The federal government buys the Indian title; surveys the lands; opens land offices, and offers the lands for sale, at the minimum price of $1.25 per acre; sells them mostly to actual settlers; organizes territorial governments for the government of the country and the protection of settlers; makes liberal grants of lands, to erect territorial buildings, make roads, improve the navigation of rivers and watercourses, establish and maintain schools, colleges, and universities, and aid in making canals and railroads.

Congress granted to the new States—admitted prior to 1840, a section or mile square of land in each surveyed township of thirty-six square miles, to establish and maintain common schools; and grants of two sections in each surveyed township have been made for common school purposes, to each new State admitted into the Union since 1840.

Our federal government derives a considerable revenue from the sale of the public lands, over and above all expenses attending them; and yet it retains the control of all the lands, until sold, or granted for useful purposes, and disposes of them as a general rule, (some few improvident grants excepted,) to the utmost advantage, for the promotion of the settlement and improvement of the country, and the welfare of the people of the United States. What would Illinois and Iowa, the Upper Peninsula of Michigan, and the States of Kansas and Nebraska have been to-day, without the aid of Congressional grants of lands for railroads and other public improvements? Who can estimate the influence, twenty or fifty years hence, upon all the Western, interior, and Pacific States, of grants of the public lands, made by Congress? While other countries have thrown away the most of their public lands, by giving them to a few favorites, Congress has made the public lands of the United States a source of revenue—a great national power, and bond of union between the States; and also a great civilizing agent, for aiding in settling, improving, and developing the resources of the interior and of the western portion of the continent, and of educating and promoting the general welfare of the people.

Our land laws and land system tend to promote the rapid settlement and improvement of the new States and Territories; to produce an independent, educated, industrious, and energetic people, as nearly equal in condition as the Providences of God will permit—living upon and cultivating their own lands, with no landlords to demand rents, or share their crops with them—the federal, State, and local governments, to which they must pay taxes, being their only landlords. Such a system tends to promote justice and equality of condition, education and intelligence, industry and energy of character, extended commercial and industrial intercourse, public spirit and patriotism—and to make a people fit for self-government—a nation of high-spirited Republicans, and law-abiding constitutional Democrats. Our public land system may, very properly, be regarded as a model of excellence; and when fully appreciated, it will become the admiration of the civilized world.

Postal System and Laws.—The postal system of the United States and the laws regulating the same, have been gradually increased and matured, during more than three-fourths of a century, and improved in accordance with the suggestions of experience, in this country and in England. Our system will now compare favorably in magnitude and facilities, in extent of accommodations, safety and economy, with that of any country of Europe.

Pension Laws.—The pension laws of the United States constitute a noble and philanthropic system—to promote and secure the comfort of disabled soldiers, and of the widows and minor children of those that have lost their lives in the service of their country. They do justice, as far as is practicable, to the soldier and his family; and have a salutary influence in encouraging enlistments to support the government and the flag of the country, in time of war.

Military System and Laws.—The military system of the United States is anomalous, Congress having power to provide for calling forth the militia of the several States, to aid in executing the laws of the Union, suppress insurrections and repel invasions; and also power to provide for organizing, arming, and disciplining the militia, and for governing such part of them as may be employed in the service of the United States, reserving to the States respectively the appointment of the officers thereof, and the authority to train the militia according to the discipline prescribed by Congress. The federal government has fully exercised all the military powers granted by the constitution; passed numerous acts upon the subject; kept but a small standing army; and relied mostly upon the militia and volunteer forces—to be raised quickly in time of war and invasion, or insurrection.

Congress has matured a military code for the government of the army and navy, and the militia also, when called into the actual service of the United States.

The States also have power to pass laws not inconsistent with the laws of the United States, to provide for organizing, arming, training, and calling out the militia; and all of them have exercised such powers; and depend entirely upon the militia, and the United States army, in case of an emergency, to aid in executing their laws. The organization of the militia in most of the States, in time of peace, is only nominal.

The military Academy at West Point, on the Hudson river, and actual service in the army during the great rebellion, have educated a large number of military men, and fitted them for officers; so that the United States can raise in a few months, officer efficiently, and organize as large military forces as any country of Europe, except Russia. The immense field which our country offers for civil and mining engineering and other business avocations, give our officers employment, in time of peace; but the government can command their services again, whenever they may be needed. Our military expenses are, therefore, very small, in time of peace, when compared with our very large military resources and powers, which can be called into existence and made available, in a few months. Considering the military spirit and patriotism of our people, our military system may be regarded as the best in the world, for such a country and such a people, living under such a government.

Common law of the United States.

Congress has enacted a great body of laws of a national character; and in interpreting and executing the constitution and laws of the United States, great numbers of decisions have been made and opinions given, by the Attorney-Generals, heads of department and bureau officers, as well as by the courts; and the heads of department and bureau officers have made rules and regulations, prescribed forms of procedure, and issued circulars from time to time, to give interpretation to the laws and aid in executing them; under which, usages and systems of practice have grown up, become established customs, assumed the force of law, and now form what may be properly termed, *the common law of the United States.* It embraces the usages, customs, and practice of the departments and bureaus, the decisions of the courts, and the opinions of the Attorney-Generals, upon the subjects of commerce and navigation, revenue and finance, the public lands and postal matters, pensions and military affairs, bankruptcies and fugitives from justice, and to a limited extent, practice in the federal courts, and interpretations of the criminal laws of the United States. It cannot therefore be denied, that *the United States have a growing common law, upon such national subjects and questions*—though they have *no municipal common law*—no common law upon the subject of property, personal rights and obligations, contracts, police matters, morals, religion, education, nor the poor. All such subjects of legislation and law, fall within the exclusive jurisdiction and domain of the State governments.

SEC. 11.—*Territorial governments and laws.*

Congress has absolute and unlimited power to legislate for the Territories of the United States, and the District of Columbia; but has delegated the power mostly to territorial governments, and neglected to exercise it sufficiently to promote the best interests of the Territories. The ordinance of Congress adopted July 13th, 1787, for the government of the territory northwest of the Ohio river, was not only an organic law, charter, or constitution for the organization and regulation of the territorial government; but it also contained some of the germs of a civil code of law—including as it did a prohibition of slavery, a general rule for the descent of property, and the modes of executing and attesting wills and testaments, and conveyances of property. But acts of Congress passed during the last fifty years, for the organization of territorial governments, have been simply Organic Laws, or constitutions, leaving the people of the Territories, through the agency of territorial legislatures, to legislate for themselves, upon all subjects of a municipal and police character.

Nine-tenths of the men who usually emigrate to a new territory, are in some sense adventurers, and may be included in the following classes: 1st, young and inexperienced men; 2d, fugitives from justice, and fugitives from their creditors; and 3d, men of shattered fortunes and small means, who have not been successful in life. The settlers in new territories comprise but few experienced, first-class men, who are fit for legislators and lawgivers, and qualified to frame a code of laws for a people; and hence the importance of Congress framing and adopting the outlines of a code of laws for all the Territories—regulating the descent of property, the mode of conveying and transferring property, and executing wills and testaments; marriages and divorces; the domestic relations and guardianships; securing to married women their own property and earnings; regulating bills of exchange and promissory notes, and the rate of interest on debts and contracts; establishing absolute freedom of religious worship, freedom of speech and of the press; prohibiting any discrimination or distinction in legislation or taxation, between persons, on account of race or origin, color or religion, or any distinction in taxation between the property of residents and non-residents.

The success of the Territories has been owing to the great natural wealth and resources of the country, the virtues of the public land system and the munificent donations of Congress, and to the energy of the people; rather than to any great wisdom in their territorial legislation. The shocking election frauds and abuses, and the barbarous legislation in Kansas while a Territory, involved the Territory in civil war, and showed that the heterogeneous mass of people, that settle new territories, are poorly qualified to make good laws, and to maintain order and peace.

But the most despicable government that ever existed on the continent of America, is that of the Territory of Utah. The Mormon settlements have been foul nests of knaves, thieves, and robbers, ever since they settled in Missouri; from which they were driven by an outraged people, on account of their crimes. They then went to Illinois, and built the city of Nauvoo. When driven from Illinois, they migrated beyond the Rocky mountains, and settled in Utah. The lusts of Brigham Young and his subordinates of the Mormon priesthood, induced the pretended revelation, authorizing polygamy, and the introduction of the practice of polygamy among them. But the government being practically a *Theocracy*, the most of the women are monopolized by the Mormon priesthood, who set at defiance the law of Congress, prohibiting polygamy in the Territories of the United States. Mormonism is the grossest, foulest, and most corrupting imposture which has been successfully imposed upon any people, since the age of Mahomet; and yet it has some virtues, and elements of progress. It inculcates order, industry, and economy.

SEC. 12.—*Our Indian system and policy.*

Our Indian system has been the least successful in its workings, of any branch of our government. Finding the Indians wandering savages, without government or law (except their chiefs and a few rude customs), and without any capacity to make laws, and to organize and administer a government for themselves, Congress omitted to subject them to laws, to form a government and a code of laws for them, and the result was, that they became corrupted by intercourse with the whites; and *for want of fixed residences and subjection to law, the most of them became outlaws and robbers.*

Much has been done to improve, civilize, and accustom to habits of industry, the few thousand Indians settled upon reserves in the State of New York; and some progress has been made in civilizing the Creeks, Cherokees, Choctaws, Chickasaws, and other Indians, who were removed into the Indian Territory, west of Arkansas and Missouri, nearly forty years since; but their improvement has been small compared with what it would have been, if Congress had organized a territorial government for them, united them under one government, adopted the outlines of a code of laws for them, appointed for them a Governor, State Officers, Judges, and Marshals, subjected them to law, appointed their chiefs and educated men to such offices as they were competent to fill, and allowed them to elect some of their own officers, and to participate in legislating for themselves, and in administering their own local affairs, within a certain narrow sphere. *Nothing can be done with wandering tribes, until they are confined upon reservations, and subjected to law.*

With our boasted free institutions, Protestant civilization, and exclusive spirit, keeping the Indians at arm's length, we have succeeded in half civilizing about 100,000 of them, during a period of 250 years; while our Spanish American neighbors, with the aid of the Catholic Priesthood, by mixing with and intermarrying with the Indians, extending to them the civilizing agencies of law and government, have subjected to law, the Gospel, Catholic civilization, and to some degree of regular industry, and raised to a higher grade of civilization than exists among the tribes in our Indian Territory west of Arkansas, more than twelve millions of the full-blooded and half-breed descendants of the aborigines of America. Truly we have no reason to be proud of our success, in promoting the welfare of the Indian race.

CHAPTER II.

WORKINGS OF OUR SYSTEM OF GOVERNMENT—OUTSIDE PARTY ORGANIZATIONS AND MACHINERY TO CARRY IT ON, AND THEIR INFLUENCES—REMEDIES SUGGESTED FOR ITS DEFECTS.

SEC. 1.—*Popular elections, and their influences upon politicians and people.*

THOUGH our form of government is the best in the world for an intelligent people, in a cold or temperate climate; yet, like all other human institutions, it is not perfect in its operation, and does not fully answer the hopes and expectations of its framers and friends. Popular elections, as conducted under our system, are by no means an unmixed good; though a large portion of the evils resulting from them arise from the defects and vices of our electoral system, and might be avoided. The pursuit of politics, in a democratic country like this, often entices men from their business and proper pursuits, and allures great numbers with false hopes and delusive expectations, and subjects them to bitter disappointments.

Frequent elections and the popular agitations attending them, stimulate the personal ambition of great numbers of persons; awaken aspirations which can never be gratified; excite the minds of the multitude to run to and fro, to attend political meetings; disturb industry and business; and by the exaggerations, falsehoods and false pretences attending them, they tend to keep a people excited, restless, and dissatisfied with their government as well as with their rulers, and to induce in many persons, indolence, trickery, and crime. Popular elections and the enjoyment of the elective franchise, have utterly demoralized the negro of Jamaica and other British West India Islands, as well as Hayti and St. Domingo, and there is great danger that they will do so in our Southern States.*

Strong and well-balanced minds are benefited by such excitements, while weak ones are often injured. They operate as healthy stimulants to some, but are very injurious to many. It may well be feared that the enjoyment of the elective franchise and the machinery and excitements attending popular elections, will demoralize vast numbers of the negroes of the South, and make them ambitious, turbulent, and disorderly; excite in them hopes which can never be realized; divert them from industry; involve them in contests with the whites and with each other; and do the race vastly more injury than good. What the social and political status of the colored man will be hereafter, must depend upon his capacity for improvement and self-government, and upon the farther development of his intellectual, moral, and industrial character. But it is said, the freedmen have been denied their rights, and sorely oppressed; and that universal manhood suffrage is necessary, to enable them to protect themselves. That they have been oppressed is very true; but all history and experience shows, that they are incapable of protecting themselves. They must secure the good-will of the whites by patient industry,

* Ex-Governor Perry of South Carolina describes the negro as "no longer that industrious, useful and civil laborer which he once was, but an idle drone. Inflated with his new and marvellous political importance, he has abandoned his former industrious habits, and *spends his time in attending public meetings and loyal league gatherings, by day and by night.* This whole race seem disposed to quit their work, and resort to the towns and villages, where they may eke out an idle and wretched existence, in pilfering and begging."

and Congress, under the fourteenth amendment to the constitution, will protect them from unequal and unjust State legislation, more effectually than they can protect themselves by the ballot.

There are many evils incident to popular elections, which cannot be avoided; but they are greatly increased in number and magnitude, by the electoral system in operation with us—by which minorities are practically deprived of any representation—by the caucus and convention methods of nominating candidates for office—and by the multiplication of elective offices.

The system of popular elections which gives all representation and power to majorities, however small, and none to minorities, however large, tends to stimulate both personal and partisan ambition too highly; to excite rivalship and strife, partisan passions and prejudices; to divide a people into parties, cliques, and factions; and to increase and intensify the violence of party spirit. It offers too great temptations to resort to improper means to insure success, for poor, weak, and selfish human nature to resist; and hence it tends to stimulate secretiveness and duplicity, petty scheming and trickery, falsehood and fraud,—and to encourage social drinking and prodigality, as a means of popularity and of getting votes. It tends to stimulate and sharpen the intellect; but to paralyze the conscience and the moral feelings; to foster demagogism and a despicable scramble for office, and to demoralize politicians, and great numbers of the people. The elective system should be so organized as to stimulate party spirit as little as possible, and the personal ambition of as few persons.

SEC. 2.—*Partisanship, and its influence upon the mind, and upon the conduct of man.*

To attain truth, in the investigation of a moral or religious, political or financial question, or complicated question of any kind, it is necessary to examine it in all its aspects and bearings, from several standpoints, and from every practicable point of view. Every fair-minded judge hears, patiently considers, and weighs properly, the arguments and views of the case presented by both parties, before he decides the cause. Every legislator should, in like manner, hear and consider the views of public questions presented, with the appearance of candor, by the members of both political parties, and by men of all shades of opinion. Legislators should also consider the views of executive officers, and of petitioners and remonstrants, who are often deeply interested in the questions before them. This is necessary to the attainment of truth, and to enable them to act wisely.

It is the characteristic of zealous political partisans, to look at every measure presented, and at every political or national question, from the standpoint of their party; and to see it and examine it on one side only. With the eyes of the understanding nearly closed, they listen to the arguments of their opponents—not for the purpose of learning what truth they may contain, and what weight should be given to them; but for the purpose of finding defects in them, or what they may distort and make appear erroneous—in order to destroy their influence. Being accustomed to hear the merits of their own party extolled, and its principles, policies, and measures held up to view as tending to promote the best interests of the country, and the general welfare of the people; and accustomed to hear the opposite party and its principles and policies reviled—as tending to evil, and to evil only, political partisans usually take one-sided and partial views of all questions and measures of a political or public nature. They seldom view a question in all its aspects and bearings; and hence they get only partial and imperfect views, and in their reasoning upon them, they necessarily arrive at conclusions more or less erroneous. They often become imbued with enthusiasm in relation to the merits of their own party and party creed, and inclined to attribute all the prosperity of the country to its principles, policies, and measures. They can see no good in the other party—either in its principles or its policies, —its leaders or its measures—and attribute to the federal and State constitutions, to our popular system of government, and to the virtues of the people and the laws previously enacted, all the prosperity which the country enjoyed during the administration of their opponents.

The first object of many partisan legislators, is to promote the success and secure the ascendency of their party. To promote the general good and welfare of the country, and of the whole people, is with them a secondary consideration—being regarded by them rather as a means of promoting the success of their party, than as the proposed end and object of their legislative action. They may be patriots in a certain vague and general sense, attached to their country, and wish it well; but can see no merit or virtue in either the men, measures or policies of the opposite party; and expect to work out the good of the country, as well as their own personal good, only through the agency of their party.

Party spirit has become so violent and intense in this country, that it tends to blind the understanding, to fill the mind with prejudices and false assumptions, and to pervert the reasoning powers. In the view of violent partisans, every public good must be worked out through partisan agency, and partisan agency only; and they are seldom if ever willing to do anything for the public good, which will tend to expose the frauds or abuses of their party, or endanger the success of their party or party friends. Registry laws, intended and well adapted to prevent fraudulent voting, and to secure the fairness and purity of elections, have been opposed on partisan grounds only.

Zealous partisans are inclined to look with a jealous eye upon the leaders of the opposite party, and all their measures; to suspect their motives as selfish and sinister, —to regard their measures and policies as designed to promote the success and increase the power of their party, without regard to the public good—and to attribute to the corruptions, the abuses of power, the erroneous principles, and the bad measures and policies of their opponents, all the evils and misfortunes which have befallen the country.

Looking with an eye single to the principles, purposes and policies of their own party—always regarding them favorably, as tending to promote the best interests and welfare of the nation; and looking with suspicion and prejudice upon the leaders of the opposite party, and regarding their measures and policies as having evil and pernicious tendencies, they look forward with hope and cheerfulness to the triumph of their own party, and often regard with fearful forebodings the success of their opponents; and hence they are inclined to look with favor, and to regard as a sort of pious fraud, almost any kind of organization, management and trickery, deception and falsehood, which may tend to defeat their opponents, and promote the success of their own party ticket. Partisan newspapers and speakers, addressing the people at political meetings, are expected to present in bold relief, and to magnify the merits and successes of their party, to palliate their shortcomings, misdeeds and reverses—to seize hold of and magnify the errors, corruptions, and abuses of power of their opponents, and to paint in as dark colors as possible, the tendencies of their measures and policies, and the dangers which would result to the country from their success.

The tendency of party spirit is to tolerate no man as a leader, who is not blind to the faults of his own party, and to the merits of his opponents. Men of sound understandings, who look at both sides of political questions and judge fairly and impartially of their merits, soon lose the confidence of violent partisans, are distrusted by them, and no longer recognized as leaders. A fair-minded man, who looks at both sides of political questions, and considers them carefully, with a view to judge of their merits, is unfitted for a party leader, and must stand in the background. Partisan enthusiasts, and men who have one blind side, and are accustomed to see and appreciate the merits of one side only, must occupy the front seats.

The violent party spirit and party organizations of the present day, tend to make sharp, one-sided, and narrow-minded men, and cunning politicians—but not statesmen. They tend to discourage freedom of inquiry, freedom of thought, and freedom of speech upon political questions; to destroy freedom of action; and to unfit men to become statesmen, however long they may be in public life. Party spirit is, in fact, so wedded to temporary partisan expedients, that it can hardly tolerate sound statesmanship.

The power of party organizations and the intensity and violence of party spirit, have greatly increased during the last fifty years, by reason of—

1. The election of Presidential electors by the people, by general ticket.

2. The election of Sheriffs and other county officers directly by the people; and

3. The election of State officers and Judges of courts of record, by the people.

The changes, whereby all such officers are elected by the people, were made from time to time, since the year 1820. Such changes have greatly increased the importance of State and county, as well as Presidential elections—but more especially the latter. Under the general ticket system of electing Presidential electors, the party casting a majority of votes, however small such majority may be, get all the electors, and the other party get none. A very few votes sometimes turn the scale in favor of one party or the other, and give such party the whole vote of the State. Hence the great anxiety and efforts to get votes in the doubtful States, and the large expenditures of money, trickery and fraud, to carry elections—accompanied very often by abuses of power, by officers authorized and required to register voters, and by officers who receive and canvass the votes. The temptations to corruption offered by such a system, are often greater than human nature can resist.

Sec. 3.—*Party organizations and nominating conventions —how managed.*

Parties and party spirit will exist in all free countries. They are incidents to free institutions—and arise from honest differences of opinion among men, as well as from ambition for the honors and emoluments of office. They become evils only when party spirit is carried to excess.

Party organizations, such as we have in this country, exist in no other, and are not necessary in a well-organized government. They were invented long since the organization of our government, partly to supply the defects of our system of elections, and partly to promote the success of party, and party leaders (as is shown in the first chapter of this work); and they can be dispensed with when those defects are supplied by law. The principal evils of our system of government, grow out of these organizations, nominating conventions, and other party machinery, devised to stimulate party spirit, to secure success at elections—either by fair or foul means, and to control the destinies of the country.

Party organizations and machinery consist of national, State, county, city, ward and township committees, and committees for each Congressional district, for each political party; and township, ward, and city meetings, county, State, district, and national conventions—for making nominations, discussing political questions, adopting resolutions, party creeds and platforms, and appointing committees for the succeeding year or term. The committees call the meetings and conventions; provide for holding them; procure and disseminate documents, addresses, political tracts, and other information among the people; procure and distribute tickets at the polls; and do various other things, to obtain votes and carry elections—some of which honest men will do, and some of which they will not do.

The primary meetings of each party, which nominate township and ward officers, and appoint delegates to city and county conventions, are generally composed of from ten to about fifty persons, who are mostly politicians and aspirants to office, or the friends of aspirants, and seldom comprise more than from five to twenty per cent. of the voters of the party, for which they assume to act. The county conventions nominate persons for county officers, for the State legislature (in most of the States), and appoint delegates to State and Congressional conventions.

The State conventions nominate persons for State officers and Presidential electors, and appoint delegates to national conventions. Thus the system of party machinery is complete—all depending upon the action of the little handful of party politicians attending the primary meetings, and upon the delegates to county conventions, appointed by them—the most of the voters having no voice in selecting the candidates, or adopting the creed of either party.

The primary meetings are attended by so few persons, that it is generally easy for two or three leaders to rally their friends, and secure the appointment of such delegates as they wish; and conventions are easily packed, to procure the nomination of men, who could not be nominated by the voice of the party, fairly expressed.

It is not generally difficult for a shrewd politician, by the free use of money, and the employment of agents in several towns and wards, to rally his friends and procure the appointment of a sufficient number of friends as delegates to the county, city, or district convention, to secure his nomination for such office as he may desire. This is often accomplished, by the expenditure of considerable sums of money, and the profuse use of promises. *The process is called packing a convention.* Nominations to Congress and other offices are often secured in the same manner—by the expenditure of large sums of money; the profuse use of promises and pledges to support the applications for office of a large number of active politicians, as a compensation for *their* services; and by packing conventions.

By the caucus and convention system, everything is arranged in secret by a few leaders, without any public discussion in convention, of the resolutions presented, or of the merits or relative merits of the candidates named; and when they come to vote, a silent vote is cast, without any reasons being assigned. Conventions come together simply to record the decisions of the leaders, when they are united; and to determine by vote, which faction or section is the strongest, when they are divided.

SEC. 4.—*Corrupting tendencies of bad party practices and theories.*

Looking at the usages of political parties as they are, many politicians conclude that there is very little (if any) honesty in politics; that it is mostly brag and bluster, false pretences and sophistry, bribery and corruption—to get votes, promote party success, and carry elections; and that as their opponents resort to foul and corrupt means to secure success, it is necessary for them to do likewise. Partisans on both sides, reason and manage in the same way.

Regarding politics as a game, partly of chance and partly of skill and management, and starting with the proposition that no one has any inherent natural or legal right to office—except by virtue of an election or legal appointment; politicians easily persuade themselves that no wrong is done to any man, or class of men, when their party are enabled to carry an election by false pretences and sophistry, deception and trickery, or by a perversion of law, in excluding or admitting voters.

Political partisans often justify themselves, and quiet their consciences, in practising deception and falsehood, and other corrupt means, to promote the success of their party, by alluding to the fact, that their opponents do likewise; that to do so is sanctioned by custom, and necessary to success. Criminals of all grades reason in a very similar manner, to apologize to themselves, for their crimes.

The bad practices of each party tend to corrupt the other; and unless some remedy can be devised, to correct the corrupt practices and evils which have grown up under our system of party organizations, nominating conventions and caucuses, and electing public officers, there is great danger of such wide-spread corruption and distrust of all public officers, and of legislation and the administration of law, that we shall sink into anarchy, and a chronic state of revolution and civil war—as Mexico has done.

SEC. 5.—*Objects and purposes of party organizations, creeds, and platforms.*

The first and most obvious purpose of party organizations, is to furnish the machinery to bring together delegated conventions, to nominate candidates for office; and secondly, to work the machinery and carry on political campaigns effectively,—to secure party success at elections. The machinery consists of a series of committees, primary meetings, caucuses, and nominating conventions, —comprising National, State, County, City, Township and Ward committees, meetings, and conventions. The most effective and legitimate means of operating upon public opinion and upon voters—to secure party success, are party creeds and platforms, mass meetings and addresses, and the dissemination of political tracts and documents, public speeches and newspapers. But in addition to this, a large amount of *intrigue, trickery and fraud are practised, through the agency of such machinery.*

Party leaders, deeply imbued with ambition and party spirit, desire an organization, frequent meetings and addresses, a party creed and a political faith, and also the establishment of some political dogmas—to distinguish them from other political parties, and to unite their friends and followers, and stimulate their zeal. By such means they can determine what should be recognized as political orthodoxy, and are enabled to restrain freedom of opinion and individual liberty, from endangering the unity of the party; and they can also maintain rigid party discipline, and confine the patronage of the party to the most zealous and active of the faithful; one of the main objects of party leaders being to secure party zeal and fidelity,—and activity and capacity to promote the success of the party, rather than the best interests of the country;—moral character, qualifications and fitness for office, being very generally regarded by them, as matters of secondary consequence.

Another object is, to enable them to reason from party creeds and dogmas, and to appeal to partisan prejudices, —to alarm the fears of their followers for the success of their opponents, to keep them faithful to party nominations, and prevent them from straying from the party fold. Instead of seeking after truth, and appealing to a healthy public sentiment, party leaders very generally reason from party dogmas, and appeal to partisan prejudices. A still further object is, to form public opinion, and to educate and mould the public mind, in accordance with the creed and dogmas of the party,—in order to secure permanent success, and party domination. The objects are mostly selfish, rather than patriotic—to promote personal and party aggrandizement, more than the public good; and yet they cannot be dispensed with, until we have a change in our electoral system, and its defects are supplied.

Sec. 6.—*The party cry of principles, not men, is delusive.*

Party men often raise the cry of principles, not men—to induce voters to support candidates whom they know to be extremely selfish, unscrupulous, and not very honest

—and console themselves with the delusive idea, that they go for principles, not men, and that the only way to promote the success of their principles, is to vote for the nominees of their party.

The true rule is, to go for principles and men of principle, character, and fitness. Principles cannot be carried into practical effect, without men; and selfish, ambitious partisans, who have but little regard for honesty, can pervert and bend to their own selfish purposes, the principles of any party. Honest, patriotic, public-spirited and fair-minded men, who are not violent partisans, will discharge their duties faithfully; and the public interest will seldom suffer in their hands—even if their political principles are not in all respects sound; but no confidence can be safely reposed in a dishonest and ambitious man—no matter what principles he may profess. A dishonest man will frequently use the power vested in him as a public officer, to promote his own personal interest, or the interest of his friends—regardless of justice and the public good. Such men can be swayed by bribery, favoritism, and the expectation of personal benefits to result to themselves, when they think detection and exposure are impossible, or very difficult and improbable.

When unfit, dishonest, or reckless and unscrupulous men are nominated for office, no man should vote for them because they were nominated by his party, and profess the same principles that he does. Dishonest men have no regard for principle, and it is of no consequence what they profess. Voters should not support such nominees, but cross their names off the ticket, and insert better names from the ticket of the opposite party, if there be such, or put on names not in nomination, or vote in blank—to show their disapprobation of the nominees. There is no other way to save a country from official corruption, and abuse of power. *Men should not delude themselves with the idea that they are supporting their principles, when they are voting for ambitious politicians, who have no principle.*

The object of the cry is, not principle—but to acquire power and patronage, and the emoluments of office.

The general principles which usually divide great political parties, have very little bearing upon the duties of subordinate executive offices, or upon local legislation; and hence the questions which should be propounded in relation to all candidates for office, are those suggested by Mr. Jefferson: Is he honest? is he capable? is he faithful to the constitution? These questions should be propounded and answered in the affirmative, in addition to the usual question—Does he belong to our party?

The masses of the voters in our country can have no reasonable expectations of deriving any personal benefit from office, or public contracts and jobs, and are interested in the election of good officers and in good government; and yet they are so blinded by party spirit, and deluded with the idea that their own good and the public good also, is inseparably connected with, and depends upon, the success of their party, that they often support men whom they know to be personally selfish and dishonest, or otherwise unfit for the stations they aspire to. They deceive themselves with the idea, that *they go for principles—not men;* and that it is better to elect bad men who have sound political principles, than good and honest men, whose political principles are not in all respects sound. Deluded mortals! They do not seem to know, that there is generally very little difference between the political principles which govern the two great parties of our country; and that the principal difference between them, consists in the difference between two or three of the leading measures advocated by them respectively. Such political delusions, generated by party spirit, are productive of very evil consequences.

When political partisans flatter themselves that they go for principles, not men, they mean *political principles and partisan expediency—not moral principle.* Moral principles are very generally well ascertained, and certain in their character; while political principles are very uncertain in their nature. Men may easily deceive themselves in relation to the latter; and are often misled and governed by very unsound principles. Those who disregard moral principle, to follow an assumed political principle, very generally follow false principles, and not sound principles of any kind. When a rule of action, in accordance with assumed political principles, is not in harmony with moral principle, the assumed political principle must be more or less unsound; and when electors vote for dishonest and bad men for office, under the assumption that they are going for principle, because the persons voted for are nominees of their party, they deceive themselves. Extremely selfish, dishonest, and bad men, generally have no regard for principle of any kind, either political or moral; and "*when the wicked rule, the people will mourn.*"

All or nearly all the differences between the great political parties of our country, during the last century, have related to our national government and foreign affairs, national policies and slavery. There have been no differences, or rarely any, involving questions of principle, in matters of local government. Local elections generally involve no differences of principle between the political parties of the day, but merely preferences for men; and hence as a general rule, in local elections, the questions should be as to the honesty and fidelity to the government, and the qualifications and fitness, of the candidates—without much reference to their partisan associations. But to keep their party organized, party leaders strive to draw party lines closely at local elections—on account of the influence which local elections and local officers have upon State, Congressional, and Presidential elections. The leaders endeavor to impress upon their followers the duty of voting for the party candidates as a matter of political principle—often at the sacrifice of moral principle—when in fact there is no political principle involved in the election—nothing but moral principle, the differences in the character and fitness of men, and party policy. Religious and moral men should always look to the character of the candidates they support for office. There is less difference between political parties than is generally supposed; and more importance should be attached to the character, qualifications, and fitness of candidates—and less to party associations and party creeds, than has been, heretofore.

SEC. 7.—*Both parties should be represented upon every administrative, corporate, and election board of officers.*

To secure fairness and impartiality, it is necessary that each party should be represented upon every board of officers; and this can be done only by the representation of minorities, as well as majorities.

All prudent persons wish to live in harmony with their personal and partisan friends; which they cannot do, in the present state of partisan organizations and feeling, if they express their opinions freely, in criticizing the measures and policies of their party, and party friends. To oppose any party measure is generally regarded by party leaders as an unpardonable offence; and even to question the propriety of a party measure, tends to lessen a man's influence in his party, and often subjects him to attacks and abuse from his party friends.

Members of the same party, associated together on boards of directors of corporations, and on election and other official boards, are, from prudential considerations and delicacy, very generally disinclined to oppose each other, or to express their opinions freely of any scheme, measure, or policy presented to promote the interest of their party, however unjust it may be, and inconsistent with the letter and spirit of the law. Such prudential considerations and delicacy very often induce public officers to overlook and wink at acts and iniquities perpetrated by their partisan associates, which they would expose and denounce at once, if committed by their opponents.

When all the members belong to the same party, abuses of power, frauds and iniquities, are often cloaked and concealed, because the persons who disapprove them are restrained by partisan and prudential considerations from exposing them; but such is not the case when the members belong to different parties. On the contrary, when men of different parties are associated together as public or corporate officers, they rarely have any false delicacy in expressing their opinions freely, of the acts, measures, and policies of their opponents, and in criticizing them severely. Such expressions of opinion and exposures bring all partisan schemes and official acts before the public, and subject them to the searching eye of the newspaper press and of numerous critics, and to the test of public opinion; which tends to hold party leaders in check, and to deter them from carrying into effect many partisan schemes and contemplated abuses of power.

Secrecy is the cloak of much iniquity and fraud, in public matters, which it tends to foster and encourage;

and hence secrecy in most public matters (except those of a military or police character) should be avoided, and the utmost publicity should be required. Secrecy favors intrigue and fraud, corruption and crime. Fairness and honesty can be secured, only by action open to the public view, and by the publicity of all acts and proceedings of a public character. The utmost openness and publicity should attend the proceedings of courts of justice—of administrative boards of officers—of boards for registering voters, holding elections, canvassing and certifying votes, and of all legislative bodies and councils and committees.

To subject the acts and proceedings of all such official boards, as well as legislative bodies, to a proper degree of publicity, and to the salutary influence of public opinion, it is necessary that both parties should be represented in each, so that the public may have reports from both sides.

SEC. 8.—*Necessary qualifications of public officers and of voters.*

We want for public officers, honest men. Honesty is the first requisite; and in most situations, nothing will compensate for the want of it.

2d. We want patriotic men, who can overlook personal considerations and the success and interest of party, and devote their minds and energies to the faithful discharge of their duties, and to the promotion of the best interests of the country. An honest and patriotic party will be strengthened by the faithful and proper discharge of their duties, by its officers. It is impossible for excessively selfish and extremely avaricious men, to be either scrupulously honest, or very patriotic, and devoted to the public interest. Nor is it possible for a violent partisan, to be practically very patriotic. We should have honesty and patriotism first; and party spirit should come afterwards and be secondary—that the former may temper and moderate the tendency of the latter, to become too strong.

3d. A public officer should have sufficient intellect and acquirements, education, training and discipline, for the place he is to fill, and some practice and experience in the same or some analogous employment or pursuit; and for all the higher offices, men should have a superior intellect, a sound understanding, large acquirements, maturity of mind, and considerable practice and experience.

4th. All public officers should have industry and energy of character, and habits of attention to business, above the common order of men; or else they are not well fitted for their places.

We want for public officers the best of men—taking their intellect and moral character, education and habits, acquirements and experience, energy of character and industry, all into consideration. Such men partisan politicians, caucuses and nominating conventions, generally do not want. They want active, pliable, and devoted partisans. We should have no inferior, nor very common men, in any official station—though it is not to be expected that very talented and experienced men, of large acquirements, can be procured to fill the common and lower offices. More common men, or young and inexperienced men, must fill them. But we want the best men that can be procured for all public stations; and should get rid of a system which ignores moral character and standing, experience and fitness, and regards cunning and tact, activity and partisan servility, as the principal passports to party favor.

Under the most favorable circumstances, and under those only, man is a progressive being; and there is still room for progress, not only in mechanical and natural science, but also in the science of law and government. Our system of government is but an experiment, of comparatively short duration; and as its defects are exhibited in practice, efforts should be made to correct them. We want for legislators, and for all the higher grades of office, wise and prudent, moderately progressive men—who keep pace with the rational progress of the age, but do not run in advance of it. As science, industry, and society progress, law should progress to keep pace with them. We do not want for such offices rash and fanatical reformers, nor men so bigoted to the laws and institutions of our forefathers, that they think it is impossible to change them, except for the worse.

Voters can judge of the fitness of candidates for office, only by their acts and reputation; by their education, pursuits and habits; in a word—by their history. And hence men should be brought forward as candidates, who are known; men who have some antecedents, some history, character, and reputation, among their fellow-men; and men are not qualified to vote properly, unless they have some knowledge or reliable information, of the education and character, of the pursuits and habits, and of the history and successes or failures, of the men whose names are presented for their suffrages.

In an elective system of government like ours, where the most of the officers are elected for short periods of time, the voters should be reading, observing, and thinking men—capable of thinking for themselves, and forming proper estimates of the character, qualifications, and fitness of men for office; and of the candidates, from their own knowledge, or from reliable information of their acts, and history. As a general rule, men should be brought forward who are known, and have a history, not obscure men; and the voters should have some knowledge or reliable information of the history of the candidates, to enable them to judge of their merits and fitness.

Such is the theory of our elective system of government; but unfortunately, by reason of the defects in the modes of nominating and electing public officers, the practice and workings of the system are far different.

SEC. 9.—*Elements of character, which commend men to the favor of party politicians.*

Success being the primary object, and the permanent good and welfare of the country only a secondary consideration with zealous party politicians, they want for public officers, and recipients of party favor, men of pliable temperaments and pliable consciences, who will submit to the dictation and cater to the wishes of party leaders; men of no great firmness of character or fixed principles, but such as habitually swear by the last-published creed of the party; men who have no independence of mind, and who profess no opinions differing in the slightest degree, from the last edition of the party creed; men of versatile talents, and subtle and shining, rather than sound reasoning powers; men who can see no errors in the creed, dogmas and policies of their own party, and no good in those of their opponents; men who are nearly blind to the vices, corruptions, and abuses of power of their own party, and party friends, and keen to detect the slightest errors and misdeeds of their opponents, and to turn them to account; men who are partial to their own party and party friends, as far as they can be, without positively disgracing and destroying themselves; men who are ready to interpret the constitution and laws, so as to favor their own party and party friends, whenever it is practicable to do so; and men who sympathize with the party, in all its acts and measures, creeds and policies. In all these respects, party politicians of all political parties, are essentially alike. They differ in other particulars, but not in these, except in the degree of the strength and intensity of their partisan feelings.

Party politicians generally comprise a majority of nominating conventions; but such is not always the case. Some men go there who have no interest or feeling, but to select the best men, and to promote the public good. Hence nominating conventions generally prefer and nominate for their representatives and standard-bearers, politicians who fully sympathize with them—men of the character indicated in the last paragraph. But such is not always the case. Men of high character, who are not active party politicians, are sometimes nominated, because it is supposed they will poll a strong vote, and draw voters to the party.

Many good men are nominated and elected to office, under the caucus and convention system of making nominations; but the tendency of the system is, to keep nature's noblemen, and all high-toned and conscientious men, in the background, and to elevate to place and power, pliable, trading politicians, of easy virtue. Austere and rigid morals, very rarely commend a man to the favorable consideration of a party caucus, or nominating convention. Good and unselfish men are generally too quiet to be very efficient politicians; while those that are very selfish and ambitious, are usually bold and enterprising, active and energetic, in canvassing for themselves.

SEC. 10.—*Tendencies and effects of party organizations; creeds and platforms, and party discipline.*

Party organizations tend to foster party spirit, a spirit of exclusiveness and intolerance. By means of party creeds and platforms, adopted without debate or much consideration, to fan the flames of class interests, and the prejudices of race and party, and to catch votes, they tend to create and perpetuate artificial distinctions between parties, for mere party purposes. They furnish rules and tests of party faith, by which to determine the fidelity of the members, and to discipline or denounce as unfaithful, those that presume to think for themselves, contrary to the party creed.

Party organizations and machinery have become so complete, party spirit so intolerant, and party discipline so rigid and efficient, that if a party man, having any position or influence, presumes to express opinions differing from the creed or the policy of his party, the party leaders combine against him, charge him with deserting his friends and the principles of his party, and denounce him as a political heretic. Very few men have popularity and strength sufficient to withstand such attacks, and maintain their position. The result is, that most of the public officers of our country are the mere slaves of party and party leaders—without much freedom of action, or freedom of speech—being accustomed and required, to speak and act, in accordance with the creed and policy, and the supposed exigencies of their party; and if they fail to do so, they are usually denounced as traitors.

The New York *World*, after commenting in May, 1869, upon the treatment of President Johnson by the Republican party, said:—

"Two other notable examples of the despotism of party—which, for obvious reasons, we mention together—are William H. Seward and Thurlow Weed. They formed, organized, drilled, and led to victory the Republican party. Yet because, in course of time, they ventured to question the policy which the majority determined to adopt, though continuing to labor for the success of the party, they were promptly ostracized and as bitterly reviled as they had been lavishly praised. Senators DIXON, of CONNECTICUT, and DOOLITTLE, of WISCONSIN, who enlisted in the Republican party when its first call for recruits was sounded; who fought with it and for it throughout the war, when it needed all the help that it could get; who blinked or boldly defended some of its most questionable deeds;—these men, the very moment that they dared to question the wisdom of what was known as the Congressional policy of reconstruction, were branded as traitors to their party, and, almost against their will, were fairly driven into the Democratic ranks. . . .

"What is the moral of all this, but that in American politics to-day, there is no place for middle-men? He who would achieve political success must ally himself with a party, abide by its fortunes, and endorse its policy, whether or not it commends itself to him. There can be no hope for promotion in any other line of action. There was once in England a class of men known as 'trimmers,' who held themselves free to advocate such measures as they might approve of, irrespective of the party in which they might originate. Some such remain, among whom may be mentioned Lord STANLEY and ROBERT LOWE. But, with the enlargement of the elective franchise, party lines are drawn more tightly than once they were. Mr. GLADSTONE, as Chancellor of the Exchequer, allowing freedom of opinion among his followers, was beaten on the Reform bill. Subsequently made Prime Minister he adopted a more vigorous party discipline, and carried the Irish Church bill through the House of Commons by a triumphant majority. To-day, he allows no stragglers in his forces. The day for middle-men is past; the field for those in this country or in England, who would win power without the sacrifice of independence, is closed. Henceforth, the successful men in our politics are to be the partisans who will stick at nothing which is avowed by the party to which they belong."

The torrent of abuse, that was poured out by party friends upon the Republican Senators who voted against the conviction of Andrew Johnson, upon the impeachment trial, was terribly vile and demoralizing.

Party organizations and creeds, and party spirit, tend to magnify the importance of many questions of but little real consequence, and to encourage the formation of immaterial issues, in order to multiply the differences between parties,—to enable them to maintain party lines as distinctly as possible. They lead men to study the success of their party, and their own success connected with it, rather than the interests of the country; to consider every question from a party standpoint; and to regard principally, its bearing upon the future success of the party. In legislative bodies, they induce party leaders to oppose, as a matter of policy, the measures of their opponents,—even if good; rather than lend their efforts to improve and perfect them—for fear they may inure to the future success of their opponents.

Party organizations have become so strong, and their machinery so extensive, far-reaching and powerful, that they dictate interpretations of the constitution, the creeds and political faith of the people, and the leading measures and policies of the government; and in a great measure control the action of the government. They have checked and restrained freedom of inquiry and freedom of thought, freedom of speech and freedom of the press; increased the intensity and violence of party spirit; engendered political intolerance and tyranny; and nearly destroyed all freedom and independence of official action.

Party conventions often nominate and endorse men of bad or doubtful character, and put them upon a level with those of high moral character and standing. By means of the party endorsement the system tends to put all candidates for office upon the same level; the inexperienced upon a level with the experienced; the unqualified upon a level with those of high qualifications; and the tricky, selfish politician upon a level with the honest man. All are put upon the same ticket, and commended as worthy of support. By such means, an artificial character is given to bad and worthless men—whereby they are often elected to important offices; when they could command very few votes, if they stood upon their own character alone,—not endorsed by a political party.

By giving effect to combinations and political management, they facilitate intrigue; tend to multiply aspirants for official stations of all grades—to produce a despicable scramble for office—and to aid in elevating to place and power, men distinguished for craft and devotion to party, who are adroit politicians, and talking men, and often men of bad or doubtful character —in preference to thinking and sound-minded men, of good character. The system tends to the proscription of honest, firm men—as unfit for party instruments, and unavailable for party purposes.

The machinery and influence of party organizations, tend to form and mould the opinions of the people, in accordance with party creeds; to form narrow-minded politicians; and to prevent the development of enlarged views, and a high order of statesmanship—which can spring only from freedom of action, freedom of thought, and very mature deliberation. They are inconsistent with the formation of great statesmen, and noble-minded, self-sacrificing patriots. The great civil war through which our country has passed, developed and formed some great commanders; but very few statesmen have been produced in our country, during the last forty years. Under our advanced system of party organizations, and party discipline and intolerance, statesmanship is dying out.

By electing to office, through the agency of party organizations, and subjecting to the domination of such organizations, and to the temptations to bribery and corruption, great numbers of politicians of pliable consciences and easy virtue, and many of bad or doubtful character, the legislation of the country, all the departments of the national, State, and city governments, and nearly all branches of the public service, have been more or less corrupted. Even the judiciary have not always escaped the taint of party influences, and partisan prejudices and partialities; nor even the suspicion of bribery, in some instances. The whole tendency of such a system is, to corrupt politicians and office-holders, and to demoralize the people. If the evil be not arrested, it will undermine and destroy the stability of our government.

Sec. 11.—*Practical Sovereignty—how exercised.*

The practical sovereignty of this country is vested in the dominant party, and is exercised by the leaders, to a very great extent, in committees, party conventions, and caucuses. A few party leaders, at State and national conventions, draw up and submit a series of resolutions—which are adopted by the conventions; generally without any debate or discussion, and without sufficient time for careful examination. The resolutions so prepared and adopted, are received and published as the platform, embracing the outlines of the creed of the party; and any man who presumes to question their soundness, is regarded and treated as unfaithful to the party. Woe be to the candidate for office, or the aspirant to party favor, who does not subscribe to every jot and tittle, of the last platform of his party. It expresses, to some extent, the interpretation given by the party to the constitution; declares the powers of the government in relation to some leading measure, and the policy which Congress and the Administration should pursue; and constitutes, for the time, the *supreme law of the party*—more potent than the constitution itself, or the practical construction given to the constitution—and more obligatory than a decision of the Supreme Court.

Partisan creeds and platforms, adopted hastily, and with but little consideration, merely to unite the party and get votes, exercise a very pernicious, and often dangerous influence over the action of Congress and State legislatures, and over the action of the President also—on the one hand restraining their action, and on the other impelling them on, to devise and carry into effect extreme party measures—sometimes of a revolutionary and dangerous character.

The New York *Weekly Times* of May 9th, 1868, very truly said: "The practical *working of our Government is simply a Government of parties. It is the will of the dominant party—not the will of the people—which controls and directs public affairs. Those of the people who do not belong to the dominant party, have no more voice in the Government, than if they lived in France or Algiers.* They are aliens—not in view of the law, but in view of the actual government of the country. A necessary result of this is, that *the officers of the Government must be agents of the dominant party;* and if they cease to be such agents, if they attempt to act for themselves instead of for their employers, they must be got rid of."

On referring to the appointment of Robert Lowe, as Chancellor of the Exchequer of England, in December, 1868, notwithstanding he had opposed the policy of the Liberals on the reform bill, the *New York Times* said:

"Yet Mr. *Gladstone appreciates so highly his talents and the influence which they give him*,—and would so much rather have him for a friend than a foe,—that he tenders him the very best position in the Cabinet, under his incoming administration. . . .

"Mr. GLADSTONE is evidently under the *impression that the strength of a party does not consist wholly in the number of its votes—that talent, debating power, sagacity, and high personal character, still count for something, even to a party which is largely in the ascendant.* We have got over all such obsolete ideas in this country. When a party has a large majority of votes—it can do anything it likes. It needs nobody's support—*and scorns to look outside its own party lines for help.* All it has to do is, to feed its own followers well, and see to it that *not even the smallest 'nubbin' of patronage falls to anybody who is outside the party fold.*

"In this country *party is the ruling power.* The Government is nothing but the party. Whatever aids the party, aids the Government. The only proper and legitimate mode of aiding the Government, therefore, is to aid the party. Whatever does that is all right; whatever don't do that is all wrong. This fundamental principle of popular government evidently has not yet penetrated the British mind. *Parties in England especially, think it worth while to conciliate the confidence and support of their opponents, as well as of their stanch supporters.* The *general sentiment of the whole country, seems to them worth something;* and they try to get it on their side.

"This will probably be regarded as proof of the slight progress England has actually made in the science of party government, in spite of the Reform bill, as compared with the United States. That the party which is successful in the election, and which thus has absolute control of all the patronage and power of the Government, should actually give a high position to a man who refused to go with it, on a cardinal measure of party policy, shows how little that party knows of the *cardinal maxims of party rule, or the real secrets of party strength!*

"If such things are to be done with impunity, what becomes *of the well-known principle,—adopted now by all parties in this country,—that 'to the victors belong the spoils?'* How can a party be expected to maintain itself, if it is to be thus cut off from the full breasts of Government patronage? What encouragement have politicians to work for a party victory, if they see so large a slice of its rewards coolly handed over to a renegade,—to one who deserts the party because he cannot endorse its acts? *What right has any party man to a judgment or a conscience of his own? What business has he to 'set up for himself,' —to act upon his own convictions of duty,* instead of following in the train of his party,—content to obey its behests, and to ask no questions?"

Should a legislator or other public officer regard his official oath; or should he submit to the dictations of party caucuses, and party leaders?

The modern mode of legislation, in the State legislatures, as well as in Congress, is, for the members of the dominant party to meet frequently in caucus—to discuss matters of party policy, to prepare and agree upon bills, resolutions, and reports to be acted upon and passed—so that the members of the party may be united, and when the measures are brought up for action in their respective houses, they may be put through by the party leaders, under the party lash, without much discussion—whereby the members of the other party, and the people they represent, are deprived of any substantial participation in legislation.

Such are the methods by which the independent action of legislators and other public officers, is shackled, and by which the substantial practical sovereignty of the country is controlled and exercised—the people having very little voice in it. Are such practices and methods wise and safe, for any country? If not, is there any remedy, and if so, what is it?

The Congressional *coup d'état* of 1867, in springing upon the country, *in obedience to a party caucus*, the first of a series of acts, known as the reconstruction acts, was the most audacious legislative act ever attempted in this country. It not only took the people by surprise, but the audacity of the act produced such a shock of the public mind, as to nearly silence opposition for a time. In its boldness and revolutionary character, it would compare with the acts of the British House of Commons which brought Charles I. to the block, for the purpose of revolutionizing the government of England. *It was a revolutionary act, intended to change the basis of power, and the very foundations of our government*—by conferring political power on three-fourths of a million of colored men and disfranchising half a million of white men—to put the balance of power in ten States, and the absolute control of several of them, permanently into the hands of the negro race.

It should be remembered, however, that the Southern people, under the reconstruction policy of President Johnson, had very generally elected their old secession leaders to their State conventions and legislatures, and to nearly all the most important offices in the rebel States; and while they ratified the 13th amendment to the federal constitution, *they ignored and denied some of the most important civil rights of the negro;* they employed their wits in forging new chains for him, and refused to ratify the reasonable and important provisions contained in the 14th amendment—to secure the civil rights of the negro, and give peace to the country. They showed, in various ways, a rebellious spirit—hostile to the Union and to the new order of things—growing out of the war, and the emancipation policy of the government.

The attitude assumed by the legislatures, leading men, and people of the South, threatened the country with anarchy, and endangered its future peace, as well as the civil rights of the negro race; which alarmed even the most conservative portion of the Republican members of Congress, satisfied them that it would be better for the country to throw the political control of the ten States, then lately in rebellion, into the hands of the negroes, than to allow it to relapse into the hands of the secession leaders, who had once plunged the country into the most terrible war of modern times. The attitude and conduct of the Southern people united the Republican party in Congress, in support of the violent acts known as the reconstruction acts, and formed a strong apology for their adoption; which was approved and sanctioned by a majority of the people of the United States. The advocates of negro equality embraced the measure *con amore*, while the more rational and conservative republicans regarded it as only *a choice of evils*, which party spirit, party organization, and the bad conduct of the Southern people, had forced upon them.

Peculiar and critical circumstances sometimes furnish an apology, if not a full justification, for violent measures. The only legal justification for the reconstruction acts (if there be any), must be based upon the theory that those States, by their own voluntary and revolutionary acts, were *de facto* out of the Union, and while so out, waged war upon the United States and were conquered; and being so conquered, it was just and legal to treat them as conquered provinces or subject territories, and to govern them under the provisions of the constitution in relation to Territories.

There is no such apology for the impeachment and trial of President Johnson, in *obedience to the decree of a party caucus*, for pretended high crimes and misdemeanors. If they had impeached him for a terrible abuse and prostitution of the pardoning power, in pardoning great numbers of murderers, mail robbers, counterfeiters of bonds and securities of the United States, and persons who had been convicted of defrauding the revenue, and of other high crimes and misdemeanors, there would have been good grounds for convicting him and removing him from office. But party passion and ambition blinded the leaders—so that they overlooked the real grounds for impeachment, and the proper means of attaining their ends, and could see nothing clearly but the exigencies of the party.

A special despatch from Washington, published in the Chicago *Tribune*, in May, 1869, says:

"The State Department has just prepared a list of counterfeiters convicted and pardoned during Mr. Johnson's term. The total number of cases was 142. Pardons began with the remission of two sentences on the day of Mr. Lincoln's burial, and the last was on the last day of his term. A list of pardons of those convicted of violating the internal revenue laws shows 91 cases."

Sec. 12.—*The exercise of the appointing power, and party services to be rewarded.*

It is right and proper, that executive officers, invested with the appointing power, should appoint to office their political and personal friends, who are qualified, in preference to their enemies or opponents. They need friends —men in whom they have confidence, who approve their measures and policy, and will aid in carrying them into effect. As a general rule, they should not appoint opponents, who disapprove their policy, and may secretly exert an influence to thwart it. It is therefore expedient, right and proper, that they should prefer their personal and political friends, and appoint them only to office, in preference to their opponents. A public man who does not know who are his friends, or does not discriminate between them and his opponents, will soon be destitute of friends.

But it does not follow, that they should appoint friends, regardless of their qualifications and fitness; or that they should refuse to appoint any, who have not professed to belong to the same party. In this age of general education, there are so many educated and good men, so many who have had a business education and experience, so many professional men, and so many men who have had more or less official experience, that there is no justification nor apology for the appointment of unqualified and unfit men, or men of bad or doubtful character.

There are also exceptions to the general rule, that an administration should make its appointments from its own political friends. Military and naval officers, and civil as well as military engineers, should be appointed for their professional learning, experience, and ability—without much reference to their political or party associations; and men of high character and standing, and eminent fitness for particular stations, who are not active partisan politicians, should be acceptable to either party. The public good would often be promoted by the appointment of such men, without regard to their slight party affinities. They always make good officers, and faithfully carry out the measures and policies of an administration, and give them a fair trial. It is upon the same ground that the most of the experienced and faithful bureau officers and clerks at Washington, are generally retained in office, when a different party comes into power.

There has been a great cry against party appointments, and removals from office, to make room for such appointments; and there is much reason for the cry against the party abuse. But the evil does not consist in such appointments, when proper and good men are appointed, to fill vacancies. It consists in *the appointment of unqualified and unfit or bad men—because they have been active partisans, and to reward them for party services.*

The American people do not believe in a life tenure of office of any kind; and hence the most of our federal officers are appointed for only four years, and at the end of their term, there is no wrong nor evil arising, in most instances, from filling their places with other good men, equally well qualified, except as to experience—which they will acquire in a few months.

To have two armies of politicians, nearly all of them aspirants to office, or for public patronage, contracts, or jobs, operating upon the public mind in various ways, for weeks and months before a contested election, with the hope and expectation of being rewarded for their services, if their party succeed, must necessarily have a very corrupting influence; and induce much falsehood and deception, intrigue and fraud—to carry elections. *Hence it has a corrupting influence to appoint men to office, as a reward for party services. Men should be appointed for their political principles, party affinities and fitness; and not as a reward for their partisan services. They should be appointed for what they are, and what they are capable of doing for the public; and not for what they have done for a political party.* But with the present electoral system and party organizations, the evil cannot be avoided. It is inherent in the system. We should change our electoral system, and get rid of party committees and party caucuses, party nominating conventions, and all the present party machinery; and let the people select their candidates for office, and elect their own rulers, without the dictation of party committees, caucuses, or conventions; and then we should not have many partisan services to reward. An administration would then come into power, with but few persons claiming appointments, as rewards for party services; and at liberty to bestow the patronage of the government, upon the best and most fit men of their party.

In this age of general education and pretty general extravagance, in which prodigality has become so very common as to demoralize great numbers of our people, and tempt them to acts of dishonesty, there are perhaps ten men fitted for office, where there is one such of rigid honesty and true moral courage; both of which are necessary to render men safe depositaries of power in important situations. There is no great difficulty in procuring educated men, of experience in business, who, with practice, can soon make reasonably good officers—if men of easy virtue be acceptable, and no regard be paid to honesty and moral character. The difficulty is, in uniting honesty, energy, and firmness of character, with other qualifications and experience. Our system of elections and party organizations has an unfavorable influence upon the character and honesty of politicians, which increases the difficulties of filling the executive and administrative offices of the country, with good, honest, and well-qualified men.

But with all the evils attending our present system, and

the cry against the abuse of the appointing power, it is safe to say, that the appointing power is exercised with more care and discretion, and with more regard to the character, honesty, and qualifications of the appointees, and the public good, than is used in making nominations for elective offices; and that, as a general rule, the class of men appointed to offices are quite as good, and perhaps better—and quite as honest, as those elected. When appointees show themselves unqualified or inefficient, neglect their duty, or are even suspected of dishonesty, there is generally an outcry against them from some quarter, and they are very soon removed; but an election by the people is regarded as an approval of ignorance and inefficiency, neglect of duty and abuse of power, and any dishonesty short of bribery, stealing, or embezzlement of the public funds.

Some attach great importance to a system of competitive examinations of candidates for appointments, by commissioners appointed for that purpose; and by giving the Senate a check upon removals from office. But it does not appear to me that much good cán arise from such machinery and checks to executive power; and certainly some evil would spring from it. The main difficulty is, to obtain men who unite honesty and fidelity, and firmness of character, with sufficient acquirements and business qualifications. If such commissioners could examine candidates phrenologically as well as intellectually, and ascertain their grade of honesty with as much accuracy as they can their intellectual capacity and acquirements, such a system would be invaluable. But you cannot determine by any such means, whether a man be trustworthy or not. All you can judge from is his previous acts and character, habits and associations. You never need look for scrupulously honest men, among gamblers, gambling speculators, idle and prodigal, or extravagant and fast men.

Some mistakes will be made in making appointments under any system; and if there be any reasonable ground to suspect the honesty or fidelity of a public officer, he should be removed at once. Any check to executive power in making removals, will aid in keeping bad men in office, and tend to encourage dishonesty. The power of removal has a salutary check upon appointees, which does not exist in relation to elective officers.

SEC. 13.—*Differences of race and language, religion and manners, are all sources of clannishness and discord.*

Sameness of race and language, origin and national history, manners and customs, moral sentiments and religion, are all bonds of sympathy and union, between individuals and communities; and generate preferences for them over those of a different race and language, or who profess a different religion. Where persons of the same race and origin, language and religion, associate mostly together, but in their pursuits and business are thrown into contact with persons of a different race and religion, their associations with each other beget mutual sympathies, and induce a clinging together, which is properly denominated *clannishness.* On the contrary, their business and industrial intercourse with persons of a different race and language, or different religion, is generally of a formal character, and excites no feelings of sympathy. It is mostly an intercourse of men with men; and not a social intercourse between families—in which both sexes participate, for social enjoyment. It is not an intercourse which often leads to marriage between persons of different race, language, or religion. Where such differences exist, there is, very generally, too little sympathy between the sexes, to induce marriage, or to render it either agreeable or desirable; and hence, with the wonderfully mixed population of the United States, perhaps ninety-nine hundredths of all the marriages, are between persons of the same race, language, and religion. There is so little difference between Protestants, that persons of different Protestant sects, of the same race, do sometimes intermarry; but even such marriages have their discords and disadvantages.

The word clannishness is used as a common and expressive term, to express the preferences of people of the same race and language, religion and customs, for each other; which leads them to cling together. I do not use it in a sense which ought to be offensive. It applies to Protestants as well as to Catholics; and to Yankees from New England under certain circumstances, as well as to Irish and Germans, Scotch and English, and other emigrants from Europe.

This spirit of clannishness has affected the settlement of both country and city. The sons of New England and of Ireland, the Catholic Germans and Protestant Germans, and the emigrants from each other nation, have as a general rule, settled by themselves—each occupying nearly whole townships in the Western States, and whole neighborhoods in cities — having their own churches, their own societies and associations, their own peculiar amusements, and in some cases, their own schools. Those that belong to different races, or profess different religions, have but little intercourse with each other, except of an industrial or business character.

It was so in the colonial settlement of the Middle States. The first settlers of New York and New Jersey were Hollanders, and the first settlers of Maryland and Virginia were from England; but there were large and distinct settlements of Germans, comprising nearly whole townships and counties, on the Hudson and Mohawk rivers, in the State of New York, and in Central Virginia as well as in Pennsylvania. The English language and common schools, a common government and the Press, railroads and commercial and industrial intercourse, have melted the descendants of the revolutionary population of the States of New York and New Jersey, into one homogeneous mass; so that, at this day, you can scarcely tell the descendants of a Dutch Burgher, or of a German, from those of the Pilgrim fathers. The spirit of clannishness which existed among them during the revolution, and for two generations afterwards, has disappeared, and no longer exists among their descendants. The spirit has been perpetuated only by immigration from the old world. Even religious antipathies have been softened down, and have nearly disappeared, between different Protestant sects; but can never be entirely extinguished between Catholics and Protestants.

The causes in operation are gradually Americanizing the descendants of European emigrants, who have come to our country during the present century—amalgamating them to a large extent in opinion and feeling, with the American people, and forming a national character for the whole white population; but the sons and daughters of Africa, can never be amalgamated with the white races, and must ever remain a distinct people.

There is no clannishness, (as a general rule) but a cosmopolitan spirit, among scholars and well-educated men —the world over. The more illiterate a people are, the fewer bonds of union they have with races and peoples other than their own, and the stronger their proclivities to clannishness.

The Germans who come to America are mostly an educated people—embracing mechanics of nearly all kinds, farmers and gardeners, merchants and teachers, as well as laborers; and have sufficient diversity of employments, to form communities among themselves, and to live independently, in a great measure, of their neighbors.

The Catholic Irish who come to America, are a very different people from the Germans. Having been oppressed as a people for centuries, the most of them are destitute of any school education whatever, and are poor and dependent laborers, who have made themselves useful in digging our canals, grading our railroads, and doing the most of the common and coarse labor in our cities and villages. But few of them are mechanics, manufacturers, miners, farmers, or gardeners. Though farm laborers, and accustomed to the spade and to farm labor as it is done in Ireland, they are not accustomed to the modes and varieties of American farming; and are not well fitted to make good farmers or gardeners, or to form distinct communities among themselves, as the Germans do. Hence they have mostly collected in the cities and villages, as common laborers, carmen, porters, and keepers of saloons and small shops and stores—very few of them rising to the learned professions, or to the higher grades of business of any kind. By attaching themselves almost universally to one political party, and acting together, they have had a very great influence in that party, in many villages and wards of cities. Having as a race or class of men the least education and intelligence, and being the most prone to intemperance and clannishness of any white race, they have had a disturbing influence upon the politics of our country. In many of the cities, and particularly in the city of New York, they have been charged with having a demoralizing and corrupting influence —by opposing men of high character and standing, and supporting and electing to office many men of low character and standing, and often very unscrupulous men, and men of bad or doubtful character. They have often held the balance of power in a State, and generally given it to one political party. The alleged pernicious influence which they have exercised upon elections, has formed one of the strongest apologies given by leading radical republicans, for forcing negro suffrage upon the country, that the negro vote may balance the Irish vote as well as the rebel vote.

The alleged abuses and inefficiency of the police in New York and some other cities, have been so great, as to form an apology for taking the whole power of appointing police officers and regulating the police, from the local government, and vesting it in commissioners, appointed by the Governor and Senate. It may well be doubted, if police officers and constables elected by universal suffrage, will ever be very efficient.

There has been some clannishness among the Germans; but much less than among the Irish. The former have generally taken a much less active part than the latter, in the politics of the country.

During the last thirty years, we have had party organizations, party committees and caucuses, party conventions and mass meetings in all the States; Irish clubs and clans in most of the cities; German societies and clans in many cities and districts of country; and now we have negro clubs and clans, with negro clannishness at the South, as a still further disturbing political element. What the result will be, nothing but time and experience can determine.

SEC. 14.—*Uses of negro suffrage, and of the exercise of political power by the negro, as an experiment.*

Man's understanding and reasoning powers are so imperfect in their operations, that his theories and political knowledge are never certain and reliable, until they have been confirmed by practice and experience, and verified by history.

Looking at the extension of political power to the illiterate freedmen of the South, by the light of history, it must be regarded as a doubtful and dangerous experiment; but it will have its uses, whether it succeed or fail. It may be useful to other nations, if it injure this. The experiment must be a failure, unless the sons of Africa in the United States have been so improved by climate and circumstances, as to be greatly superior to those in the West India islands.

The disastrous failure of the governments of Hayti and St. Domingo,—the anarchy and insurrections, civil wars and revolutions, devastations and massacres in that unfortunate island, and the experience of Jamaica and other British West India islands, do not seem to furnish evidence sufficient to satisfy many of our people, of the unfitness of the negroes as a race, for the proper exercise of political power. The majority of the dominant party can never be convinced of the weakness of the masses of the negro race, and their incapacity for the safe and proper exercise of political power, until the experiment has been fairly tried under the most favorable circumstances, and proved a failure. Nor can the pro-slavery portion of the democratic party ever be convinced that the negro has any capacity for self-government, until the fact has been established by experiment. Nothing but experience and practice, under the most favorable circumstances, and during a period of sēveral years, can test fairly, and determine, to the satisfaction of all reasonable men, the strength and weaknesses,—the capacities and incapacities, of the negro race; and their fitness or unfitness for entire self-government, and the exercise of political power.

Such is the confused state of public opinion upon the subject, that it seems necessary to try the experiment. If the experiment prove entirely successful, all will be well; opposition to the measure will gradually disappear; and a great and new principle in our system of government, universal manhood suffrage, will be established. If the proposed Fifteenth Amendment to the constitution be adopted, and the experiment fail, there will be a terrible reaction upon the subject, which will sweep the radical negro-equality party out of existence, and a violent agitation will be commenced, to repeal the obnoxious amendment, and amend the negro constitutions of the South; and the agitation will be continued, until the objects are attained, or we are again involved in civil war.

There is a large number of educated colored men at the South, from one-half to seven-eighths white, who have inherited a large share of talent from one, two, three or more white ancestors. Some of that class would make good officers; and if the negroes would generally select their leaders from the best and most intelligent of that class, and from white men of the highest standing, and elect them to office; instead of following the lead, and electing cunning and ambitious but illiterate men of the full African type, there would be much less objection to negro suffrage. But the very inception of the system has excited political aspirations in the minds of many of the most illiterate of the race; and the colored voters have generally shown no capacity to discriminate between the educated and the uneducated—between the sound-minded and good on the one hand, and the visionary and reckless on the other. A spirit of clannishness has often excited the suspicion in their minds, that none but full-blooded negroes, as illiterate and poor as themselves, fully sympathize with them.

Negro suffrage has been forced upon the white inhabitants of the eleven seceding States, and established by their new constitutions,—formed under the reconstruction acts of Congress. Let the experiment be fairly tried; and if it should prove a success, it will be time enough then, to force it upon the States that have refused to incorporate it into their State constitutions. The public good does not require that it should be forced upon them now, and firmly established, by the adoption of the proposed Fifteenth Amendment to the federal constitution.

SEC. 15.—*Party committees and political societies and clubs, and their influences.*

Party committees not only call party caucuses and conventions, and make arrangements for holding them and carrying on political campaigns; but they discuss, and often agree upon nominations in advance, present them to the conventions, and secure their adoption; and in a great measure direct and dictate the proceedings of such conventions—so that the most of the delegates of the party have but little influence in them. Such committees sometimes exert considerable influence upon legislation for partisan purposes. They exercise great influence with the appointing power, in making removals as well as appointments to office; and especially in the appointment of the assistants and subordinates of collectors of customs, marshals, postmasters of cities, and other officers. They also exercise an influence upon the letting of government and municipal contracts and jobs. In all such matters, *they assume to dictate what the interest and success of the party requires;* and their recommendations are often received as if they had the right to dictate.

If such committees were always composed of clear-headed, high-minded, and disinterested men, who had no personal nor improper ends, to attain by their action, their influence would be good; but zealous partisans and aspirants for office, do not wish, and will not have such men appointed—they want strict party men, politicians who belong to their clique or coterie, and will favor them and their friends; and hence such committees very generally use their influence to secure nominations and appointments, contracts and jobs, only for the members of their own clique or ring, and their immediate friends and dependents, without regard to the public good. Party committees and caucuses have been hotbeds of ambition and faction, as well as of intrigue and corruption.

Public officers act under the sanction of an official oath, and are responsible for their acts; which must soon be known to the public, and be subjected to the criticisms of the newspaper press, and to public opinion. On the contrary, party committees do the most of their acts, make recommendations, write letters, and exert their influence, in secret, and unknown to the public. They act in secret, without the sanction of an oath, and cannot be made responsible for their acts; and hence the people have no such check upon them, as they have upon public officers. Their influence is great, and sometimes good; but often very pernicious.

In the large commercial cities of New York and Boston, Philadelphia and New Orleans, there is a large corps of federal officers, and an army of local officers also; and if one party has the control of the State and local government, and the other of the national government and its patronage, the committees of each party exercise great power and influence. Jealousies and divisions are apt to arise from the exercise of power by such committees, in the division of the spoils,—where the patronage is large. The Republican party in the city of New York has been divided for some years—each division having its committee known as the Radical Committee and the Conservative Committee. The Democratic party has also been divided, and had its Tammany Hall Committee, and its Mozart Hall Committee, and sometimes a third clique or faction, with its committee.

The character and influence of such committees may be judged of by what the Press, and particularly the Press of their own political party, say of them. The New York *Times* (semi-weekly), of July 27, 1869,—referring to remarks of several other Republican papers of the State, in relation to the Republican committees in the city of New York, says:—

"They have expressed the all but universal feeling in regard to the condition of the party here,—the mismanagement which has *weakened and disgraced it, and the intolerable pretensions of the men who in its name assume the right to regulate conventions and nominations according to their pleasure.* . . . . While divisions lasted, the consequences of mismanagement were ascribed to the conflict between 'Radical' and 'Conservative,' rather than to the true cause. But with the pretext for division, forbearance toward its promoters has ceased. *The infamy as well as the impolicy of the squabble for office, which has been carried on by rival committees, has attracted attention* to the character and aims of the individuals composing them. . . .

"But one course can be advantageously followed. *These city committees must be swept out of existence, and a new organization effected, that will command the respect and confidence of city Republicans, and enable them to develop the full measure of party strength.* It is idle to talk of compromise in the premises. The present committees, 'Radical' and 'Conservative,' are simply nuisances, *kept up for the purpose of enabling certain men to acquire plunder. They are corrupt from beginning to end.*"

The same paper, of July 30th, says:—

"'What we want, as a party, above everything else, both in the city and country,' remarks the Newburg *Journal*, 'is a little *more honesty among leaders, and toleration everywhere.*' The truth could not be more tersely stated. The party in this city has *been run in the interest of combinations of individuals, who, by sheer impudence and pertinacity, have secured from successive conventions an indorsement of their pretensions.* Of *bonâ fide* title to leadership they have not a particle. Neither by ability nor character, neither by service nor by the possession of popular respect, are they justified in claiming the prominent positions they have held. *By persistent bullying and intriguing, however, they have contrived, year after year, to be intrusted with the party management, and this power they have used for corrupt personal purposes.* The welfare of the party has not entered into their calculations. The effect of their action upon the reputable members of the party and upon the popular vote, they have not cared to consider. It has been enough that, invested with the symbols of party authority, *they have carried on a system of bargain and sale;* so that while the city Republican vote has steadily declined, *their opportunities for carrying on the traffic in offices and plunder, have continued undiminished.*

"Now, the ability of these schemers and jobbers *to manipulate conventions* and promote their own ends has been in good part derived from the prevalence of an intolerant spirit. . . . . We have seen in this city the most *trustworthy Republicans branded as enemies, and their excommunication demanded, simply because they refused compliance with the sinister requirements of ward politicians,* who care nothing for the party except as an *agency for distributing offices.*"

Such are the remarks of one of the most candid and reliable papers in the United States; and there is no reason to doubt the correctness of its views. Selfishness and party spirit generally rule supreme, in such committees.

The numerous forged naturalization papers procured and used at elections, and the common practice of certain classes of reckless men, repeating their votes, and voting in several wards of the same city—by the procurement of Democratic committees, shows that they have been still more corrupt than the Republican committees. More corrupt, because they have had more material, and more pliable material, to operate upon—to carry elections; and more facilities to perpetrate fraud—having a unanimous election board on their side, in nearly all the wards of the city.

The Columbian Order, or Tammany Society, was formed about the year 1790, and was designed as a patriotic political league or society, to sustain the State institutions, and resist the supposed tendency to concentration of power in the federal government, and preserve the balance of power between the federal and State governments. Mr. Hammond, in his history of political parties in the State of New York, says: At first "there was no party politics mixed up in its proceedings. But when President Washington, in the latter part of his administration, rebuked self-created societies, from an apprehension that their ultimate tendency would be hostile to the public tranquillity, the members of Tammany supposed their institution to be included in the reproof; and they almost all forsook it. The founder William Mooney and a few others, continued steadfast."

Perhaps the great political power and influence exerted by the affiliated societies and clubs of Paris, suggested the idea of using the Tammany Society for party purposes; and Colonel Burr and his friends used it with effect, to operate upon the Democratic party, and upon elections in the city of New York. When it was incorporated I am unable to say; but it has long been an incorporated institution, with the usual powers of a corporation, including power to hold property, and have a hall to meet in. Its corporate powers gave it a more complete organization; and its hall and other property served as a nucleus to hold the society together, and make it permanent. I am not aware that any other society for political purposes, has ever been incorporated in the United States. The tendency of such societies is to increase the power of their officers and leaders, and to promote the aggrandizement of the members, without regard to the public good; and it is scarcely possible to promote the public good, by giving them the powers and privileges of a corporation.

The Tammany Society has exercised great power and influence in the Democratic party, and over nominations, elections, and appointments to office in the city of New York, for nearly three-fourths of a century;—which has often given the party the balance of power in the State, and the control of the State government, and sometimes given it the balance of power in the United States. But the loyal leagues, established of late years by the Republicans, have been so numerous and well organized in the most of the States, have acted in such perfect harmony and concert, and their influence has been so extensive—

pervading almost every district in the United States, that they have been an overmatch in the Union, for Tammany Hall, whose powers are local. The Tammany Society and its officers and committees have also exercised great influence over the legislation of the city, and of the State, so far as it relates to the city, as well as over public contracts, jobs, and the local administration.

The influences of party committees and political societies, are generally selfish, and very rarely disinterested, pure, and patriotic. They are designed to promote the success of a party, or the interest and aggrandizement of a member or members of the party or society; and the general good of the country is seldom considered. They answer for war, and for revolutionary and military purposes, better than for peace.

It is very desirable, that our system of elections should be so amended and reconstructed, that party committees and nominating conventions, party machinery and political leagues and societies, may all be rendered unnecessary, and dispensed with—as not consistent *with a free and unbiassed* exercise of the elective franchise; nor with the right of the people to choose their own rulers; nor with a fair and upright administration of the government. The people have more reason to repose confidence in responsible public officers, either elected or duly appointed, and acting publicly, under the sanction of an oath, than in irresponsible party committees and political societies, whose operations are carried on in secret, for party purposes.

SEC. 16.—*The Newspaper Press—its party dependence—intolerance—slander and abuse of public men.*

Nearly all the newspapers in the United States are dependent, for the principal part of their support, upon either a political party, a religious sect, or some particular order or class of men. Such is the violence of party spirit, the discipline of party organizations, and the clannishness of sectarian feeling, that it is very difficult,—much more difficult in this country than in England, to support a newspaper without such aid;—and to obtain it, it is necessary to sacrifice the independence ot the paper and its character for fairness and impartiality, and to make it the servant and instrument, as well as the organ, of a party or sect; and most editors and publishers feel their dependence, and the necessity of conciliation and subservience so strongly, that they make their papers very servile instruments of the party or sect upon which they depend for support.

At the seat of government of each State as well as at the city of Washington, the Legislative and Executive patronage is large, and goes far towards supporting the organ of the dominant party; and in each county, the patronage of the sheriff and other county officers, is very considerable, and contributes largely to the support of the organ of the dominant party in the county. The advertising and other patronage of members of the bar, and of merchants and business men, aids greatly to support the local newspapers; and as a general rule, professional and business men give their patronage whatever it may be, to the organ of the party which they severally prefer. Party fealty is not only expected, but exacted; and if the least independence is exhibited in criticising or questioning the propriety of any of the measures or policies of the party, or any article of the party creed, the patronage of the party, to a greater or less extent, is withdrawn, subscribers fall off, and sometimes a new organ is established to supplant it.

Such is the state of things which makes nearly all our

newspapers, mere party organs, one-sided mouth-pieces—blind and dumb to the merits of the measures and policies of the opposite party—subservient to, and frequently lauding the leaders of their own party, and often shamefully abusive towards the leaders of their opponents. The papers are placed in the same situation as politicians are, who are seeking promotion. *They are not allowed to be fair and impartial, in the presentation and discussion of public questions, partisan measures, policies and platforms;* but are expected and required to paint in brilliant colors, and to magnify the importance of the acts, measures, and policies of their party, and the necessity of its success, to the prosperity and welfare of the country,—and to paint in sombre colors, the acts and policies of their opponents, and the evils which would follow their success.

There is less party dependence, and more independence in many of the papers in large commercial cities, which have a lucrative commercial patronage, than there is usually in country papers. Commercial and business men are more in the habit than farmers and mechanics are, of reading papers of both parties, and of patronizing, as advertising mediums, those that are the most enterprising, and have the largest circulation. By such means commercial and business men become more liberalized in their views, opinions and feelings, and better prepared to appreciate a paper that fairly presents and discusses public questions, and the creeds, measures, and policies of both parties, and criticises and condemns some of those of its own party, and expresses an approval of some of those of its opponents. The *New York Times* and *Tribune*, *Herald* and *Journal of Commerce*, *World* and *Post*, and many others, as well as the London *Times*, are all more independent in their character, and fairer in presenting and discussing both sides of public questions and policies, than party papers, in small cities and villages, are allowed to be. The *World* says:—

"What opening is there for men who, while working with a party, can hold themselves free to criticise its action? There can be but one answer, and that is the Press. Journalism alone offers an opportunity for the exercise of an honest independence, linked with an intelligent support of party. It is a curious fact that, while mere politicians have lost caste with their party associates by declining to accord with them in some points, the influence of journals has increased in proportion as they have shown themselves independent of the mere dictates of party. Mr. Greeley was soundly berated by his party confrères for becoming a bondsman for Jefferson Davis, while the same men at the same time secretly admired as well as diligently read the *Tribune*. As a politician, Mr. Greeley has been unsuccessful; but the *Tribune*, in which all the peculiar vagaries of its editor have found expression, is conceded to be the most influential organ in the country, of the Republican party. On the other hand, the journals which heed the beck of party with unquestioning docility, exert but little influence. The independence which ruins the politician, makes the journal—provided, of course, that the latter display ability, as well as independence."

The reasoning of the *World* applies only to papers in large cities, which have a lucrative commercial patronage, as well as a large circulation; but as the country grows older and the cities increase in size, it will apply to a constantly increasing number; and if party organizations, party committees and nominating conventions, party creeds and platforms, can be dispensed with, the reasoning of the *World* will apply to nearly all the papers in our country, and we should soon have a much healthier state of public opinion and feeling, than we have now.

The organs of each political party have, to a very great extent, been converted into instruments of slander and abuse, to defame the leading men of the opposite party, who are either office-holders, candidates for office, or leading politicians. Our system of elections and party organizations engenders such a violent party spirit, and such jealousies and hatred towards the opposite party and its leaders, that many regard it as the special business of party newspapers to abuse and defame their opponents. The object seems to be, to excite a sensation, and to effect some partisan or personal end, without regard to truth or propriety.

Party organs are made the conduits for pouring upon public men and candidates for office, torrents of abuse and vile slanders, by anonymous writers, and by persons furnishing incorrect information to editors and publishers, —for which the system and party spirit, and not the editors, are properly responsible. They are made the instruments of pouring defamation and abuse upon office-holders and candidates to such an extent, as to lessen greatly the influence of such organs—by rendering it difficult to ascertain the truth, and destroying confidence in their statements.

Such slanders and abuse are almost unknown in English papers, and in newspapers upon the continent of Europe; and they are pointed to by Europeans as evidences of the corruptions of American politics, and of the tendencies of our institutions to corruption and anarchy. There can be no doubt of their demoralizing influences.

The slander and abuse poured out upon public officers and candidates for office, has pernicious influences of various kinds. In three cases out of four, it is undeserved and unjust; and when the statements made have some foundation in fact, the facts are often so exaggerated, distorted and colored, and the explanatory circumstances omitted, that they make false impressions, and really convey more falsehood than truth. The practice of almost indiscriminate abuse, tends to confound the innocent with the guilty, and to enable the guilty to escape in the general confusion—to destroy confidence in party papers—to induce many persons to believe that there is no honesty in public men—to deter many honest and high-minded men from becoming candidates for office, as the only means of escaping newspaper abuse—and to throw the government of our country more and more, into the hands of men who make politics and party management a trade, and their principal study.

A large portion of the corruptions and evils of the press in the United States, results from our system of elections and party machinery; and will be obviated by correcting our electoral system, and dispensing with the most of our present party machinery.

SEC. 17.—*Corporations, and the abuses of power by their officers.*

Corporations other than municipal corporations, religious societies, colleges, hospitals and charitable institutions, were few, and little known, either in this country or in Europe, until within a century past. Prior to the discovery of America, all the great enterprises of the world were carried on by Governments. Now they are mostly carried on in this country, in Great Britain, and in other countries to some extent, by corporations—by joint-stock companies incorporated—by what may be termed private corporations—managed for the benefit of the stockholders; and yet nearly all of them are of a public character, and tend to promote industry and the prosperity of a country.

Being organizations of capital and labor—organized under and in accordance with law, and managed by directors elected by the stockholders, independently of the government and of party politics also, in most instances, they are bulwarks of property and of business—of industrial liberty and self-government. Their business and the property vested in them, being exempt from the arbitrary interference of the government and protected by law—and their business carried on by their own officers, under the control of the directors, they operate as schools, to aid in educating the people in the arts of self-government. When fairly and properly managed, they may be reckoned among the most beneficent institutions ever invented by man; but when selfishly and corruptly managed, they become terrible engines for filching from the public, defrauding their own stockholders, and stimulating gambling speculations in their stocks.

We have in the United States, a very large amount of capital invested in the stocks and bonds of incorporated companies; and the amount is rapidly increasing. The demand for railroads has been so great, during the last twenty years, and railroad corporations have thrown so many bonds upon the market at high rates of interest, to raise the means to construct and equip the roads, that it has had a very palpable effect upon the rate of interest, and raised the rate of interest from six and seven per cent. per annum, to from eight to ten per cent.

The amounts invested in the stocks and bonds of incorporated companies, may be estimated in round numbers, as follows:—

In Railroad Corporations nearly..........	$2,000,000,000
In National, State, and Savings Banks over	500,000,000

In Manufacturing and Mining Corporations	$1,000,000,000
Canal and Navigation Companies about...	100,000,000
Fire, Marine, and Life Insurance Companies over	100,000,000
Gas, Turnpike, Bridge, Water, Telegraph, Express, and other incorporated companies over	100,000,000
Total probably about	$3,800,000,000

—equal to about eighteen per cent. of all the private property in the United States. The amount invested in stocks and bonds of such corporations, at the end of the year 1860, amounted to about $2,500,000,000, and at the end of the year 1850 it did not exceed $1,100,000. The increase in manufacturing and mining corporations as well as in railroad companies, has been very great and rapid. The tendency of the public mind has been and is, to seek the forms and powers of corporations, as the best means of organizing capital and labor, to make them effective.

Though wonderfully efficient agencies of good, when fairly, honestly, and wisely managed, corporate organizations and powers are sometimes productive of terrible frauds and corruptions, and alarming evils, when they fall into the hands of reckless and unscrupulous men, and desperate speculators in stocks. Our system of organizing corporations, and particularly railroad companies, and electing directors,—giving the holders of the majority of the stock combining together, all the directors, and the minority none;—the loose legislation in relation to such corporations;—and the very extraordinary powers exercised by the judges, under the laws of the State of New York, of issuing injunctions and appointing receivers for corporations upon *ex parte* affidavits, without a hearing of the defendants, and without giving bonds to secure the injured parties, in case such injunctions and proceedings are not sustained;—have all contributed to engender tendencies and evils, some of which are of a very alarming character.

1st. They have encouraged and induced scheming and unscrupulous stock-jobbers, to form combinations to buy up the majority of the stock of a company—to enable them to elect all the directors, appoint the officers, and take the whole control of the road and its franchises and rolling stock, its books, business, and incomes; to manage the whole in their own way,—and very often for their own selfish ends, and fraudulent purposes; and to exercise their powers, and use the finances of the company, in secret, and without much responsibility.

2d. By the unity and secrecy of their action, they can use the incomes and credit of the company without check; can issue bonds, new stock and scrip dividends, to almost any extent, for speculative or other purposes; can use the funds of the company to employ lobby agents, to beset legislative bodies, and influence members by means, often corrupt,—to vote for acts, granting improper and dangerous powers, and powers without sufficient guards and checks; can use corrupt means to procure judicial action, and the judgments of some judges; and may, in many ways, deceive and defraud the public, and swindle the stockholders who are not in their secrets.

The management of the Erie Railroad, and some of that of the New York Central during the last three years, and the stock-jobbing operations and judicial action to get and keep the control of these and some other roads, and some of the legislation in relation to them, have been of a very demoralizing character,—tending to destroy all confidence in corporate officers, in legislation, and in some of the judges of the city of New York. They finally culminated in a judicial warfare, mobs and violence—to get control of the Albany and Susquehanna Railroad, and rendered it necessary for the Governor of the State to call out the militia—to keep the peace, and to appoint a superintendent to take charge of the road, until the controversy could be settled, or decided by the courts.

The gross income of the New York and Erie Railroad and branches, has been from fourteen to over sixteen million dollars annually, for some years past. The amount of its stock has been reported in the *Merchants' Magazine and Commercial Review*, as follows:—

End of 1867, Common Stock......	$16,574,300
" " " Preferred "	8,536,910
Total......................	$25,111,210
1869, Sept. 11th, Common Stock...	$70,000,000
" " " Preferred " ...	8,536,910
" " " Total...........	$78,536,910
Increase in two years........	$53,425,300

The funded debt was increased some during that period—being less than $23,000,000 in 1867, and over $23,000,000 in September, 1869. How such an immense amount of new stock and the proceeds thereof were disposed of, I am unable to learn. It is left to a large extent, to the public to conjecture. The management of the affairs of the company, in connection with the issues of new stock, and the disposition of the stock and the proceeds thereof, appear to the public like the most gigantic swindle, which the history of the world presents. The action of the legislature and of the courts, in relation to that company, seems equally extraordinary.

Speculating and swindling officers of great corporations, having large interests and millions of money under their control, have learned the art of procuring the nomination and election of their own friends, for legislators and judges, prosecuting attorneys and sheriffs, and of controlling both legislative and judicial action, by the expenditure of large sums of money. What may not be effected, by the expenditure annually, of millions of dollars, in employing politicians, lawyers and lobby-agents, letter-writers and newspapers—to corrupt, and in corrupting legislators, judges, and jurors, as well as politicians and voters! If large sums of money be used for purposes of bribery and corruption, what frauds and swindling operations may not be committed with impunity, under a partisan elective judiciary, and our lax and defective codes of criminal law! Our system of nominating judicial and executive officers by party conventions and caucuses, and electing them by universal suffrage, has produced in the city of New York, a sort of millennium for knaves and swindlers; and there is great danger that it will gradually weaken and demoralize the administration of justice in most of the States.

There is a lamentable want of honesty in too many of the managing officers and employés of railroad and banking, mining and manufacturing corporations, and of other incorporated companies, as well as in the officers of the national, State, and city governments. Managing officers are too much inclined to cloak and conceal the financial condition and acts of such companies, to enable themselves and their friends to speculate in the stock.

When the interests and usefulness of a corporation require additional legislation, let the officers be paid their travelling and personal expenses for going before legislatures and legislative committees, to procure such legislation. Nearly all other expenditures for such purposes, are corrupting in their nature and tendency, and therefore improper.

Legislation seems necessary to define and limit the powers and duties of directors and other officers—to prohibit the use of corporate funds for improper purposes; to increase their responsibility to the stockholders; to prohibit them from increasing the capital stock, making stock or scrip dividends, issuing bonds or contracting debts, except for current and ordinary expenses, without the action and assent of the stockholders, taken at a stockholders' meeting—to require full and accurate reports to be made annually, or semi-annually, under oath, of the proceedings and business, income and expenditures, and the financial condition of each company—to punish as a crime, any fraudulent act or violation of law, by the directors, or any director or other officer of an incorporated company—and to impose some restrictions upon courts and judges, to issue writs of injunction, and appoint receivers for corporations, upon *ex parte* proceedings. The judges of most of the States, and of the federal courts, have no such extraordinary and dangerous powers. The administration of justice in the city of New York, in relation to railroad corporations, has ceased to command the confidence of the American people, and become a subject of jest and ridicule, as well as of suspicion.

The practice of railroad directors and other officers, secretly issuing millions of stock, and keeping it themselves, or disposing of it to friends, without accounting for the proceeds,—for the purpose of controlling elections of directors and keeping themselves in office, cannot be tolerated much longer in this country. How long shall the corrupt practice continue, of defrauding stockholders of a large portion of the earnings of railroads, and using them to pay lobby agents, bribe legislators and judges, and other corrupt purposes? Stringent criminal laws are necessary to punish such swindling and abuses of power; and more publicity in the management of corporations, is necessary to avoid them.

All corporations have special privileges, and are monopolies to a greater or less extent, except those organized for manufacturing or mining purposes; and the legislature should have some control over the charges of railroad corporations and some others, and should retain power to reduce them as their business and net profits increase—or to compel them to pay into the State Treasury half of their income, over and above a certain percentage, as a substitute for local taxation, and a compensation for their special privileges.

The tendency now is, to consolidations of railroads, and the formation of trunk lines from Lake Michigan, and the Ohio, Mississippi and Missouri rivers, to the seaboard—to enable them to monopolize freights and travel, as much as possible, and to keep up prices, by mutual arrangements between the several lines.

There is reason to apprehend, that the numerous trunk lines with their connecting roads, and the great Pacific roads, with capitals eventually ranging from ten to nearly an hundred millions each, may, at no very distant day, exercise a very dangerous influence over the legislation of many of the States, and of Congress also,—unless public opinion can be more enlightened upon the subject, and laws be passed to define and limit the powers of directors and other officers, with more precision, and to regulate their action much better than it has been heretofore.

SEC. 18.—*Prominent party abuses of power.*

Among the most glaring and corrupting abuses, conceived and devised by cunning politicians, to carry elections, secure party ascendency, or enrich party favorites, are the following:—

1st. Importing and colonizing voters from other States or districts, to vote the party ticket, in towns and wards where the members of the boards of election all belong to the same political party. The ballots of such imported voters are, in such cases, generally received without being challenged; but when challenged, the persons offering them usually swear in their votes—and thus add perjury to fraud, in the full belief that the crime cannot be ferreted out, that the party will protect them, and that they shall escape punishment, and get the reward promised.

2d. Repeating votes—the same persons voting two, three, or more times, in different wards,—and often swearing in their votes, in the belief that their party friends will conceal the crime, and shield them from punishment.

3d. Forging naturalization papers, and voting upon forged papers.

4th. Ballot-box stuffing—putting into the box ballots not voted; and sometimes taking out votes of one party, and putting in an equal number of votes for the other party.

5th. Making out false certificates of the results of elections, and concealing the ballots and the poll-lists—to avoid detection; and sometimes making additions to the poll lists, to make them correspond with the number of votes certified to.

All such partisan abuses and frauds have been frequently practised; and it is impossible to prevent them without registry laws, the careful registration of voters, and the representation of both political parties upon every board of election, and upon every board for registering the names of voters, prior to each election.

The adoption of the general ticket system for the election of Presidential electors, gave an additional stimulus to party efforts to carry elections by fraudulent means, in doubtful States, where a few thousand, or even a few hundred fraudulent votes might determine the result, and give to the successful party all the votes of a State.

6th. Gerrymandering, and other unfair means in forming Congressional, Senatorial, or representative districts—so as to give the dominant party more members than they are fairly entitled to.

Gerrymandering is effected by making irregular-shaped districts, for the purpose of putting together into one, two, or three districts the most of the counties giving the minority party large majorities, and so distributing the other counties giving majorities to the minority party, as to overbalance them in each district, by majorities of the dominant party; and thus give the dominant party small majorities in two-thirds or three-fourths of all the districts in the State.

7th. The perversion of both law and fact, in passing upon cases of contested seats in Congress and in State legislatures—for the purpose of increasing the power and the ascendency of the dominant party.

8th. Legislation has often been used by party leaders, as a means of speculation.

Party domination has led to great abuses in legislation—in Congress as well as in State legislatures—to furnish rich jobs, contracts, and charters, to party leaders and favorites. Granting subsidies in lands and bonds to railroad companies, has been the means of enriching a great number of the leaders and influential men of the dominant party; and there is reason to believe that great speculations and corruptions have grown out of such grants, and in the management of the corporate powers and property granted.

Perhaps no dominant party ever exercised power with more moderation and partisan wisdom than the dominant party in New York did, from thirty to forty years since—

when under the management of what was called the Albany Regency; and yet the legislative power was often used for partisan purposes. Banks were then monopolies; the business of banking was carried on by corporations, under special charters granted by the legislature; and bank stocks were generally from ten to twenty per cent. above par. The legislature chartered from one to three banks annually; appointed party men as commissioners to receive subscriptions for, and to distribute the stock; three-fourths or more of the stock was usually assigned to men of the dominant party—a large share of it to leading partisans, as a reward for party services; the banks were organized, mostly owned, controlled and managed by men who belonged to the dominant party, and were made a means of party power as well as of profit. When money was scarce, party friends were preferred to political opponents, in making loans; which tended to draw, and did draw many business men into the party, as a matter of interest, and prevented others from being active in their opposition to the dominant party.

Railroad charters and stocks were in like manner, though to a less extent, made the means of party power, and of enriching party leaders. No very great evil grew out of that mode of party tactics and use of legislative power. The banks, railroads, and other corporations, were as useful to the people of the State, as if they had been in the hands of the opposite party; but the tendency was corrupting in its nature. More liberty would have been allowed to business men and borrowers, if the banks and banking capital of the State had been more equally divided between the two great political parties of the day. The passage of the general banking act by the legislature in 1838, put an end to the banking monopoly in the State of New York, and to speculations in bank charters and bank stocks, and to the use of the banks, as engines of party power.

It seems to me the public good requires that party spirit should be moderated and party power checked, by a division between parties of all the powers of government, except that of the Chief Executive and the military power; that it is not desirable for one political party to have the entire control of the Executive department and of both houses of Congress, except in time of war, insurrection or anarchy; that legislation should be for the equal good, as far as is practicable, of the whole people, and not for the special benefit of the leaders of the dominant party; and that every legislature, every legislative committee, every election board, and every board for levying taxes, auditing accounts, or administering the affairs of counties, cities, towns or villages, should be composed of men of both political parties—to secure publicity and fairness.

SEC. 19.—*Remedies suggested for political evils.*

There are corruptions and evils incident to all forms of government, which cannot be entirely avoided—because they arise from the natural selfishness of the human heart; and from the imperfections of human nature, in its best aspects. But many of the political evils with which our country is afflicted, arise from the defects of our representative and elective systems; from the outside partisan organizations and machinery, developed to supply the defects; and from the violence of party spirit—fostered and intensified by party machinery, nominating conventions and caucuses, and by party creeds and platforms. Evils that are developed or increased by artificial causes, may be either avoided or mitigated. To do so, it is necessary to supply the defects, and correct the errors of our system, and to moderate the intensity and violence of party spirit. As a means to attain the ends desired, the following changes in our system are suggested:

1st. Give to minorities, as well as to majorities, a representation in legislative and administrative bodies and councils, and also in corporations of all classes.

2d. Allow cumulative voting.

3d. Hold double elections—the first election to be held three or four weeks before the second, to determine who shall be candidates for office, to whom the votes at the second election shall be confined.

4th. Prohibit caucuses and conventions for the nomination of candidates for office.

5th. Go back to the old system of appointing judges and State officers by the Governor of the State, by and with the advice and consent of the Senate; or elect them by a joint convention of both houses of the legislature.

6th. Make the President of the United States ineligible to a re-election, until he has been out of office four years or more—for the purpose of avoiding any temptation on his part, to use the appointing power improperly, to promote his own re-election.

7th. Provide by amendments to the State constitutions, that State senators, sheriffs of counties, constables and police officers, assessors of taxes, and some other officers, shall be elected exclusively by taxpayers, having $250 or or more taxable property.

The mode of arranging representative, senatorial, and Congressional districts, to give minorities as well as majorities a representation, and the subject of cumulative voting and double elections, are presented and discussed in Sections 15, 20 and 21 of the next chapter.

Under our party machinery and present system of electing officers, judges and sheriffs, constables and police officers, are all too dependent for their nomination and election upon non-taxpayers, roughs and rowdies, keepers of whiskey and lager-beer saloons, gambling houses and other places of amusement, to secure good officers, a faithful administration of law and justice, or an efficient police. Men who have no taxable property, and nothing at stake in a community, generally feel very little interest in an efficient police and a good administration of justice. Having no property to protect or to be taxed, their feelings upon political subjects are mostly of a partisan character; and they are not inclined to pay much heed to the moral character of the men they vote for. There is no remedy for such evils, except to require a property qualification for voters, for such officers; or to provide for their election or appointment, otherwise than by popular elections.

Judges may better be nominated by the Governors of the respective States, and appointed by and with the advice of the Senate; or elected by the two houses of the State legislature in joint convention, than to be nominated by party conventions, and elected by the people.

Under our present system of nominating and electing State officers by the dominant party, each has his duties to perform, independent of the Governor, and of each other—the Governor has no authority over them; each acts in accordance with his own individual views, without any policy being established by a Cabinet Council, and without concert of action. The Governor has in fact, no Cabinet Council or confidential advisers; and there is no unity of policy in the executive department of the State governments. To secure to a Cabinet Council, unity of policy and concert of action, it is necessary that the State officers should be appointed upon the nomination of the Governor.

CHAPTER III.

BASIS OF SOCIAL AND POLITICAL POWER—OF GOVERNMENT, AND OF THE ELECTIVE FRANCHISE.—THE VARIOUS SYSTEMS OF REPRESENTATION AND MODES OF VOTING, AND OF NOMINATING, ELECTING AND APPOINTING OFFICERS.—SUGGESTIONS OF OTHER MODES OF REPRESENTATION, VOTING, AND NOMINATING CANDIDATES FOR OFFICE.

SEC. 1.—*Basis of social and political power, and of government.*

THE basis of social and political power and of government, is the same. It is said in the American Declaration of Independence, that *governments derive their just powers from the consent of the governed.* This is not strictly correct. Political power is derived from the same source as social power; and the government of a community or State must have the same source and basis as the government of a family. No one will pretend that the right of the parent to exercise power over and to govern the child, is derived from the consent of the child. From whence is such right and power derived? The answer must be, the power of the parent is derived from the nature and constitution of man, the helpless condition of the child, and its dependence upon the parent. It is derived from the laws of nature, and the necessity of government—to maintain order, and to promote the welfare of the child. The government of States and nations has the same basis;—not the consent of the governed, but the nature and condition of man; the laws of nature established by the Creator; the necessity of law; and the necessity also of government—to make and administer law,—to the end that the rights of individuals may be protected, crimes punished, remedies furnished for wrongs, and peace and order maintained.

It is desirable that the government of a country should be of such a character, and be so organized, as to be sanctioned by the whole people, or nearly the whole; and that the laws and policy of the government should also meet the approval of the whole people; or all but the vicious and criminal,—who cannot be expected to approve proper and rigid laws to restrain vice, and punish crime.

The sanction and approval of the people, or the most of them, gives additional power and stability to a government, and aids greatly in the execution of the laws;—and more particularly those laws that are made to restrain vice and punish crime. But it can hardly be seriously pretended, that it is necessary to have the consent of the vicious, to give validity to law for the restraint of vice, or the punishment of crime.

While the just powers of government are derived from the laws of nature and the necessity of law and government; the form of government must be selected by man, and the distribution of its powers must be determined by him; and they should be so determined, by the best and most intelligent classes of the community. When there are differences of opinion, the majority must, from the necessity of the case, determine the question, in preference to the minority. But a majority cannot rightfully confer upon a government *powers which are not within the legitimate ends and purposes of government, and not necessary to promote the welfare of the people;* and whenever a monarch or an aristocracy, an ecclesiastical body or a majority of the people, exercise extreme powers, not consistent with the laws of nature and with a reasonable degree of human liberty, and therefore not within the legitimate ends and purposes of government, they are guilty of usurpation of power, and of tyranny and oppression.

Consent or election does, or should, designate the officers to exercise the several powers of government prescribed by law, either by human law or custom, or by the laws of nature; but consent alone cannot confer power, and is not the basis of power. If laws be just and proper, the rights of persons who have not consented to them, are not infringed by their execution. If laws be unjust, the fact that a majority of the people may have consented to them, does not alter their character—nor lessen their injustice towards the minority, who have not so consented.

If the validity of laws and of government depend upon the consent of the governed, then females have the same right as males to participate in the government; and to deny them the right of suffrage—to participate in electing officers and in making laws, is gross injustice; and all governments and laws, so far as they exercise power over women, are without any just foundation, despotic, and tyrannical.

If my reasoning be correct, the oft-repeated declaration, that the just powers of government are derived from the consent of the governed, is but an assumption, and does not form a sound basis for universal suffrage.

Sec. 2.—*Intellectual and physical inequalities of men, and inequalities of fortune.*

The influence of the general laws and powers of nature and of mind,—produce great inequalities in the mental powers and capacities of mankind; in their moral characteristics and propensities; in their physical powers and capacities ; and in their powers of endurance. These are inequalities in the constitutions of men ; inequalities produced by the Supreme Being, through the agency of general laws and providences. What God has made unequal, cannot be made equal by human laws and regulations.

Though all men have equal natural rights, (each being entitled to liberty and the products of his own labor and industry)—as the capacities of men are not equal, the fruits of their industry are not equal, and their acquired rights of property are very unequal. If one man, by means of superior strength, activity, or skill, can and does do twice as much in the course of a year as another, and they both spend the same amount, the former may in the course of a quarter of a century or more, become rich, while the latter remains poor. So, if one man, by reason of superior intellect, education, and experience, can direct the industry of twenty others, and make it as productive as thirty such men would be, if they worked separately, or in combination under the direction of any one of themselves—then, in the case supposed, the directing man, by his superior knowledge and capacity, causes an increased production equal to ten common men. This increased production is the fruit of his intellect and superintending labor and attention ; and he is as fairly entitled to it, as the common laborer is entitled to the products of his own industry.

The accidents of fortune also—of good or bad health—of fire and flood—of dearths and fruitful seasons—of the rise or fall of goods and other property, make some rich, and others poor. The natural instincts of parents—planted in them by God, prompt them to give their property to their children. This is not only right in itself, but as a general rule it is a matter of duty, which is sanctioned by the laws and customs of all countries—among barbarians, as well as civilized nations. Hence some inherit wealth, and others poverty. From these various causes the acquired rights and the property of persons are very unequal in every country; though their natural rights may be equal.

SEC. 3.—*Equality—civil, political, and social.*

The watchword of the French Republicans has been, liberty, equality, fraternity. Many in England and also in America, couple equality with liberty, and think the latter is necessarily imperfect without the former. This is a great error. The law may establish civil equality; that is, it may allow the same civil rights to all citizens; it may protect all alike, and may extend the right of voting for public officers to all adult males, and even to females—and so far as the law is concerned, all may be regarded as politically equal; but it cannot make them equal in influence in political matters, and therefore it cannot make them in fact, politically equal. The equality would be only nominal—not real.

In this country, where we have no nobility and no class of persons who enjoy special and superior privileges—except such as are conferred by wealth and official station; the laws make no social distinctions; but they cannot make all persons and classes of persons socially equal. That is impossible.

SEC. 4.—*Civil equality.*

The object of governments and laws is to protect the persons and property, the natural and acquired rights of the whole community, equally. It is not the business of a government to take property from one man and give it to another, in order to make them equal in worldly possessions. Such laws would be very unequal and unjust in their operation; they would tend to discourage industry and economy, and to encourage idleness and prodigality; and would shock the moral sense of mankind.

The words civil equality mean no more than that the law protects equally the rights—both natural and acquired—of all persons; that it protects all in the enjoyment of personal liberty, so long as they do not commit any crime nor offence; that it protects them in their employments and their business; in their contracts and their property; and that it allows them to make contracts, and to acquire and hold—to enjoy and transfer property—and to transmit it to their heirs or friends.

The law regards contracts made voluntarily by adults of sound mind, and not tinctured with fraud, as valid and obligatory—and enforces them. It cannot protect men from improvident and foolish contracts, without violating their civil liberty, and doing in the aggregate more mischief than good. The most it can do is to protect innocent persons from contracts into which they have been drawn by fraud. Equal and just laws protect all classes of persons in the enjoyment of all they can acquire honestly, by contract and business, as well as by labor. And hence equal civil rights—equality before the law, does not imply equality of fortune, political equality, nor social equality. I can see no good reason why colored persons of African descent, should not enjoy civil equality with our white inhabitants—both at the North, and at the South. The rights of citizenship and civil equality are secured to our colored people, by the first section of the fourteenth amendment to the constitution of the United States.

Sec. 5.—*Political equality.*

The phrase political equality means that all adult males of sound mind are allowed the same political rights and privileges—including the privilege of voting for all officers elected by the people. Legislation and the administration of the government being greatly influenced by public opinion, which is formed and guided by men of intellect and intelligence—political equality does not imply that the uneducated and ignorant have or should have, equal political influence with the most intellectual and best-informed men in the country. Nor does it imply that inexperienced and unfit men have the same right to hold and exercise the powers and influence of high offices, as those that have large acquirements, experience, and fitness for such stations. On the contrary, it is an abuse of the elective franchise and of the minority, for a majority to foist upon them unqualified and unfit men.

Nor does political equality extend in this or any other country, so far as to make the elector and the officer elected, politically equal. Governments and laws are necessary to preserve order, and to protect persons and property; and it is necessary to have legislators to make laws, and officers vested with power to execute them. The best qualified men, who are honest and faithful, should fill all public offices—and when duly elected or appointed, they have powers to exercise, and public duties to perform, and are no longer on a political equality with the mass of the people.

SEC. 6.—*Social equality.*

We hear much said in these days, about social equality. It is often said that injustice is done to the poor, because the rich do not invite them to their houses, and associate with them on terms of equality; and great complaints have been made by a large class of philanthropists, because colored people of African descent, are not received into society by our people as equals. All such complaints are based on false conceptions. Social equality never did exist in any country, and never can exist. Even among savages and barbarians, the Chiefs are raised to a social level above the masses of the people.

Social intercourse is purely voluntary. It is nowhere regulated by law; not even in England, nor on the continent of Europe. It is influenced everywhere by custom and public opinion—but by custom which is advisory only, and has not the force of law. In ancient times, the laws of Hindostan and some other Eastern countries forbade intermarriages between persons of different castes—and the early laws of Rome forbade intermarriages between the patricians and plebeians. But all such laws, disappeared in Rome and in Europe nearly two thousand years since, and never existed in our country—except in the case of the laws of Massachusetts, Michigan and some other States, which prohibit intermarriages between white persons and negroes. That is the only legal restriction to social intercourse and intermarriages between persons of different races, which exists in our country.

People meet together socially, to enjoy themselves in social intercourse; to promote their own pleasure or interest—and not for purposes of benevolence—to promote the enjoyments of persons inferior to them in intelligence and social position. In a sparsely settled country and in small villages, there are very few distinctions in society; nearly all meet together in one society, on terms of equality; but in cities and densely peopled countries the case is very different. All cannot unite there in one society; and hence they divide off and form numerous societies, partially separate, but more or less intermixed—association depending on similarity of education and opinions, tastes and conditions of life—sympathies of nationality and race—and on interest and business intercourse.

The educated, intelligent and refined, generally have no motives to associate with the ignorant and rude. They can derive neither enjoyment nor profit from such association. The rich have no motives, as a general rule, to associate with the poor. They have associates enough of their own class, and cannot possibly in cities, associate with all in their vicinity. If they invite the poor to social entertainments at their houses, the latter cannot reciprocate the compliment, and have no means of interesting them. Hence it is impossible for the rich and the poor to associate together on terms of equality. Thousands of people in moderate circumstances have been utterly ruined by ambitious efforts to associate with persons of wealth, and to dress and live in style—to accomplish that object.

Social equality is not in accordance with the natural differences among men, nor with the condition of things in any country. Official station, differences in natural talent, in education and opinions, in nationality, race, and language, in tastes and habits of life, in employments and business, and in wealth and style of living—all naturally tend to form distinctions and divisions in society, and to render social equality impossible. To these may be added many *prejudices, which cannot be easily overcome.*

Distinctions and inequalities in society being produced by natural causes, cannot be overcome by human laws. Such being the case, the colored people of our country must for a long period, and perhaps for ages to come, form societies among themselves, distinct from the whites—both for social intercourse and for religious exercises. They can derive no advantage as a race of people, from efforts to force them into the society of the white inhabitants. The discussions and efforts of philanthropists at the North to raise the status of the negro to a condition of civil, political, and social equality with the white man, formed one of the principal causes of the rebellion; they prolonged and rendered more fierce and bloody that terrible war; and they may disturb the peace and harmony of our country, for half a century to come.

Pope, the most philosophical of English poets, said,

> "Order is Heaven's first law; and this confess'd,
> Some are and must be greater than the rest;
> More rich, more wise—but who infers from hence,
> That such are happier, shocks all common sense."

What the Providences of God have made unequal, it is vain for man to attempt to equalize, by arbitrary laws, and forced customs.

SEC. 7.—*Theory of pure democracy, and how it works—Political equality impracticable.*

A pure democracy in its strict sense, means a government in which all the adult males of the community have equal political rights and equal political power, and participate equally in the practical business and administration of the government in all its branches, legislative, executive, and judicial. This is the case in the Baptist church, where each distinct body of worshippers constitute an independent church and government; and being few in numbers, and the subject and proper jurisdiction of ecclesiastical government being very limited, such a system and form of government can be carried into effect; but it is utterly impracticable when applied to a State or a country. But if *a representative democracy*, instead of a pure democracy, is intended, and every one is to have equal political rights, and equal political power, in order to carry this principle into effect, as each man has the same right as his neighbor to hold office, without regard to character or qualifications, all officers should be elected by lot, as many officers in Athens were, and not by choice and favoritism; and no man should be elected to, or hold office more than one year, until all his fellow-citizens have had their turn, and the circle of rotation was completed. And in legislation, the representative should be bound in all cases by the will of the electors of his representative district, and all laws should be a compound of the opinions and wills of the electors of the State or nation; so that the opinions of each and every elector should have the same amount of influence upon the legislation and government of the country.

This is the theory of a pure representative democracy. It is a beautiful theory; and if all men were virtuous and none excessively selfish—and all were endowed with equal natural talents, had equal acquirements, intelligence and abilities, or were inspired by the Deity with equal wisdom and goodness, it would be equally beautiful in practice as it is in theory. But unfortunately such is not the case, and hence the theory is impracticable. In filling the offices of a country it puts vice and extreme selfishness, ignorance and inexperience, on a par with virtue and intelligence, and with experience and fitness for official station. It would necessarily fill nearly all the offices with inexperienced and unfit men. Any country would soon be reduced to anarchy under such a system; it would be impossible to hold society together. Men would soon find it necessary to resist the exactions, corruptions, and tyrannies of ignorant and bad officers—and to defend their own rights, and redress their own wrongs by force. Even savages have their most talented and able men for chiefs; and are not so simple as to recognize that all are equally entitled to official station, and equally qualified for the exercise of official power.

The theory of the entire political equality of men, and

that all have an equal right to hold office and to exercise official power, if they can procure an election or appointment, by means of party tactics and clanship, is radically unsound; and the time has come when the American people must suffer from it, if they do not recognize its unsoundness, and provide a suitable remedy. Governments should be so organized as to secure (as far as is practicable) virtue and intelligence, patriotism and fitness, in all public offices; and to secure men of experience, high qualifications, and the highest order of talents, for high official stations.

No man has any just claims to office, nor any right to be a candidate, unless he has a good character, and qualifications and fitness for the office to which he aspires. Men of character and high qualifications for office have a just claim and right to have their fitness considered by their countrymen; and men of acknowledged merit, who have talents and fitness superior to their opponents, have some just, though imperfect right to the offices to which they aspire; while those who are not qualified have no right whatever to official station—and it is an abuse of power to elect or appoint them. When the majority of the electors reject the superior and best men who are candidates, and elect bad or inferior men, they abuse the power vested in them as voters, and do injustice to the minority of the voters, and to all the non-voting class.

The elective franchise is not designed as a personal privilege, to be sold by the voter, nor to be exercised to gratify his personal or partisan prejudices and partialities—regardless of the public good; but it is vested in the voter as a trust-power, to be exercised for the public good, and also to enable him to protect his own rights; and whenever the voter does not so exercise it, he abuses the power vested in him. No one is justly entitled to the elective franchise who has not sufficient intelligence and public virtue to exercise it for the public good. There have been, until recently, in all the States, and still are, in the most of them, more or less restrictions and limitations to adult male suffrage. Any system of universal manhood suffrage, where there are two or more races, and a majority of the voters are illiterate and ignorant, must necessarily lead to demagogism and corruption, and to anarchy and civil war, as it has in Mexico and other Spanish-American republics. The reason why nearly universal suffrage has practically obtained in some of the States, is the difficulty of discriminating and determining the true rule, and of applying it to all persons claiming the right. Persons who have no correct information upon political subjects, no definite opinions upon political questions, cannot be expected to exercise the elective franchise very wisely; and yet many of that class judge pretty soundly, from the acts and history of candidates, of their abilities, as well as of their character; and hence such men are proper electors for certain officers, though not for all. Partisan influences and clannish prejudices and partialities have done more to pervert the exercise of the elective franchise, than all other causes.

SEC. 8.—*Basis of the right of suffrage.*

Political self-government can be exercised only by means of representatives elected at comparatively short periods. Representation by election, and the exercise of the elective franchise, are the means, and the only means, of exercising the right and power of political self-government; and it may be affirmed as a self-evident truth, that persons of so feeble intellect and little intelligence, that they cannot participate in the election of public officers advantageously to themselves and the community, have *no natural right nor just claim to the right of suffrage.*

The elective franchise (the basis of political power in our country) is not an inherent right, which belongs to all persons; nor to every man, as a natural inheritance. On the contrary, it is, to some extent, a trust power, to be used for the good of all; and no one is entitled to it, who has not sufficient intelligence and public virtue, to exercise it with some degree of propriety, and for the public good. It is an acquired, not a natural right. It is acquired by education; by the acquisition of knowledge of men and things; by maturity of mind and experience in life; and by public services, by discharging the duties of a tax-payer, head and representative of a family, or by bearing arms in support of the government.

Persons and classes of persons and races, who are incapable of political self-government when they form whole communities by themselves, are equally unfit to exercise the powers of self-government, by voting properly and independently, when they form a portion of a community, with persons or races, who have more vigorous intellects, and more energy of character. It has a corrupting and pernicious influence to confer the elective franchise upon men who cannot think and judge for themselves, and who necessarily become the mere instruments of party leaders, and often of crafty political demagogues.

Some of the features of political self-government grew up spontaneously in Greece and Italy, France and England, the Netherlands and Germany, Switzerland and other countries in the temperate climates of Europe; where the people have elected a portion of their local and municipal officers, even under the monarchical system of government. Such peoples have shown themselves capable of using advantageously the rights and powers of self-government, and the most of them are justly entitled to it; and by reason of their character and intelligence, *have a right to elect their own officers, and to make their own laws, through the agency of representatives elected by themselves.* But none of the customs and institutions of self-government have ever grown up among any people in the torrid zone; and the descendants of Europeans who have settled in tropical countries, have shown very little capacity for self-government,—so little that it is still a problem, whether it be possible to maintain an elective representative system of government, with frequent elections, in any tropical country.

Among savages and barbarians, their chiefs (some elected and some hereditary) are the representatives of their respective tribes. The Patriarchal system of government is one of the most ancient in the world. The Patriarchs were the heads of the great and wealthy families, and the representatives as well as the heads of their respective tribes or clans. The fact that the patriarchal system grew up spontaneously in nearly all pastoral countries, and temperate climates of the Old World, furnishes conclusive evidence that it is well adapted to such countries and climates. When the representative system of government arose in England in the 13th century, the Archbishops and Bishops were summoned to Parliament, to represent their respective dioceses and churches; and two knights were at first elected by the county court of each county, and afterwards by the freeholders of the county, as deputies to represent the counties. Long afterwards, the privilege of voting was conferred by various statutes, upon *householders* who rented a tenement of a certain amount. The voters were all *either freeholders or householders, and acted in some representative capacity*—as representatives of families—of wives and children, whose rights it was their duty to protect—or they were owners of property subject to taxation, and should therefore have a voice in legislation and taxation.

In ancient Greece and Rome, freemen, who were neither householders and heads of families nor property holders, were allowed to vote; but such has not been the case to any considerable extent in Europe, for nearly two thousand years, until universal adult male suffrage was established in France, by the Revolution of 1848. In fact, the insurrections and revolutions of that year, furnished the germs of nearly all the popular elements in the governments of Italy, Prussia, and Austria, at the present time; all of which were borrowed from the laws and institutions of the United States.

The first American constitutions, and all those adopted during the 18th century, limited the right of suffrage very considerably, and allowed none but property holders and tax-paying citizens to vote; but the tendency has been towards universal manhood suffrage, ever since the election of Mr. Jefferson to the Presidency, in the year 1800.

The true basis of the elective franchise is as follows:

1st. That the elector is a citizen and the head of a family, whom he represents, and whose rights it is his duty to protect; or

2d. That he is the owner of property subject to taxation, and therefore directly interested in matters of taxation, and in all matters of legislation relating thereto; or

3d. That he is an adult male, and has done military duty within a certain time; and

4thly. That he has sufficient intelligence to judge for himself, of the character and general capacity of candidates for office, and has opinions and a will of his own upon such subjects; and

Lastly, That every such elector is a loyal citizen, not a

pauper depending on the public for support, and has not been guilty of any high crime.

The property of the married woman should be secured to her, subject to her control, and exempt from the control of the husband, except so far as he acts as her agent, and with her assent; and when that is the case, the laws and legislation of the country will bear upon husband and wife equally, and he can be safely trusted to act as her representative in political matters. To allow a married woman to vote, would often lead to contentions between husband and wife, and disturb the harmony of families, without effecting any adequate good, to compensate for the evil consequences that would result from it. But there is no good reason why widows and other single women, who are householders and heads of families, and also tax-payers, should not vote.

Such has been the delusion upon the subject of universal manhood suffrage, that paupers and criminals of all grades are allowed to vote in the most of the States. But it is very obvious to my mind, that there is good sense and justice in much of the old British law upon that subject, as laid down by Blackstone in his Commentaries; and that paupers, who are not tax-payers, but dependent on the public for their support, have no just claims to participate in the legislation and government of the country. It is equally obvious that persons who have been guilty of violating the laws, by the commission of high crimes, have no right or just claims to participate in the election of officers to make or to execute the laws; for they feel interested in electing to office their friends and sympathizers, and men of the same vicious class with themselves.

To give the elective franchise to persons who have not sufficient understanding and intelligence to think and judge for themselves of the character and general capacity of candidates for office, gives them no real power; but confers additional power on aspiring men and party leaders, who make feeble-minded and ignorant voters mere instruments to carry out their wishes, and vote as they advise and direct. The tendency of such a system is to degrade the elective franchise and the whole system of popular elections; to make politics a trade and a mere gambling game; to invite appeals to party spirit and clannish prejudices; to encourage party trickery and demagogism; to elect managing and unscrupulous politicians to office; to corrupt the legislation of the country, and the whole administration of the government; and to demoralize the people. The anarchy and demoralization of Mexico and other Spanish-American countries, tend to illustrate the natural tendency and effect of lowering and degrading the elective franchise; and the corruption of ancient Rome, during the last half-century of the Republic, also shows the tendency and effect of such a policy.

SEC. 9.—*Colored suffrage—its tendency and effect at the South.*

That the Southern freedmen are greatly inferior to the colored people of the North in intelligence, capacity for self-government, and fitness to exercise the elective franchise, is very certain. That they are greatly inferior in natural intellect as well as in intelligence to the white population, is equally certain—however much we may think the race may be improved by freedom, and the education of successive generations. If intellect and intelligence are of consequence to the proper exercise of the elective franchise (as is generally believed), it furnishes a good reason why the emancipated slaves of the South should not be put upon a political equality with the loyal white inhabitants. The reasoning which would extend to them civil equality, does not apply to political powers and privileges.

To disfranchise great numbers of the white men of the South, and give emancipated slaves and all free colored men equal political privileges with the loyal whites, is nearly equivalent to putting the entire control of several of the State governments, and of a majority of the counties of South Carolina, Georgia, and all the Gulf States, into the hands of colored men. It will put the government of those States into the hands of the most ignorant and improvident class of the population, and subject the more intelligent white classes to their domination. It will encourage demagogism, foster rivalships and bitter dissensions between the whites and blacks and their respective leaders—and must, sooner or later, produce anarchy, seditions and riots, insurrections and murders.

In discussing the subject of Negro Suffrage, the *New York Times* in November, 1867, said:—

"If the question were free from 'side issues,' it would be easily and promptly settled. If it were simply this—'Are *the negroes of the South*, as a body, *qualified to take part in* the reorganization of the Southern *State governments;* is it *wise or safe to leave them to decide what principles shall be embodied in the State constitutions*, what shall be the form and *powers of the State governments*, and what shall be the securities for life and property under them?'—there are *not ten men out of a thousand in the Republican party who would not say no. Nobody believes they are.* How should they be? The great mass of them have been kept in the most *stolid ignorance all their lives;* they can neither read nor write; they have heard nothing of politics and know nothing of the simplest facts of our history or our government; they have *neither the capacity to form opinions* nor the material to form them from; and as matter of necessity, as well as of fact, they will be and are *simply tools in the hands of party leaders* and wire-pullers, on the one side or the other. Circumstances just now throw them into the hands of the Republicans. The weight of their votes can and will be thrown into the Republican scale. And it is *this fact which leads the Republicans to accept for them the principle of universal suffrage*, and which, we may add, leads the Democrats to oppose it."

Conferring political power on all the colored men at the South, where they are numerous, and especially where they form a majority, will tend to make them vain and insolent, ambitious and clannish; and to make many of them idlers—seeking office, when they should be at work. It will encourage them to form political combinations and party organizations among themselves; to hold meetings and nominating conventions; to nominate candidates wholly or mostly of their own race; and to support each other for office, in opposition to the whites—in States and counties, cities and districts, where they have a majority. They will do at the South, as they have done in Hayti—except so far as they may be restrained and influenced by the whites, by law, and by the federal government. There is no reason to doubt that it will tend to foster political ambition and a spirit of restlessness—to divert their minds from honest industry—and have a very demoralizing influence.

The disposition to combine among themselves, to act together, and to support their own men for office, will grow upon them, as they feel more and more their own power, acquire experience and skill in managing conventions and party machinery, and learn that they can achieve success by such means, and by no other. They will nominate and elect more and more their own men, until they assume the entire control of the governments of many of the counties and cities, and of some of the States also. Can it be safe to the country, or useful to the colored population of the South, to confer such powers upon such masses of ignorant and weak-minded men? Should there not be some limitation to adult male suffrage, in the Southern States?

The high wages and demand for laborers in the Pacific States and the adjacent mining territories; the low wages and depressed condition of hundreds of millions of the people of China; and the facilities offered by steam navigation to the poor Chinese to come to our country, have already brought here 100,000 or more; and the probability is, that before the close of the present century, we shall have several millions of that race of people; and that in many districts and counties they will constitute a majority of the inhabitants. They may eventually constitute a majority in all the States west of the Rocky Mountains. Will it be safe to our country to confer upon them equal political powers and privileges with an American population of European descent, and thereby give them, eventually, political control of the Pacific States? Being Pagans, of a low grade of intellect, and a low standard of civilization, have they any right to claim equal political powers and privileges with our superior, educated and Christian peoples, of European descent?

SEC. 10.—*Delusions relative to the effect of the elective franchise upon laborers, and the price of labor.*

Strange delusions have crept into the minds of many of our people, in relation to the influence of the elective franchise, and the ballot. Some enthusiastic republicans seem to regard the elective franchise as a panacea for nearly all the ills of the country—civil, social, and industrial, as well as political. They think the franchise will raise the wages, and increase the value of the labor of the colored man; give him new courage and spirit; elevate him in the scale of manhood; and raise him from his present low, and in many cases degraded moral and social condition. Such expectations are preposterous.

Persons who suppose that the exercise of the elective franchise can have any influence upon the price of labor, can have no correct conceptions of the principles of political economy, and the laws which govern prices. The prices of labor are governed by the same laws of trade, by which the prices of agricultural products, and other products and goods, are governed—that is, by the demand for labor, and the greater or less supply in the market.

Prior to the Revolution of 1789, the people of France enjoyed no political power whatever; now the elective franchise is enjoyed by all the adult males of France. Has it raised them in morals? No one will pretend that it has. The new code of laws (the Napoleon code), religious toleration and some degree of religious liberty, the extinction of the oppressive powers and privileges of the ancient noblesse, the division of the great estates of the old nobility, the modern system of railroads and other internal improvements, modern science and inventions, have all contributed, with the elective franchise, to increase the industry and commerce, and improve the condition of the people of France; and there is no reason to doubt, that the elective franchise has aided in raising them in the scale of manhood; because they had intellectual capacity to use the franchise with some degree of wisdom. But no well-informed person will pretend, that the elective franchise has raised the people of Mexico or Hayti, either in the scale of morals or manhood.

SEC. 11.—*Is liberty, equality, or law and justice, the great desideratum of civilization?*

The question may be asked, "Is liberty, equality, or law and justice, the great desideratum of civilization and progress?" If it be liberty and the nearest possible approximation to equality, then the North American Indians would stand at the head of the civilization of the world, and the people of France very near the foot. The former enjoy the highest degree of liberty—personal and civil, political and religious; but are without law,—except a few rude customs; while the latter have a good degree of civil liberty and some of the forms of political liberty, but enjoy an admirable system of laws—generally well administered, and an efficient police—which gives them a grade of personal and civil liberty as perfect as it exists anywhere in the world, upon all subjects except matters of government. The Indians are miserable and degraded savages, gradually sinking in numbers and power—their liberty, and approximative equality without law being of no service to them; while the people of France, with restricted liberty regulated by law, are in the front rank of civilization,—keeping pace with the progress of the age. This illustration is sufficient to show, that a good system of laws, properly administered, is of ten times as much consequence as political liberty, to the welfare of the human family, and the cause of civilization. Liberty without law has very little value; but on the contrary law, without political liberty or the elective franchise, is of immense importance to a people.

Even arbitrary, unjust, and oppressive laws,—such as the laws of primogeniture, laws which authorize the entailment of property, laws which give a nobility unjust and oppressive powers and privileges, and laws and customs which authorize serfdom, are better than no laws at all. A system of law and government embracing such unjust and oppressive laws, serves to organize society, to preserve peace and order, and is better for even the laboring poor, and the oppressed classes, than the uncertain and wandering condition of savages and barbarians, who have no laws, except a few rude customs.

We want law and justice, and so much liberty, and no more, than is consistent with law and justice. Liberty without law, and without regard for justice, tends to license and rowdyism, vice and corruption, confusion and anarchy.

Political liberty, which is the enjoyment of the right to elect their own officers, and to make their own laws, is of no consequence to any people or class of people, who have not sufficient intellect and intelligence to elect the best men to office; and to judge, with some degree of wisdom, of the soundness and importance of the leading measures and policies of government. Political liberty has not increased the wages nor the industry, nor improved the physical or moral condition of the Indians and mixed races of Mexico. On the contrary, they remain as poor and ignorant, depressed and degraded, as they were when under the dominion of Spain.

SEC. 12.—*Antagonisms between laborers and employers—trades unions and strikes.*

All persons have rights, to a greater or less extent, to protect; and therefore all are interested in good laws, and in a good administration of the government. Hence it seems right and just that all should be represented in making and administering the laws, who have sufficient intelligence and wisdom to use the elective franchise properly, and with safety to the country. The chief difficulty is, to determine how far political power should be trusted to the uneducated classes, who have no property to protect, to legislate for and to govern the educated classes, and to impose taxes to an unlimited extent upon property and business. This difficulty has been regarded as very great in Great Britain, where the laboring classes are mostly uneducated, have little or no property subject to taxation, and yet constitute a large majority of the whole population of the United Kingdom.

All persons are laborers and belong to the laboring classes, in the most general sense of those words, who do more or less manual labor; but in the restricted and technical sense in which it is commonly used, the word laborer includes only those *persons who sell their labor to others* by the day or week, month or year, or work by the piece for wages—and does not include small farmers and gardeners, mechanics and manufacturers, who labor for themselves, and sell their products instead of their labor. The word laborer is also mostly confined to those who do common labor for wages. The words laboring classes have a broader signification, and include all persons who do either common or mechanical labor for hire, or for themselves. In our Northern and Western States, there are great numbers of small farmers, and also numerous mechanics, who work for themselves and do a small business without employing much hired help. Such persons belong to the laboring classes, though they are not commonly called laborers.

Almost everything is done in Great Britain on a large scale—by capitalists and business men, employing great numbers of laborers and mechanics. There are in that country very few small farmers, mechanics, or manufacturers, who labor for themselves. The number of small shopkeepers is much larger; but a very large majority of the people are laborers, mechanics, and servants, who sell their labor to others; belong, strictly speaking, to the laboring classes, and have an interest in keeping up wages; while their employers have an interest in reducing wages, and keeping them down. There is a strong antagonism in Great Britain and nearly all old countries, between the laboring classes and their employers. The same kind of antagonism is beginning to show itself to a limited extent in the manufacturing and mining districts of the United States, and in some of the commercial cities, as well as in the cotton, rice and sugar producing districts of the Southern States, since the abolition of slavery.

The mechanical, manufacturing and mining laborers of Great Britain, have formed societies, extensive combinations and trades unions, for the purpose of aiding each other, communicating information, establishing, raising, and keeping up the prices of labor. Many of those organizations have been long in operation—some of them more than half a century. They have inaugurated numerous strikes to raise wages, and resorted to violence and crime to compel laborers to submit to them; and while they have produced good in some instances, by communicating information, aiding persons out of employment, and procuring a proper standard of wages by negotiations with employers, they have often disturbed industry, and been the cause of an incalculable amount of evil.

Trades unions have been organized, and strikes inaugurated to a limited extent in the United States, with similar, though less injurious consequences; less injurious, because the unions here are not so strong as in England; the field for labor, in proportion to the number of laborers, is much greater; wages are higher; the inducement to strike is much less; and the difficulties between laborers and employers are generally compromised very soon, or otherwise the laborers look elsewhere for employment.

Laborers and servants, and the small shopkeepers depending upon them, constitute three-fourths or more of the whole population of England, and there is antagonism of feeling as well as of interest between the laborers and employers; and hence the educated and business classes, as well as the great landholders, feel that their rights and property would be unsafe, if the whole political power of the House of Commons were vested in the laboring classes, by a system of universal manhood suffrage, and frequent elections.

Sec. 13.—*Single and plural voting.*

The educated, wealthy, and aristocratic classes of England fear the effect of universal suffrage,—believing that it would throw the whole power of the House of Commons, and the virtual control of the government, into the hands of the representatives of the laboring classes, and endanger their rights and interests; and yet many of them realize the importance of extending the elective franchise, equalizing the representation in the Commons, and making some great reforms in the government. To secure the advantages of an extension of the elective franchise and of some reforms, and avoid the dangers of universal manhood suffrage, reflecting and ingenious minds have invented a system of single and plural voting—single voting for uneducated laborers having no property subject to taxation, and various grades of plural voting for educated, business, and professional men, and property holders; allowing a laborer or mechanic, and every man, an additional vote for a common-school education,—another or third vote for a classical or scientific education,—another or fourth vote for taxable property of a certain amount,—and an additional vote for a professional or business education, of a certain grade.

Such is the outline and substance of the plan of plural voting. It is presented here as an ingenious theory, for which there is more apology in the United Kingdom of Great Britain and Ireland, than in any other country. The system does not recognize political equality—though it admits that all adult males have political as well as civil rights and privileges.

John Stuart Mill, in his work on Representative Government, says: "I regard it as wholly inadmissible that any person should participate in the suffrage without being able to read, write, and perform the common operations of arithmetic. . . . Universal teaching must precede universal enfranchisement. No one but those in whom an *à priori* theory has silenced common sense, will maintain that power over others, over the whole community, should be imparted to people who have not acquired the commonest and most essential requisites for taking care of themselves; for pursuing intelligently their own interests." Again he says: "It is also important, that *the assembly which votes the taxes, should be elected exclusively by those who pay something towards the taxes imposed. Those who pay no taxes, disposing by their votes of other people's money, have every motive to be lavish, and none to economize.*"

Speaking of the effect of universal suffrage, Mr. Mill says: "The great majority of voters in most countries, and emphatically in this [England], would be manual laborers; and the *twofold danger*, that of *too low a standard of political intelligence*, and that of *class legislation, would still exist in a very perilous degree.* It remains to be seen whether any means exist by which these evils can be obviated."

"In all human affairs [he says], every person directly interested, and not under positive tutelage, has an admitted claim to a voice; and when his exercise of it is *not inconsistent with the safety of the whole*, cannot be justly excluded from it. But though every one ought to have a voice—that every one should have an equal voice, is a totally different proposition. . . . Entire exclusion from a voice in the common concern is one thing; the concession to others of a more potential voice, on the ground of greater capacity for the management of the joint interests, is another. . . . An employer of labor is, on the average, more intelligent than a laborer; for he must labor with his head, and not solely with his hands. A foreman is generally more intelligent than an ordinary laborer; and a laborer in the skilled trades than in the unskilled. A banker, merchant, or manufacturer is likely to be more intelligent than a tradesman, because he has larger and more complicated interests to manage. In all these cases it is not the merely having undertaken the superior function, but the successful performance of it, that tests the qualifications; . . . for which reason the occupation should have been pursued successfully for some length of time (say three years). Subject to some such condition, *two or more votes might be allowed to every person who exercises any of these superior functions.* The liberal professions, when really and not nominally practised, imply a still higher degree of instruction; and wherever a sufficient examination, or any serious conditions of education are required before entering on a profession, *its members could be admitted at once to a plurality of votes.* The same rule might be applied to graduates of universities; and even to those who bring satisfactory certificates of having passed through the course of study required by any school, at which the higher branches of knowledge are taught. . . . The plurality of votes must on no account be carried so far, that those who are privileged by it, or the class to which they belong, shall outweigh, by means of it, all the rest of the community."

Again Mr. Mill says: "Until there shall have been devised, and until public opinion is willing to accept, *some mode of plural voting*, which may assign to education, as such, the degree of superior influence due to it, and sufficient as a counterpoise to the numerical weight of the least educated class: for so long the benefits of completely universal suffrage cannot be obtained, without bringing with them, as it appears to me, a *chance of more than equivalent evils*. . . . It is *not useful, but hurtful, that the constitution of the country should declare ignorance to be entitled to as much political power as knowledge*."

Such are the views of some of the leading minds of England—of men who are in the front ranks of the liberal party. They apply with great force to our country, and particularly to the Southern States; where a large proportion of the people are of African descent, bred in ignorance as plantation slaves. My reading and observation, concurring with the history of the world, lead me to the conclusion, that the mode of electing or appointing officers, directly by the people or indirectly, and the frequency or infrequency of elections, should be adapted to the condition, grade of intellect, and education of the people, and to the climate in which they live. The higher their grade of intellect, the greater their intelligence, the greater their self-restraint, and the more they are accustomed to the exercise of political power, the greater the number of officers that may be advantageously elected by the people, and the greater may be the frequency of elections; and that there may be a nearer approximation to a pure democracy, in temperate and cold climates, than in hot and tropical countries.

The number of laborers in proportion to the whole population being small in our Northern and Western States —(except in the mining districts, and in the large manufacturing and commercial cities)—and there being no such antagonisms between laborers and employers, as there are in England, there is no necessity here for such a system of plural voting, as ingenious Englishmen have suggested, to obviate the evils and dangers of universal suffrage in England; but the intolerance and tyranny of party spirit, and the domination and evils arising from party organizations and nominating conventions, are such, that we need other modifications of our system of elections, much more than they do even in England. We need a system of limited and full voting, such as was provided for in the first constitution of the State of New York—adopted in 1777; we want also the representation of minorities, double elections, and cumulative voting.

SEC. 14.—*Limited and full voting.*

The first constitution of the State of New York, adopted in 1777, provided that every male inhabitant of full age, who personally resided within one of the counties of the State for six months immediately preceding the day of election, should be entitled to vote for representatives of the county in the Assembly; if during the time aforesaid he had been a freeholder, possessing a freehold of the value of twenty pounds within the county, or had rented a tenement therein of the yearly value of forty shillings, and been rated and actually paid taxes to the State.

That constitution provided that the Senate of the State of New York should consist of twenty-four freeholders, to be chosen by the freeholders of the State, possessed of freeholds of the value of one hundred pounds ($250), over and above all debts charged thereon; and that the Governor and Lieutenant Governor should be elected by the same class of voters. No State, county, nor judicial officers were elected—all being appointed in various ways. Representatives to Congress were elected by the two houses of the State legislature, prior to the adoption of the constitution of the United States.

Under that constitution, there was a large class of small freeholders, and householders also, who paid taxes, and enjoyed the limited privilege of voting for members of the Assembly only—not being allowed to vote for State Senators, nor for Governor and Lieutenant Governor; while the freeholders of the State having freeholds worth more than $250 each, over and above all encumbrances, were allowed to elect the State Senators, Governor and Lieutenant Governor, and to vote also for members of the Assembly. The former enjoyed *the privilege of limited voting only*, while the latter had *the privilege of full voting, or voting for all elective officers.* The idea was that one branch of the State legislature should be elected and controlled exclusively by freeholders—by men having landed property subject to taxation, as a security for property; and that the small freeholders and householders should have a voice in the lower house only, and should not have the power to control both houses, and to impose taxes to an unlimited extent upon the property of others.

There was still a large class of men in the State, mostly single men, in the employ of others, who were not allowed to vote at all, for members of either house of the legislature; and were subject to laws, in making which they had no participation. The mistake in the constitution was, in not extending the limited suffrage, for the election of members of the Assembly, to nearly all the adult male citizens of the State; and in making so broad a distinction between the owners of landed and personal property, both being subject to taxation.

All persons are subject to the laws, have rights to protect, and are interested in the government, and in the legislation of the country; though all are not equally interested, nor equally capable of participating in the government, nor in the election of officers. Hence there is great propriety in allowing a limited suffrage, to participate in the election of members of the lower house of State legislatures, and members of Congress, to all adult male citizens, except criminals and paupers, idiots and lunatics—to allow them some participation in the government, for the protection of their rights. Under such a system, giving to the educated classes and property holders the entire control of the State senates, and the election of governors and local officers, it would be much less hazardous, and perhaps it might be entirely safe, to allow a limited suffrage to the illiterate and ignorant colored men at the South.

The proposed Fifteenth Amendment to the federal constitution will probably be adopted,—whereby the descendants of the Puritans will force negro suffrage, and the political equality of the negro, upon all the States; and if so, and if, as a matter of self-defence, the most of the States should be driven to the necessity of adopting the *system of limited and full voting*,—requiring a small property qualification for voters for State senators, governor, and many local officers, the effect of the amendment would have a compensating influence, which would overbalance all the evils that can arise from it.

Sec. 15.—*Cumulative voting, and its advantages.*

Cumulative voting is the casting of two votes for one

of two candidates, instead of casting one vote for each of them.

The tendency of party spirit and party nominations is, to put all the nominees of a party upon the same level—without regard to talents or acquirements, experience or moral character, and to induce electors to cast their votes for the whole ticket—because they cannot cut off any candidate upon the ticket without weakening their party, and adding to the strength of their opponents ; while cumulative voting would frequently enable the minority party to elect one candidate, by concentrating their votes upon him, when they could not elect two. Cumulative voting would, therefore, tend to aid the minority or weaker party, and to give them in many cases some representation, instead of giving the whole to the majority.

Cumulative voting would present an opportunity to electors, to express their preferences between candidates of their own party ; and to make them available, when two or more candidates for the legislature, councilmen, or other offices of the same class are presented for their suffrages, to give two votes for one candidate, instead of giving one vote for each of two candidates.

Under the present system, party men, who have some discriminating judgment and some conscience, are very frequently embarrassed because they cannot cut off a party candidate whom they esteem unworthy of their support, without losing a vote, or voting for a political opponent, which most party men hesitate to do, for fear of weakening their own party and adding to the strength of their political opponents. But cumulative voting would give electors an opportunity to discriminate between candidates of their own party—to increase their vote for the best men of their party, and secure their election, and to cut off those that they esteem unworthy or unfit, without voting for a political opponent, or losing any portion of their votes. It would tend to encourage electors to break in upon party tickets, to vote according to their consciences and judgment, and to cast their votes for candidates of their own party, whom they esteem the most fit and worthy.

Under the present system unscrupulous schemers and cunning tricksters have an advantage over honest and fair-minded men in getting nominations, while a system of cumulative voting would give men of high character and standing in a community an advantage at the polls over men of bad or doubtful character. A system of cumulative voting would teach the politicians of each party the necessity of bringing forward for office their best men, as the only means of securing success.

SEC. 16.— *Voting by ballot, or vivâ voce.*

The ballot has two uses in voting: 1st. To facilitate the process; and 2d. to enable the elector to conceal his vote from the public eye.

When not more than two or three, or at most half a dozen officers are to be elected, the ballot facilitates the process very little; but when a governor, State officers, members of the State legislature, county officers, and also members of Congress, and every fourth year a number of presidential electors are to be elected, the ballot greatly facilitates the proceeding; though at the same time it serves as a cloak for numerous frauds, in canvassing and certifying votes. It also renders it much more difficult to ferret out fraudulent voting, to ascertain for whom fraudulent votes were cast, to purge the poll-lists of such votes, and to determine for which candidates a majority of the legal votes were cast—so that the system of voting by ballot is not an unmixed good.

By enabling the elector to conceal his vote from the public eye, and from the knowledge of political friends and persons wishing to intimidate him, or exercise an influence over him, it tends to secure the freedom and independence of the voter; enables him to cut his ticket, and vote for those that he may consider the best men of both parties (if he wish to do so), without being known and abused by his party friends for so doing; it also tends to prevent ill-feeling between neighbors, acquaintances, and party friends, and to preserve the peace at elections, as well as afterwards. Where the *vivâ voce* mode of voting is practised, many contentions and quarrels arise after elections—growing out of the vote given by one of the parties; which would have been avoided, if the party had voted secretly, by ballot.

Voting *vivâ voce* increases the power of party spirit, party organizations, and the influence and tyranny of majorities over minorities, in an election district. Very few men, of the majority party, while subject to such influences, have the moral courage and independence to so far separate from their party friends, as to vote for one or more candidates of the opposite party, when they think them the best men. It, however, offers some safeguards against frauds. Where the vote is *vivâ voce* and recorded on the poll-books, and the poll-books are properly preserved, they furnish persons of both parties who may see fit to examine them, evidences of the real vote, and the means of purging the poll-books of fraudulent votes,—which will tend to hold the election board in check, and prevent ballot-box stuffing, and frauds in canvassing and certifying the votes.

The ballot favors the personal liberty and independence of the voter, the exercise of freedom and honesty in voting, and tends to preserve peace in the community, as well as at elections; but when fraud is committed in voting, the ballot aids in concealing the fraud. It also aids in facilitating and concealing frauds in election boards, and in canvassing and certifying the votes. Votes may be purchased with equal facility, and corruption may prevail to nearly the same extent, under both systems. Each system has its virtues and its evils; but, upon the whole, the virtues of the system of voting by ballot greatly predominate. Its virtues can be secured by no other means; while its principal evil can be guarded against, by a careful registry of voters, and by having both political parties represented upon every board for registering voters, and for receiving, canvassing, and certifying the votes.

In the Northern States, where the ballot has been universally used, there has been less party domination and tyranny over voters, than in Southern States, where the *vivâ voce* system has been practised; and there have been also fewer disturbances at elections; and contentions and quarrels growing out of votes cast contrary to the dictates of party and party leaders, have been more rare.

SEC. 17.—*Direct and indirect popular elections and appointments.*

Great changes have been made in the mode of electing officers in many of the States. During the Revolutionary war, and until the adoption of the Constitution of the United States in 1788, members of Congress were elected by the colonial or State legislatures, as our Senators in Congress now are.

Under the first New England charter, the governors of the colonies of Plymouth and Massachusetts Bay were elected annually by the freemen thereof. Under the second charter, those colonies were united in 1692, and from that time until the Revolution, the governor of the colony was appointed by the King of England. The freemen of the Connecticut and Rhode Island colonies elected their own governors, annually, from the time of their first settlement; and never had a royal governor. The other colonies had, at first, proprietary governors, and then governors appointed by the King, until the revolution. From that time until since the year 1840, the governors of the States of New Jersey, Maryland, Virginia, North Carolina, South Carolina, and Georgia, were elected by their State legislatures. The governors of the other States were elected by the people; and under the last constitutions formed, the governors of all the States are elected by the people.

All the early State constitutions provided for the appointment of judges and State officers by the governors of the States, by and with the advice and consent of the State Senate; or for their election by the legislature on joint ballot. But that salutary practice has been abandoned and changed in nearly all the States. Demagogism, blended with popular delusions, has gradually infused into the minds of the people many false and delusive ideas and maxims, including the following:—Vox populi, vox Dei,—(that the voice of the people is the voice of God, speaking through them)—that the people can do no wrong—that the majority of the people are always right—and that to secure good officers and good government, all officers should be elected directly by the people, for short periods of time, by universal adult male suffrage. Such delusive ideas (some of them originating among the Radicals and Jacobins of France, during their first Revolution) have been working in the public mind for three-fourths of a century, and gradually extending their influence from time to time, to a large number of our people; until they have wrought many unfortunate changes and evils in our system of government; and finally culminated in negro suffrage, and strong efforts to force negro equality upon the country.

Fortunately the Constitution of the United States cannot be easily changed; that it cannot be changed by a mere party majority; and that it provides an equitable rule as between the small and large States, for the election of President and Vice President, through the agency of Presidential electors, and the election of Senators in Congress indirectly, by the State legislatures; and that all judicial, executive, and administrative officers of the United States, are required to be nominated and appointed by the President, by and with the advice and consent of the Senate, by the heads of departments, or by the judges of the courts. These are conservative features, which have rendered the Federal Constitution superior to all the State constitutions now in force; and made it, to a great extent, *the bulwark of law and justice, and of liberty regulated by law; which is the only liberty of much value.* But it may well be feared that the proposed Fifteenth Amendment, if adopted, will so override the conservative features of the State constitutions, as to make radicalism and a central absolutism triumphant.

Though the exercise of the appointing power greatly increased the importance of the office of governor, and the anxiety of the people to elect the best men to fill the office, it did not produce any such popular agitation, scheming, and system of bargain and intrigue, as our present system has of nominating by party conventions, and electing judges and all executive and administrative officers by the people.

By the second constitution of the State of Mississippi, formed in 1832, it was provided that the Judges of the

Supreme and Circuit Courts, the Chancellor, the Secretary of State, Attorney-General, State Treasurer, and Auditor of Public Accounts, should all be elected by the people. This was an innovation upon the practice which had universally obtained in all the States, up to that time, of appointing all such officers by the Governor, with the advice and consent of the Senate, or electing them by the two houses of the legislature.

The Convention which revised the constitution of the State of New York, in 1846, being deeply imbued with radicalism and popular enthusiasm for the election of all officers directly by the people, unfortunately followed the example of Mississippi, and provided for the election of all the Judges, State and County officers, and Clerks of Courts, directly by the people; and the most of the States, which have formed or revised their constitutions since that time, have committed the same blunder. Time will show the evils of such a system, and suggest proper remedies.

Among an educated and reading people, the most of the electors will acquire sufficient knowledge of the acts, history and character of a few of the leading men of the State, whose names may be presented for the office of Governor, to enable them to vote intelligently for a proper man for that office; but it is impossible in a large State, for the most of the electors to have or obtain sufficient information of the character, qualifications, and fitness, of all the men in the State, whose names may be presented for Judges and State officers; and the masses of the people are generally very poor judges of the legal acquirements and fitness of men, for high judicial stations. The multiplication of elective officers increases the difficulty, and often renders it impossible for electors, who are constantly occupied with their own private affairs, to acquire sufficient information of the qualifications, characters, and fitness, of numerous nominees for office, to enable them to discriminate properly, and to vote intelligently. On the contrary, the Governor and State officers are employed and paid, to devote their whole time to the public service; and it is the Governor's duty to inform himself in relation to all candidates for office; and he has the aid of the State officers in their several departments. He is responsible for his acts; and more likely than the wireworkers and managers of party conventions, to make good selections. The reason which applies to the election of members of the legislature, local officers, and the chief executive officer of a State by the people, does not apply to the election of judges and State officers. (See on this subject section 19 of the last chapter.)

In Brazil, the Senate and Chamber of Deputies are elected indirectly by the people. The heads of every fifteen families, having an annual income from property or business of $50 each, choose one elector, and the electors thus chosen in the several Provinces, elect Senators for life, and members of the Chamber of Deputies for four years. Each of the twenty-one provinces of the Empire has a provincial assembly (like our State legislatures), elected indirectly, in the same manner as the national Chamber of Deputies —in some for two, and in others for three years. The system of indirect elections and a limited suffrage has worked well, and secured peace and prosperity to that immense empire, for nearly fifty years; while Mexico and all the Spanish-American republics, under the influence of republican governments, universal adult male suffrage, and direct elections, have all, with the exception of Chili, been frequently disturbed by factions, insurrections, revolutions and civil wars. Universal suffrage and direct elections by the people do not seem adapted to the impulsive populations of tropical climates—the masses of whom are always weak-minded, as well as uneducated.

In the Netherlands, or Holland, the system of elections is mostly indirect, and far from popular or democratic. Persons who pay a certain amount of taxes choose a certain number of electors in their respective towns; and these electors elect the members of the *town councils*, who, prior to the amendment of the constitution in 1848, were chosen for life. The *town councils* elect deputies to their provincial assemblies, which are very similar to our State legislatures. The States-General, or national legislature, is composed of two Chambers — the Senate and Chamber of Deputies. The Senate is composed of 39 members, divided into three classes—elected by the provincial assemblies for 9 years—one third part going out every three years: of which North Brabant elects 5, North Holland 6, South Holland 7, Friesland 3, Drenth 1, Gelderland 5, Zealand 2, Overyssel 3, Limburg 3, Utrecht 2, and Groningen 2. The members of the Chamber of Deputies, 68 in number, are elected for 4 years, from 38 districts, into which the provinces or States are divided, by electors who are twenty-three years of age and upwards, and pay taxes, varying in different provinces, from $8 to $65. The executive power is vested in the King. Such is the system of government of Holland, the most liberal and popular of any in the Old World, with the single exception of that of Switzerland. Our federal system of government was mostly borrowed from Holland and Switzerland.

SEC. 18.—*Good judges—How they are not secured.*

The method of electing judges by the people, in many of the States, is an anomaly—unknown in the history of the world, except in ancient Rome; which finally sank into anarchy, civil war, and despotism, under the combined influences of corruption, demagogism, and military power. Some good judges will be obtained by any system of election or appointment; but the method of electing them by the people has not proved a success. It has not improved the character of the bench, in the States which have adopted it.

A judge should be an experienced man—distinguished not only for legal learning and ability, but also for unselfishness, uprightness and impartiality, evenness of temper and firmness of character. He should not be a sensitive, nervous, excitable man—nor a man of very tender feelings, that may be easily wrought upon, and swayed by friendships, partialities, or the misfortunes of suitors; but should be constantly governed by a spirit of justice, tempered by humanity, and a due though not an excessive regard for the infirmities of human nature. He should have no special favorites at the bar; and as a general rule, the less intimate acquaintance there is between a judge and members of the bar practising before him, the better it is for the ends of justice. An active and zealous partisan politician should very rarely be appointed a judge—never unless he be a man of very superior intellect, large acquirements, high moral character, even temper, and not very avaricious nor selfish.

The masses of the people are not good judges of legal talents and acquirements, and fitness for high judicial stations—being generally too much captivated by talking talents. They are much better qualified to select men for legislative, executive, and administrative duties. To nominate candidates for high judicial stations by caucuses and conventions of partisan politicians, and elect them by the people, is a very poor method to secure good judges. It is impossible to secure impartial judges in that way.

Judges should not feel that they are dependent upon certain suitors in their court, and upon some of the members of the bar, for their nomination and election; and at the same time feel that other suitors and members of the bar voted against them, or opposed their nomination. Such feelings are not consistent with impartiality, and the fair administration of justice.

The reasoning of judges, like that of all other classes of men, is often warped by partialities and prejudices, which they are not aware of themselves. There are, in both English and American law, so many technical matters of pleading, practice, and evidence; so many nice hair-spun distinctions in the rules of law announced from the bench, (some of which are very whimsical); and so many conflicting and unsound decisions, that it requires but little partiality or prejudice, to direct the attention of a judge in one direction or another, and to sway the minds of many judges in favor of, or against either party, without much regard to the real merits of the case. Much of the proverbial uncertainty in the administration of justice, arises from such causes. Hence the importance of having upon the bench, clear-headed, pure-minded, upright, honest, and impartial men; who feel a proper degree of independence, and are animated by the spirit of justice. The creatures of corrupt men, or of party politicians, are not safe judicial officers.

Good, conscientious, and unselfish men, are too apt to be quiet and inactive—while selfish and ambitious men are generally bold and adventurous; and hence partisan nominations are very generally managed and controlled by the most selfish and unscrupulous, as well as the most active and ambitious men of the party. Make judges, prosecuting attorneys, and sheriffs, dependent for their nomination and election upon roughs and rowdies, pimps and gamblers, political rings and swindlers, partisan committees and scheming politicians, and the administration of justice, and particularly of criminal justice, will necessarily be weak, and often influenced by partiality or prejudice.

The facts stated, and the charges made in the petition filed in the Supreme Court of the State of New York, by Joseph H. Ramsey against the New York and Erie Railroad Company, —— Gould, —— Fisk, and others, show the dangerous and corrupting influences which result from the control of great corporations, by selfish, ambitious, and unscrupulous men.

In that case Judge Murray, at Delhi, in Delaware county, where the petition was filed, on the 23d of November, 1869, made an order, suspending —— Gould, —— Fisk, and several others, from their functions and authority as directors and officers of the New York and Erie Railroad Company, till the further order of the Court; and appointing a referee to take testimony, and report the evidence and proofs in the case, to aid the Court in the further exercise of its powers.

On the next day (Nov. 24th) Judge Balcom, living in another county, made an *ex parte* order in the case, that all proceedings in the action on the part of the plaintiff, including the service of any orders or papers therein, other than the summons and complaint, and also including all proceedings before Philo T. Ruggles, the referee named in the order of Judge Murray, be stayed, until the entry of an order upon the motion specified in a certain notice—such stay not to exceed twenty days. On the next succeeding day, Judge Barnard, of the Supreme Court, at a court held in the city of New York, made an order in a cross-suit, similar in terms and effect to that of Judge Balcom, enjoining proceedings in the suit before Judge Murray.

The exercise of such strange, anomalous, and conflicting judicial powers, was never before heard of in any civilized country. If the acts of New York judges in relation to railroad corporations, and the action of managing directors and officers thereof, do not disgust the bar and the business men of the country with our elective judiciary, it will be strange indeed. Several of the papers of the city of New York have commented with becoming severity upon the subject.

From The Evening Post, *Nov.* 26.

"Judge —— Balcom, of Binghamton, has issued an order staying all proceedings in the suit of Joseph H. Ramsey against the Erie Railway Company and others, and forbidding the referee to take testimony. This order was served on Mr. Ramsey's counsel on Wednesday evening.

"Yesterday, Judge —— Barnard, of the Supreme Court, in this district, issued a somewhat similar order. * * * In making these orders, both Judges directly violate the previous order made by Judge Murray, whose jurisdiction in such cases is co-ordinate and equal with theirs. By what right do they thus insult another Court, and attack an authority which cannot be impaired without disgracing themselves? If these judicial acts are done in a private interest, in order to protect bad men from exposure and punishment, they are intelligible. * * * We trust that proper measures will be taken to test these questions at once, even if it involves the suspension of a Judge from office by the Legislature, as for a flagrant crime, and the tedious trial of an impeachment."

From The Democrat, *Nov.* 25.

"Here is the Company's seat of government. Here its managers live. Here they operate in gold-stocks and bonds. Here they have, at enormous expense, purchased an Opera House for an office, in which their orders are written and accounts audited. Here they have purchased a first-class Supreme Court, on purpose to decide all matters of law in their favor; and it is an insult to the Company, its Opera House, and its Court, to compel Fisk and Gould to go out of the city. * * * Must they be forced to buy a little Supreme Court to locate at every depot along the line? Must they employ only Supreme Judges for switch-tenders, to open and shut the law, to let such and only such trains through as are marked 'Fisk & Gould,' *private!*"

From THE WORLD, *Nov.* 27.

"There have never been more disreputable scandals in the administration of miscalled justice, than those which are now, for the second time, taking place in connection with the affairs of the Erie Railway. An angry conflict between the parties to a suit, is what often takes place in litigation; but the enlisting of Judges of the same Court as contestants engaged in a struggle to thwart and circumvent one another, and resorting to expedients of chicanery in the interest of crafty and unscrupulous litigants, is disgraceful to the Supreme Court, and to the personal character of the Judges."

THE NEW YORK TIMES says:—

"The action of Judge Barnard in the suit commenced in the name of the Erie Company against Mr. Ramsey and Mr. Eaton, his counsel, to restrain the prosecution of Mr. Ramsey's action, brought in Delaware County against certain of the Erie Directors, is quite as remarkable as anything which has been done hitherto by this extraordinary Judge, in this most extraordinary litigation. The case requires no comment. * * * After a career of the most reckless and profligate management, this band of Erie adventurers found themselves confronted at last by an honest judge, suddenly suspended from office, and called upon to account for forty millions of money. Forbidden access to their books and papers, except in the presence of an unsuspended director; prohibited absolutely from making any entry therein or removing any of them from the office, and ordered to appear before a referee, that all the secrets of their shameless career should be exposed to the public view, and that the public might see and know when, and how, and under what circumstances these many millions have been disbursed,—it is not surprising that extraordinary measures should have been taken in their behalf. What may not the threatened fearful exposition have presented? Who can say what reputations, * * * would have been blasted by such a revelation?"

Sec. 19.—*The frequency or infrequency of elections and appointments.*

The character of a government is determined as much by the term of service of its officers, and the frequency or infrequency of elections, as by the mode of such elections, and the origin of its powers.

Late in the evening of November 9th, 1799, after Napoleon Bonaparte had dispersed the Council of Five Hundred at the point of the bayonet, about sixty members of the two legislative bodies met and passed a decree, abolishing the Directory of France, vesting the executive power in Napoleon, Sieyes, and Roger Ducos, as provisional Consuls, and appointing a Commission to act with the Consuls in framing a new constitution. A constitution was formed in a few days. Napoleon was made First Consul for ten years, and the whole was submitted to a vote of the citizens of France, on the 13th of December, 1799, and approved by an affirmative vote of more than 3,000,000.

In 1802 the Council of State adopted a resolution to submit to the electors of France, the question, "Shall Napoleon Bonaparte be First Consul for life?" And thereupon registers were opened in every commune, and the people voted upon the question. The result was announced in a senatus consultum of August 2d, 1802, declaring that 3,557,885 votes had been cast, of which 3,368,259 were in the affirmative, and only 189,626 in the negative.

On the 18th of May, 1804, the Senate declared Napoleon Emperor of the French, but referred to the electors of France the ratification or rejection of the decree.

The question was submitted to the people, and the decree was ratified by a vote almost unanimous—being 3,572,329 in the affirmative, and only 2,569 in the negative.

In December, 1848, Louis Napoleon Bonaparte, the nephew of Napoleon I., was elected President of the then French Republic for a period of four years, by a popular vote of 5,658,755, against about 1,500,000 votes, which were cast for General Cavaignac.

December 2d, 1851, Louis Napoleon Bonaparte, then President of the French Republic, issued a decree, dissolving the Legislative Assembly and Council of State; arrested and sent to prison about one hundred and eighty members of the Assembly, and a number of other distinguished men; with the aid of the army mowed down with fire-arms in the streets of Paris, more than two thousand citizens who opposed his revolutionary measures; made himself DICTATOR OF FRANCE; decreed universal suffrage; and issued a proclamation to the people. On the 3d of December he decreed that the people meet in their respective communes, and by their votes accept or reject the following plebiscite: "The French people desire the maintenance of the authority of Louis Napoleon Bonaparte, and delegate to him the powers necessary to establish a constitution, upon the basis proposed in his proclamation of December 2d." The affirmative votes cast November 20th and 21st, 1851, numbered 7,439,216; the negative votes 640,737; and 30,820 votes were annulled for irregularity.

In pursuance of the authority vested in him by the voice and vote of the people, Louis Napoleon formed and adopted a new constitution for France, by which he was made President for ten years, with nearly absolute power, and very slight checks upon its exercise. He was invested with the command of the army and navy, with the sole power to initiate laws, and nominate all officers—with power to declare war, conclude peace, make treaties of alliance and commerce—with a Senate and Corps Legislatif and Council of State to assist him, but with little more than advisory and nominal authority.

Like Napoleon I., not satisfied with the nominally republican constitution and Presidency, in accordance with a decree of the Senate, the question was again submitted to the people in November, 1852; Louis Napoleon was elected Emperor, by the vote of 7,824,129 of the citizens of France; and the Empire was proclaimed December 2d, 1852.

Such have been the votes of the people of France,—by which they conferred almost absolute power upon Napoleon Bonaparte, and also upon Louis Napoleon; and increased their powers from time to time, after each of them had been guilty of the most dangerous conspiracies, usurpations, and abuses of power.

When officers are elected for one, two, three, four, or six years, with powers defined and limited by law, public opinion and the criticisms of the press in a free country, have a powerful influence and check upon them. They know that they cannot be re-elected unless they satisfy their constituents; that they will be subject to trial and punishment, if they are guilty of crime, corruption, or official misconduct; and that misconduct in office is often more easily ferreted out by successors, and generally more easily punished, after they go out of office, than while they remain in. The shorter their terms of official service may be, the more dependent they are upon the popular will, and the more subject they are to public opinion. The term may be so short as to destroy nearly all independence and firmness in the discharge of official duties, and produce a timid spirit—injurious to the public weal.

If a man hold office for life, or for so long a period as he will probably want the office, he often feels too independent of the people, and has too little regard for public opinion—unless he is ambitious to obtain a higher station. Hence the importance to an educated and intelligent people, in a country of law, of electing their legislative, executive, and administrative officers, for comparatively short periods of time—to hold them in check, and compel them to study the public interest, and to pay heed to an enlightened public opinion. The Bonapartes, elected as they were, were no more held in check by the public opinion of France or of the world, than they would have been if they had been hereditary monarchs. Their election by the people for ten years, and then for life, served to foster their pride, to confirm their supremacy and power over the people, and to make them feel more independent than they would, if they had inherited their power. Napoleon was more absolute, and so is Louis Napoleon, than any of the hereditary monarchs of Europe, except the Czar of Russia, and the Sultan of Turkey; and the fact that they owed their high position and power to the votes of the people of France, gave the people no additional check upon them, and no more influence over them.

All our elective officers, State, national, and local, are elected for short, or comparatively short periods of time; and such is the case also with those appointed to office—with the exception of the judges. The officers in some of the States are elected for too short periods, to be convenient or advantageous. They render elections for many offices too frequent. The governors of all the New England States are elected annually; in each of the States of Delaware, Maryland, Virginia, North Carolina, Georgia,

Florida, Kentucky, Indiana, Illinois, Arkansas, Louisiana, Texas, California, Oregon, and Nevada, the governor is elected for four years; in New Jersey and Pennsylvania he is elected for three years; and in each of the other States he is elected for two years. The terms of service of State officers and State Senators are equally short and various—being but one year in each of the New England States, and from two to four years in the other States.

No advantages can arise from the election of such officers and county officers annually, over their election for three or four years. Frequent elections render the changes of officers too frequent, and the scramble for office too great. More experience, as a general rule, will be secured during a series of years, by electing such officers for three or four years, than for but one or two; and the expense and idleness, intrigues and other evils, attending their nomination and election, will occur less frequently in one case than in the other. If the annual election of nearly all officers has worked well in New England, it is because they are a homogeneous, educated, and intellectual people. As the foreign element increases, the system may not work so well.

Senates should be filled with men of mature minds, who should hold their offices long enough to acquire experience, and become intimately acquainted with the affairs of the State; but the members of the most numerous branch of the legislature should be elected for a shorter period, that they may feel the public will more sensibly.

Long periods of official service, and holding office during good behavior, serve to educate men for the efficient and proper discharge of official duties, and tend to make skilful officers; but at the same time that system tends to foster an *esprit de corps* among officials; to stimulate the pride of official rank; to excite class feelings and interests, and ambition for high salaries; and to produce indifference and disregard for the interests of the laboring classes. Hence the system is anti-democratic in its tendencies.

Frequent elections for short terms, bring fresh zeal and industry to the public service, but they tend to fill nearly all offices the most of the time with new men, of no official experience, or very little, if any; to foster a petty ambition in great numbers of people, and to induce a general scramble for offices of all grades, high and low. They afford very little opportunity for the proper education of statesmen, and the full development of statesmanship. They have been a great evil in our country, and that evil has been increasing, during the last fifty years.

To secure experience and efficiency in office, and maintain a republican spirit, it seems necessary to observe a proper mean between long and short terms of official service—as each system has its advantages and disadvantages. The experience of our national and State governments indicates, that the best term of service for the most of our executive and administrative officers, is four years. Many, that make first-rate officers, should be continued, and some should be promoted; while those that are not above mediocrity, should retire at the end of their term, that their places may be filled by others. The term of the President of the United States does not seem too long nor too short. It is not so long as to enable the President, by his patronage and power, to obtain an undue ascendency over Congress or the army; nor so short as to make him too weak, and enable Congress very easily to undermine the Executive power. Every President, except Tyler and Johnson, has exercised as much power over Congress, the army, and the people, as was consistent with the public weal.

8*

Sec. 20.—*The representation of minorities.*

Our present system, of giving the entire representation to the majority, in each election district, and none to the minority, is not equal, nor just to the minority. It is neither republican nor democratic, just nor politic. Every principle of equality and justice requires that minorities should have an equal representation with majorities, as far as is practicable, in proportion to their numbers. To attain that end, the following suggestions are made:

1st. Divide a large State into six or eight senatorial districts, giving to each district six senators, to be divided after the first election into two classes, and to be elected for four years;—so that half the senate, three in each district, shall be elected every two years—each elector voting for two persons, or casting two votes for one person, for senator. By that mode, the party having a majority in a district would elect two of the senators at each election, and the minority would elect one.

2d. Divide a State into districts, for the election of members of the most numerous branch of the legislature, without dividing counties,—so that each district may have two or more members, by attaching each county, not entitled to two representatives, to some other county—to form a district. In districts entitled to but two members, allow each elector to vote for but one. In districts entitled to three members, allow each elector to vote for two persons; or to cast two votes for one. In districts entitled to either four or five members, allow each elector to vote for three, or to cast three votes for one. In large cities, entitled to six or more members, let each elector vote, as near as may be, for two-thirds as many persons as the city may be entitled to members, and for not less than three-fifths, nor more than three-fourths as many; or to cast all his votes for a less number.

3d. In forming Congressional districts, if a State be entitled to less than six members, let it form but one district; if it be entitled to six or more members, divide it so that each district shall have three members, and if in so dividing, there be a remainder of one or two, attach them to one of the districts, — giving it four or five members. In States having only one or two members, let each voter vote for one; in districts entitled to three members, let each voter vote for two, or cast two votes for one; and in districts entitled to four or five members, let each voter vote for three, or cast three votes for one.

4th. Elect two Presidential electors at large, in each State, and elect the others to which each State may be entitled, by districts, in the same manner as members of Congress. Let each voter vote for one elector at large, and for the others, to which his district may be entitled, let him vote the same as for members of Congress.

5th. A plurality should elect in all cases; and on canvassing, the requisite number of persons having the largest number of legal votes, should be declared elected, and certificates issued accordingly. By such a system, the minority in each district would be represented, as well as the majority. The former would generally have one-third, and the latter two-thirds of the representation.

6th. In cities, give each ward or district three aldermen; and allow each elector to vote for two, or to cast two votes for one.

7th. In States where they have no county boards of supervisors to audit accounts, equalize and levy taxes, take charge of the county property, the county poor, and county roads and bridges, elect five county commissioners every two years for such purposes, allowing each elector to vote for three, or to cast three votes for one.

8th. For the administration of towns, elect annually a board of five officers, each elector voting for three; and in States where they have boards of county supervisors, let the electors designate on their ballots which shall be supervisor and which town clerk, the other three to be assessors; and the board elected to designate which shall be treasurer. Let the board so elected supervise and equalize the valuation of property for the assessment of taxes, audit the accounts of the town, and constitute the board for the registration of voters, and the election board for receiving, canvassing, and certifying to the votes cast at elections.

Such a system of representation and voting would remedy many evils, remove many facilities and temptations to corruption and fraud, and be productive of many advantages.

1st. It would do justice to the minority, and protect their rights much better than they are now, by giving them a representation and a voice in every election district, and in every county, city, and town board.

2d. By giving both parties a representation and a voice in every county and town, city and village council and administrative board, for levying taxes, authorizing expenditures and contracts, auditing accounts and claims, registering voters, and receiving and canvassing votes at elections, it would subject all such proceedings to a proper degree of publicity; remove the facilities for secret management, favoritism and intrigue, fraud and corruption; and thereby promote honesty and fairness in the transaction of public business.

3d. It would remove the temptation to great party efforts, fraud, and deception—to carry elections in States and districts where parties are nearly equal—because neither party could gain by success or lose by defeat, more than one-third of the representation; whereas one party now gains all the representatives and officers, and the other loses all.

4th. By dividing the representation more justly and fairly between the two great political parties of the day, and rendering it impossible for either party to get all the State senators, members of Congress, or representatives of any State or district, it would lessen the prize to be gained by successful party efforts; moderate the violence of party strife and the intensity of party spirit; and allow voters to act more deliberately and independently, and with less party restraint.

5th. By enlarging the senatorial, representative, and Congressional districts, each would comprise a larger population, more varied interests, and more men of talent and distinction; which would give a better opportunity in many districts to secure men for the State legislature, as well as for Congress, of a higher order of talent and experience.

6th. As no party would be likely to support two farmers, two manufacturers, two mechanics, two merchants, or two lawyers in the same district, all the different employments and business pursuits, professions and classes of men, would be better and more equally and fairly represented than they are now. Nor could the people of one religious denomination, if they constitute a majority, elect all the representatives, as they can now.

It may be further said, that the system suggested has been tested in the triple and fourfold districts of Great Britain and Ireland, under their Reform Bill of 1868, and that it worked well.

To prevent secret and improper management of the directors of corporations, for speculative purposes and private gain, the holders of a minority as well as of the majority of the stock, should be represented as far as practicable, upon the board of directors; and the mode of voting should be prescribed by law, in such a manner as to secure that end.

Public attention in our country has been called within a few years, to the importance of minority representation, as a means of securing fairness in legislation, and in the administration of the government; and also of securing a higher order of talent. There is usually no great scramble for nominations in the party which is in the minority, in a district or county; and hence they generally bring forward their best men.

Upon the recommendation of the Governor of the State of New York, the legislature of 1867, in providing for a *Constitutional Convention*, directed a certain number of members to be elected by districts, and that thirty-two should be elected by general ticket in the State—each elector to vote for only sixteen. The object and the effect was, to return sixteen of the ablest and best men of the State, from each of the two great political parties of the day. The Governor of Ohio, in his annual message to the legislature in November, 1868, said: "The abuses of the elective franchise require the attention of the General Assembly at the present session, and I submit the propriety of amendments to the election laws, *for the representation of minorities in the boards of judges and clerks of elections, and in the registration of lawful voters*, in each township, ward, and precinct, prior to the election."

SEC. 21.—*Double elections, and the prohibition of nominating conventions and caucuses.*

The number of elective offices in the United States is

so great, and the patriots, ready and anxious to serve the country in an official capacity, so numerous, that the practice of holding party caucuses and conventions, to designate candidates to be supported at elections, has become general, and has been developed into a system. The evils of the system have been heretofore shown ; but however great and numerous they may be, the system cannot be dispensed with, in the present state of things, until a substitute has been supplied. My suggestion is, that double elections be held ; that the first one be held two, three, or four weeks before the second, as a substitute for caucuses and conventions—to designate by the voice of the electors of both parties, the candidates to be supported at the ensuing election.

The electors should vote at the first, as well as at the second election, in the method indicated in the last section; the results of the first election to be treated as a mere selection of candidates, and the voters at the second election to be limited in voting, to a certain number of persons having the highest number of votes at the first election—perhaps twice the number for which he is allowed to vote with one added thereto—so that in districts entitled to three members, there may be five legal candidates at the second election ; each voter to be allowed to vote for two of them, or to cast two votes for but one.

Require the election board of officers of each election district, to procure a sufficient number of tickets to be printed and distributed at the polls, at the second election, on each of which the names of all the legal candidates should be inserted, in the order of the number of votes they severally received at the first election, with a proper caption—designating the office for which they are candidates. The voter would then have before him for consideration the names of all the candidates, and should strike out those that he does not design to vote for, and leave upon the ticket unerased the names only of those that he votes for—or if he wishes to cast two votes for one person, he may strike out all the names but one, and opposite that name add the words, two votes.

Previous to the first election, the names of suitable persons for candidates would be announced in newspapers, and political tracts, and handbills, and their merits presented to the people for consideration; and meetings would be held, at which the merits of persons whose names had been suggested as candidates, would be examined and discussed, in connection with the political questions of the day. Every individual would and should be allowed to express freely his choice of candidates; but no vote should be taken to determine the choice of the majority of the meeting between candidates—nor to commit the meeting to support any person or persons as candidates. After the first election the merits and demerits of the candidates selected, would be more fully canvassed and presented to the people, in public meetings, as well as in newspapers, political tracts, and printed addresses.

Such a method of proceeding would supersede the necessity and use of party caucuses and conventions to make nominations; and they might with propriety be prohibited. It would also obviate the necessity of party committees, to procure and distribute tickets; the voter would be relieved from the shackles of party, and from the undue influence of party leaders and politicians; *and the votes cast at each election, would express, as near as possible, the spontaneous choice of the people.* Under such a system, the government would be a popular government, in the full sense of those terms. It would be a government of the whole people, wielded for the benefit of the whole people; while it is now merely the government of a political party, managed to a large extent for the benefit of the leaders of the party.

The representation of minorities, cumulative voting, and the system of double elections, are not necessarily dependent upon each other, and either may be adopted and work well without the others; but all three of them combined would make the reform, and the remedy for our present political evils, the more complete.

CHAPTER IV.

WOMAN—HER RIGHTS, AND THE AGITATION IN RELATION TO THEM; HER CONSTITUTION AND NATURE; HER TALENTS, AND PROPER SPHERE OF ACTION; AND HER CLAIMS TO THE ELECTIVE SUFFRAGE, AND TO THE RIGHT TO HOLD OFFICE.

SEC. 1.—*Woman—her rights, and the agitation in relation to them.*

THE rights of woman are very little regarded by the common law of England; which, with slight modifications, became the common law of all the States of the Union, except Louisiana. By marriage her legal existence was regarded as merged in that of her husband; her personal property absolutely vested in him, became his, and was subject to his sole control, and to the claims of his creditors; her earnings belonged to him; he became tenant during their joint lives, of her real estate, and had its use; and if she had a child or children by him, he became tenant by the courtesy of all her real estate, during his life-time. She could neither sue nor be sued, nor make a valid contract, except as the agent of the husband. She had no rights of property which the law recognized and protected, during his life-time.

That was all wrong. There is no good and sound reason why marriage should not be treated as a special and peculiar partnership for life,—the wife retaining the title and control of her own property, and her earnings also, as fully as the husband does his—both contributing to the common good, according to their ability. So far as the husband manages his wife's property, he should do so as her agent, and only with her assent, and in accordance with her wishes. He should have no power to sell or otherwise dispose of her property, contrary to her wishes, or without her assent; and yet its use and income, or a proper share of it, should be devoted to the common good of the family. There is no propriety in her living in luxury and indolence upon his earnings and property—insisting that he is bound to support her—and to allow her own property, if she have any, to accumulate for her future use. Both should contribute to the common good. Nor should she be allowed to contract debts in his name to adorn her person, or for anything but the most common comforts of life, without his express assent. On the contrary, she should be allowed to make contracts in her own name, and to bind herself by her contracts, and be subject to suit, and able to sue to enforce them; and the husband should seldom be responsible for her acts or contracts. The law should give him the same share of her property after her death, that it gives her of his, and no other. This would put husband and wife upon terms of as near an equality, as their different spheres of life will permit.

Since the year 1840, laws have been enacted in many of the States, and recently in England, to secure to married women their property, and the enjoyment and control thereof, freed from the control of the husband, and from subjection to the payment of his debts. These laws are in some respects defective and imperfect, and yet they secure, in most particulars, the civil rights of married women; and with some amendments and additional provisions, will do so very perfectly. The laws of France treat marriage as a partnership for life; and not only secure to married women all their civil rights, but give the wife such a power and restraining influence over the husband in the management of his business and the sale of his property, that it checks enterprise, and often tends to paralyze his energy.

We now have a class of women who, not content with the protection and enjoyment of all their civil rights, are agitating the public mind to obtain political power—the elective franchise, and eligibility to all offices. Women now nearly monopolize the business of teaching children and youth, have become a great social power in the land, as they should be; and yet some are not satisfied because they do not exercise political power. They are becoming ambitious to hold office, and to hold the balance of power between the two great political parties. They are seeking to become a new element of power, and hence their character and qualifications should be carefully analyzed and examined, to the end that their claims to political power may be fairly considered.

SEC. 2.—*The constitution, nature, and proper sphere of woman.*

Woman's constitution and nature are widely different from man's, and fit her for a sphere of industry and duty very different from his. They are counterparts to each other, fitted to live together as husband and wife, and the heads of a family—his being the more public, and hers the domestic sphere. The difference in constitution, and fitness for different spheres of life, are the sources of the affinities of the sexes, which constitute the strongest and most permanent bond of union which exists among mankind.

Marriage and the domestic relations arise from natural affinities—from the nature, constitution, and association of the sexes, and the fruits of their union. Marriage, or the union of a man and woman for life, in the relation of husband and wife, and as the heads of a distinct family, forms the first stage of organized society. The children of such unions constitute additional bonds of union between the parents. Marriage being the consummation of an agreement for a union during life, is of more consequence to woman than to man, and therefore she should do nothing to weaken the marriage tie.

The union of a man and woman for life, in the holy relation of husband and wife, leads to the full development and perfection of the marital, parental, filial, and fraternal affections, and of all the domestic affections and sympathies; which would otherwise have only a fleeting existence. When the parties are adapted to each other, and each is contented to fill his or her proper sphere, and has capacity to do so—so that all the family duties and offices are satisfactorily discharged—without conflict or rivalship, the relation tends to produce identity of interest, of sympathy, and of hopes and fears for the future; to allay jealousies; and to develop feelings of security and happiness. But to produce harmony of action, and attain these ends, the family must have a head—a business, financial, and directing head; and as a general rule, the husband must be that head, and the wife must act as the confidential friend and adviser, being free to act in accordance with her own opinions and tastes, in all matters within her special sphere; but assigning to the husband the final determination of all matters of finance, the amount of the family expenses, and whatever relates to his own business. Whenever there is a struggle between them, to determine which shall be the head of the family, there is no chance for harmony of feeling or action, nor for domestic affection or happiness. Two heads entirely equal can seldom harmonize in action.

Woman's constitution and nature fit her to be the companion, the assistant, the help-mate of man. She is not his equal in his particular sphere, but his superior in her own sphere. She is superior to him in the delicacy of her organization and in sensibility, in the acuteness of the senses, and in refinement of feeling and sentiment; but she is *not his equal in physical strength, in powers of endurance, in courage and bravery, nor in capacity for business of any kind*—except teaching children and youth. Her constitution and nature render her more timid than man; more apprehensive of danger, and less fitted for the strifes and struggles of a business life; for bold and hazardous enterprises; for navigating the ocean, seas, and lakes; and for subduing, governing, and using animals for labor and practical business. She is not only unfitted for a seafaring life, for hunting and fishing, for military pursuits, but for agricultural pursuits, mining, or manufactures, except as the assistant of man; and she is totally unfitted to act an independent part in public life.

Having less strength and powers of endurance than man, she has less ambition for power and dominion, less inclination to inquire into the principles of science, and to fathom its depths, as stepping-stones to business and wealth—*less power to master the details and complexities of business, and to endure its disappointments, shocks, and reverses.* Having more delicacy and sensibility than man, she is more under the influence of her feelings, and is governed less by abstract rules and fixed principles; and hence her judgment, as a general rule, is not so cool, deliberate, and sound as man's.

Being less able to defend and protect herself, more timid, less fitted for out-door labor and exposure to the elements, totally unfitted for many of the rougher and harder kinds of labor, and having less capacity for nearly all business employments, *she naturally clings to man as her protector, and main support. She is fitted for domestic life, to be the companion, assistant, and help-mate of man*, to raise and educate children, and manage the household affairs. She is fitted for the domestic circle, not the political circle; for domestic life, not for official life;—not for the turmoil of politics, and the strifes and struggles of electioneering campaigns, and contested elections with politicians, roughs, and rowdies.

That woman's talents are very different from man's—fitting her for a different sphere, is evident from her history, and from the fact that, with few exceptions, she has followed different vocations in life; that she has clung to man as her protector, occupied the domestic station as his assistant and help-mate, and seldom attempted to fill a station of independence—except when it was forced upon her by widowhood, or by peculiar circumstances. Many females have been taught the rules and principles, the facts and theories of chemistry and natural philosophy, and have also taught those sciences in the schools, but they have never experimented in them to any considerable extent, and have never made any discoveries in chemistry or natural science. They have sometimes studied the principles of mechanism, and practised several mechanical trades; but they have never been the equal of man in any of them—not even in cutting and fitting clothing; and they have never invented anything of much importance.

Discoveries in natural science and inventions in the practical arts, are never matters of chance; but usually the result of experimenting for years, in accordance with *some theory or conception of the mind;* and the fact that woman has not experimented, and therefore has made no such discoveries and inventions as man has, constitutes of itself conclusive evidence that *she has not had original mental conceptions upon such subjects*, as man has had—and that her talents for mechanics and natural science are inferior to man's, and do not fit her for inventions and discoveries.

Women write interesting novels and literary essays, often give graphic views of domestic life, and sometimes of the facts of history; but they never reach the spirit and philosophy of history. Women have never distinguished themselves as historians, as discoverers in science, as inventors, nor as mechanics, manufacturers, merchants, navigators, or agriculturists; and yet there is no law which prevents them from competing with man, in all such spheres of action, on equal terms; and they would do so, if their tastes led them in such directions, and their talents for such fields of inquiry and action, were equal to man's.

Women seldom think of carrying on business except from necessity. If they inherit property, they live on the income of it, without troubling themselves to carry on business to accumulate more. Not so with man. Business, in an enlarged sense of the word, is his sphere—not hers. It is, perhaps, unfortunate for women, in this extravagant age of the world, that they are so little inclined to maintain their independence—to study and prepare themselves for business, and to exert their talents and energies to carry on business of various kinds for themselves—independent of man; *and are so much inclined to lean upon him for protection, support, and guidance.* The sphere of woman's action might and should be extended to numerous mechanical employments, and to various branches of manufactures, and to trade also; which many women might pursue advantageously; if not fully equal to the first classes of men, in such fields of action. At present they are generally only laborers in such pursuits—occupying stations subordinate to men; but I see no good reason why many of them might not embark in such branches of business as principals, acting an independent part. Such is the case much more frequently in Europe, than in America.

Within a few years past, women have commenced the study and practice of medicine, with a reasonable degree of success. They would be out of place as army surgeons; but it seems evidently fit and proper, that women and children should be treated by female physicians. The sphere for the exercise of woman's talents is wide enough, without entering the field of politics, of law, or of government. As man is the protector of woman, and she leans upon him for protection and support, and is more or less dependent upon him, he fills the primary, and she the secondary place in the family, and in society. The husband and father is legitimately the head of the family; and the guardian, representative, and agent of the wife and children, in matters of business, and also in politics and government.

Single women, who have intellect and habits of industry and economy, may make themselves independent, by their own labor and attention to business; but married women, who are bearing and raising children, cannot attend to much business outside of their own households; and hence their condition is one of comparatively helpless dependence—unless they have considerable property of their own. Marriage is, therefore, in the nature of things, inconsistent with female independence. Such is the general rule, to which there are few exceptions.

SEC. 3.—*The employments and condition, education and tastes, proclivities and ambition of women.*

The inventions of the spinning-jenny, the power-loom, and the sewing-machine, have made great changes in the employments of women, during the last hundred years. Formerly nearly all the wool and cotton, linen and silk, were spun by women, by hand, upon one-thread wheels, and woven upon hand-looms. Spinning and weaving constituted (next to house-work) the principal employment of women—and particularly of girls and unmarried women—so much so that the latter were designated in England as *spinsters*. Now all this is changed: nearly all the spinning is done, and the cloth made by machinery, and a considerable portion of the work is done by men. It was formerly done in families, and gave employment to females for a large portion of the year; it is now done in factories, and does not give a tenth part as much employment to women, as it did prior to the nineteenth century.

Women having less mechanical talent than men, and less ability to manage complicated machinery and keep it in order—men occupy the posts of superintendents in every department of factory labor: and the greatest part of the spinning upon such complicated machines as mules and jennies, is done by men. Even the sewing-machine, by increasing the facility and lessening the labor, has lessened the relative importance of sewing, and increased that of cutting and fitting garments; thrown the business of making clothing more into the hands and under the control of men; thrown females more and more into the subordinate position of executing the details, under the superintendence and direction of men; and in a great measure taken out of woman's hands a business which belongs peculiarly to her sphere of life.

The invention and general use of machinery in the manufacture of cloth, and the use of sewing-machines in making clothing, have all tended to enlarge the sphere of man, and to contract the sphere of woman; to subordinate her industry more and more to his superintendence and direction; and to make her more and more dependent upon him for employment, as well as for support. School-teaching is the principal employment of women, which has been enlarged during the present century,—the teaching of children and youth being now mostly monopolized by females, in the United States.

If woman wishes to enjoy any considerable degree of independence, she must study and practise mechanical industry, book-keeping, and business of various kinds, much more, and give less attention to music and matters of dress and amusement, than she has done heretofore. She must enlarge her sphere of industry, and do more for herself; and rely less upon man. She should carry on business of various kinds herself, and for herself. If she cannot build and manage large cotton and woollen factories, forges and rolling-mills, there seems no good reason why she should not carry on and manage establishments for the manufacture of clothing. If women cannot become shipping and wholesale merchants, and carry on such business successfully, they might keep the shops and stores, and do a large portion of the retail business of both city and country. This is done, to a very large extent, in some countries of Europe. But the women of this country seem to have no taste, and no ambition, for such employments.

Single women of full age,—maidens as well as widows, have the same rights as men—to control their own persons and industry, property and business, to make contracts without any restriction or limitation, to sue and be sued, and to pursue any occupation, employment, or business, which they may choose—except those of a military or official character, and the practice of the law. The professions of medicine, theology, teaching, engineering, architecture, and navigation, are all open to them—as is the business of banking, manufacturing, building and operating railroads; and they can pursue any of these professions and branches of business, if they can find employers, or are fitted for them, and have capital and credit to do as men do—set themselves at work, operate with their own capital and credit, employ other women or men as subordinates, and manage business for themselves. They often inherit property, and even a well-established and successful business. If they had the same capacity and taste for business that men have, they would employ their capital in business, as men do, and manage it themselves. But for some cause, which it is not considered gallant to express in plain terms, ninety-nine in every hundred that inherit property, trust it to men to manage, and do not attempt to carry on business with it themselves.

The question of admitting females into colleges and universities, and giving them the same extended education as men, and in the same classes, has been much agitated of late years; and their exclusion from such institutions has been complained of as a great hardship, and as gross injustice. But if woman's constitution and talents fit her for a different, and not for the same sphere of life as man's, why educate them together? Why not educate them separately—each for the practical duties they are intended to discharge?

Men are educated for the law and other professions—

for civil, mining, and military engineering—to fit them for building roads and bridges, railroads and canals, to open mines, and to take charge of all such works, and others of a mechanical character. The pursuits of woman are such that she needs no such education. She does not need an extended education in mathematics, nor in natural nor mechanical science; because such acquirements are not adapted to her sphere of life, and to the pursuits which she voluntarily follows. She manifests neither taste, practical talent, nor ambition, for the professions and pursuits which demand such requirements. When she builds roads and bridges, canals and railroads, factories and workshops, superintends male as well as female laborers, manages all such departments of industry, carries on commerce by sea and by land, and also banking, successfully; then it will be proper to give her the same education as man; and let her participate, not only in the exercise of the elective franchise, but also in the profession of law—in the administration of justice, and in making and executing the laws of the land. Until she shows herself able and willing to fill all such stations in life, as well as man, and proves it by actual practice, it seems out of place to educate her in the same manner, and for the same sphere of life as man.

Very few young women have ambition to obtain a collegiate education, and are inclined to make sufficient efforts to go through a collegiate course of studies. The most of them are satisfied with the course of studies pursued in our best common schools—some having ambition to acquire some knowledge of music and the fine arts, and a few desiring a more extended education, generally for the purpose of teaching. The chief end and purpose of female education among the middle and wealthy classes of our country, seems to be, to enable their daughters to appear well in society—to please and amuse gentlemen, and to get husbands who can and will support them in ease, and without much effort on their part. Young ladies are educated to spend—not to make money; to live on the earnings and incomes of husbands—not to make much effort to earn a living for themselves; *to live a life of dependence—not to carry on business for themselves and to live independently, upon the fruits of their own industry.* Young ladies and young married ladies are expected to live in ease, though the minds of their fathers and husbands may be so overtaxed with business, and the anxieties attending it, as to wear them out rapidly, and shorten their days.

The constitution, nature, and talents of woman, fit her for domestic, not for public stations; and her tastes, proclivities, and ambition, are all in harmony with domestic life. Hence she clings to man as her protector and guardian; and prefers to have him act as her representative, rather than make the effort and incur the hazard of acting for herself, an independent part. She rarely attempts to act an independent part, except when impelled by stern necessity. She very generally leans upon man more than is consistent with her welfare—or the good of her family.

SEC. 4.—*Woman's rights, the protection thereof, and the relative position of husband and wife.*

Man is the head and representative of the family. He is also the agent and trustee, as well as the protector and guardian of his wife and children, and of their rights and property. He should, in most cases, *have power to manage the property of the wife as her agent, in accordance with her wishes and directions*, and for the joint good and benefit of the two, and their children, if they have any.

He should have no other authority over her property and rights of action; and the law should furnish her an adequate remedy, if he abuse his authority as agent. So far as the English common law vests the property of the wife or any part of it, at marriage, in the husband, it is wrong. He should be regarded only as her representative and agent, with authority to act in accordance with her wishes and interests, in civil matters; but in political matters, his powers, from the nature of the case, must be of a broader character. He must act more independently of her, as her trustee and guardian, as well as her representative, and without directly consulting her wishes.

There is no conflict between the rights and interests of husband and wife, where the law secures to a married woman the control of her own property, person, and earnings, as it does to a husband over his; allows her to make contracts in relation thereto; and allows the husband to manage her property only as her agent, so long as she desires it, and he manages it in accordance with her wishes, for the joint good of the family. On the other hand, the husband often needs protection from the improvident acts, extravagance, and prodigality of the wife. She should be allowed to make contracts and purchases in his name, only as his agent, and with his express assent,—except in very extreme cases of destitution, when the necessity of the case will justify it. As a general rule, the husband should not be responsible for the acts and contracts of the wife.

There ought to be, and as a general rule there is, no antagonism between the rights, interests, and purposes of husband and wife. *They have, in most cases, a unity and an identity of interest. Such is especially the case when they have children in common, to educate and provide for; and neither of them has any other children. Children form the strongest possible bonds of union between parents;*

a bond of union which generally makes their unity and identity of interest apparent to them. The greatest diversities of purpose and of interest, arise in relation to the disposition of their property, when they have two or three sets of children, or no children at all.

The rights and property of single women are as well protected by law, in all civilized countries, as those of men are; and the courts are open to both sexes alike, to redress their wrongs. Under the Napoleon Code the property and civil rights of married women are well protected; and such is the case in most respects, under new statutes passed since 1840, in many of the States of this Union. As a general rule, the same laws which protect the property, rights, and interests of the husband, protect those of the wife also; and in addition thereto, she has, in many of the States, special laws for the security of her property—and when that is the case, she certainly needs no direct participation in the government, to protect her rights. The men may be fairly regarded as the political representatives of the women, as well as of the children, and allowed to act for all classes, where rights and interests are so interwoven, united, and in many respects identical.

Sec. 5.—*Female suffrage.*

While the subject of universal manhood suffrage (including the lowest and most ignorant of the African race) has been agitated and claimed by a great and dominant political party, as necessary to secure the rights of the negroes in our country, promote justice among men, and perfect our system of government, some intelligent and strong-minded women have very naturally conceived the idea, that educated women have higher qualifications for the proper exercise of the elective franchise than the ignorant male negroes, who were recently plantation slaves; and they too have formed what they call an Equal Rights Association, and commenced agitating the question of extending the elective franchise and the right to hold office, to women also. One class cries for universal manhood suffrage without regard to intelligence and capacity to exercise the franchise properly, and to the best interests of the country; while the party more advanced in political theories, recognizing the propriety of universal manhood suffrage, claim and insist that women are entitled to the same rights as men—political as well as civil—and demand universal adult suffrage, without regard to sex. This is demanded as not merely just and proper, but as absolutely necessary to enable women to protect their rights. In fact, some have gone so far as to denounce the withholding of the right of suffrage and political power from women, as gross injustice, the relic of a barbarous age. Such are the extreme views and theories with which our country is agitated.

If education and intelligence constitute the principal and proper basis of the right or privilege of the elective franchise, then it is undeniable that it belongs of right to nearly all the women of our Northern and Western States, and to a majority of the white women of the Southern States also; but does not belong to the late plantation slaves, either male or female.

If being heads of families and householders, acting for others in a representative capacity, constitutes a ground and the only just claim to the elective franchise, then a large portion of the adult male negroes and some women, who are widows, heads of families and householders, should enjoy the franchise, to the exclusion of others, both male and female, white and colored, who do not act in any such representative capacity.

If the ownership of taxable property of the value of

two hundred dollars or more, upon which taxes are paid annually, entitles a person to the elective franchise, as a necessary means of protecting that property from exorbitant and unjust taxation, then a small portion of our women, and a few negroes also, but very few indeed, of the latter, have a just right to vote.

If subjection to military service—to defend the country from foreign or domestic enemies in time of war, or domestic tumults and insurrections, confers a natural right to participate so far in the government of the country, as is involved in the exercise of the elective franchise, then the adult male negroes of our country, if made subject to military duty, are entitled to that right, and women are not entitled to it—unless they have other just claims to it.

If all persons are entitled to the elective franchise without regard to qualification, merely because they are subject to taxation, either direct or indirect, and have personal rights which should be protected by law, then and in that case, suffrage should be truly universal, and should include not only men of all colors and races, but women also, and children of both sexes and all ages that can walk to the polls and put in such ballots as their parents, guardians, or friends may put into their hands. But it would require much boldness and hardihood to claim that minors and children subject to their parents, or under guardianship, and not allowed to make contracts except of a certain class, have a natural right to the elective franchise, the exercise of which requires judgment and information to do it with advantage to themselves, or safety to the community; and yet many of our young men between 16 or 18 and 21 years of age, have higher qualifications for the proper exercise of that privilege, than nine-tenths of the adult male negroes of the South have.

If any class of women are entitled to political powers and privileges, it is widows, who are householders, and act in a representative capacity as heads of families—having minor children under their care and protection, whose rights and interests it is their duty to look after and protect.

The husband is the legal representative of the wife—made so by her own free choice, in accordance with the laws of nature. The rights of married women are generally united and interwoven with those of their husbands; and their husbands so fairly and fully represent them, and their fathers, brothers, and other male friends sympathize so deeply with them, that their rights and interests could be no better protected if they enjoyed the elective franchise themselves. The colored man has much greater need of the elective franchise to protect his rights, than our women have; for the latter have (as I have endeavored to show) representatives and guardians of their rights, and the sympathy, as a general rule, of the whole community; while the poor negro at the South has no such representative and guardian of his rights, and no such sympathy to aid in protecting them.

If females were allowed to vote, it is probable that single women would generally vote with their fathers or brothers, and married ones with their husbands; and thus enable husband, father, or other male friend, to cast practically two votes instead of one—some females voting with one party and some with the other; so that the general result, in most cases, would not be materially changed by female votes. But some females would think and act differently from their husbands and male friends, and would vote in opposition to them;—which would be the cause of dissensions and discords in families, and of contentions and quarrels between husband and wife, and become a more fruitful source of separations and divorces, than all other causes. Domestic peace and harmony are of vastly greater importance to married women, than the personal exercise of the elective franchise. If they cannot trust their husbands, as the heads of their families, to act for them, in the election of public officers, there can be no confidence, and no harmony in the relations of husband and wife; and we should soon get down to a system of temporary domestic unions—in accordance with the agreement and mutual consent of the parties, like other co-partnerships. Women can never profit by claims to political power.

If the women, aspiring to be office-holders and to obtain a share of the offices of the country, should combine together, form associations and political parties among themselves, hold their own separate caucuses and nominating conventions, and canvass for votes as men do, and as they would do very soon, they would hold the balance of power between the two great political parties of the country; and as they would have, in most of the States, as many votes as the men, and in some of the old States they would have a majority of all the votes, they could dictate terms to each party, and would make their own nominations, of a third or fourth ticket, if their terms were not acceded to. Husband and wife, mother and sons, brothers and sisters, and even mothers and daughters, would often be arrayed against each other; and the result would be, that we should have more violent and bitter political contests than we now have; the peace of many families would be destroyed, and we should have the most perfect domestic, as well as political pandemonium in our country, which ever existed on the earth. The bargaining and intrigue, sale and purchase of votes, corruptions and evils, which would necessarily grow out of such a system, would overbalance any possible good that could arise from the change.

Women, whose husbands or fathers have sacrificed their lives or their health in the public service, are entitled to public consideration; and it may be well to appoint them to clerkships, and to post-offices in country villages, when circumstances are favorable. But the idea of encouraging women to dabble in politics as electors and candidates for elective offices, does not strike me favorably. I do not believe public morals or the public good, can be promoted by such means.

The right to vote at municipal elections in England, having been conferred upon certain classes of women by act of Parliament, approved in August last, (1869); and the right to vote at all elections in the territory of Wyoming, having been conferred upon adult females equally with men, by the territorial legislature, the experiment of female suffrage will soon be tried, both in England and America; and its influence upon society and the domestic relations, as well as upon elections and the government, will be tested and ascertained. If it should have a salutary influence upon elections and governments, without disturbing the harmony of families, it will be extended from one Territory and State, province and country to another, until it becomes the established law, among all English-speaking people. On the contrary, if it should have a disturbing and disorganizing influence, and prove a failure, as is generally believed, it will be given up, and the agitation for its extension will cease. In any case, its influence in practice will aid in settling social and political questions of great importance to the cause of civilization, in the only method by which they can be fairly and satisfactorily determined. Theories upon such subjects are often found delusive—when reduced to practice. Until fairly tested by practice, they are uncertain and blind guides—compared with the facts of history, and the results of practice and usage.

SEC. 6.—*Duties of women, and their business in special cases.*

The views presented in this chapter apply to the many of the female sex—to at least ninety-nine in an hundred; and partially, though to only a limited extent, to the remaining few, who have been characterized as the strong-minded. There are but few high prizes in the great lottery of life; and no matter what men's education and talents, acquirements and social position may be, but few of them can possibly obtain high official positions—either in the government or in the great corporations and associated industrial establishments of the country. The mass of men, let their acquirements and capacity be whatever they may, must fill the middle, common, and lower stations of life; and must content themselves with such stations, or be discontented, restless, and unhappy. So with women. Nearly all of them must, from necessity, occupy the middle, common, and lower stations in life; and must cling to their husbands and families, and conform to the condition, rank in life, and social position, in which the Providence of God—birth, marriage, and good or ill fortune, have placed them,—if they wish to fill the spheres which God designed them for, and to enjoy a tolerable degree of contentment and happiness in this world.

As a general rule, a married woman must follow the fortunes of her husband, and move in the same social circle with him, and with the wives of his peers; should conform herself and her industry, her habits of life and style of living, to his business, condition in life, and income; act as a help-mate, to manage discreetly and economically, the family and household affairs, and instruct and aid in educating her children. If she cannot make money, she should study and manage to save as much of his earnings and income as is consistent with the comfort and general good of the family, and do her part to improve their condition, and to accumulate something for the future use and benefit of herself and husband, and their children after them; and not, by a style of living beyond their means, drag herself and her family, as well as her husband, all down together into the slough of bankruptcy and poverty.

The cases where women carry on business, or manage property themselves, are exceptional—in which they fill, to some extent, the usual sphere of men. They may be classed as follows:—

1st. Married women that have inherited or otherwise acquired fortunes or property, and retain the control and management of it themselves, independent of their husbands.

2d. Single women, who carry on business or manage property themselves; and married women, who carry on business independent of their husbands.

3d. Married women, the health of whose husbands has failed, and, by reason of the necessity of the case, and uncommon energy of character, they continue to carry on the husband's business, under his advice—with the aid of employés.

4th. Widows left with children, who continue to carry on the farm, workshop, store, tavern, or other business of the deceased husband, or some other business, with the aid of her children and employés, and for the support and maintenance of herself and family.

In these exceptional cases, women must superintend their business, or some portion of it, keep books of account, make out and settle accounts, make contracts, employ men, settle with and pay their employés, sometimes borrow money and give their obligations, and do many things which properly belong to the sphere of men; but which some women learn, and do successfully. Very few women, however, are inclined to attend to such business, until stern necessity compels them; and when such is the case, the exercise and the attention to business, very generally improve their health, strength, and activity, of both body and mind. Exercise and practice are necessary to develop and give strength to the brain and mental faculties of woman, as well as to her muscles, and other physical organs.

It seems obvious that there should be an enlargement of the sphere of industry for women, and an increase in the number of female employments in this country; but it must depend upon public opinion and the voluntary action of females themselves, and not upon legislation, to make the necessary changes; and hence the elective franchise would be of no use to them, in that regard. The wages of females employed in cooking and household work may be too low to be in keeping with wages in other employments; but neither wages nor employments can properly be regulated by law. The wages of labor depend partly upon custom, but mostly upon demand and supply.

SEC. 7.—*Cooking and household work—Aversion to, of American girls.*

About half of the women and girls in this and all countries, are required for common household work—such as cooking and baking, washing and ironing, nursing, &c., &c.; but owing to the fact that higher wages are paid to females employed in factories, or in teaching, and other causes, there is very generally a great aversion, on the part of American girls, to going out to service to do household work; so much so that the people of the North and West are obliged to depend for such help, mostly upon Irish and German girls—and at the South upon colored women and girls.

When American girls get married, the most of them are ready to conform to their circumstances, and to do housework for themselves, when necessary; but have a great aversion to doing the same kind of work for others. And many of them are not inclined to bring up their daughters to do the same kind of work and drudgery, even at home, which they do themselves for their own families; and they will work beyond their strength, often injure their own health, to save their daughters and bring them up in comparative ease and indolence. Such feelings and aversions to doing housework, are the effects of an unsound public opinion among women; which result in bringing up a large portion of our American girls, without such an industrial education and habits of industry, as are necessary for the future good of themselves and their families.

The want of sufficient female help, and the difficulty in many cases, of getting good help in this country to do housework, is the great bane of housekeeping and domestic life. Housework must be done, and if not all done by females it must be done by men. Who should do it? Many educated and well-bred women who have families and children, and need help to do housework, and are able and willing to pay for it, are compelled to go into their kitchens, for days, and sometimes for weeks in succession, and to work often beyond their strength, to do the necessary cooking and housework for their families. If it were not for the immigration from Europe, and the great numbers of Irish and German girls and women, who are willing to go into the families of others, to do housework, American ladies, in our cities and villages, would very generally be compelled to do the most of their own work, or hire men to do it.

Though housework is a healthy employment, it is mostly solitary work, and therefore unattractive. Sewing, and work in shops and factories, where several females are collected together, gives an opportunity for sociability, and is more attractive on that account. Hence there are thousands of women in cities who attempt to live by the use of the needle, some of whom are compelled to resort occasionally to vice, to eke out a very poor support with the wages of sin, when they could get an honest and much more comfortable living, if they would go into families, and do housework, sewing, and such other work as the circumstances of the family might require.

By reason of great numbers of females becoming teachers and seamstresses, those employments are overstocked, and wages depressed. Complaints are often made, that females are wronged and oppressed, because their wages are so much lower than those of men. In seasons of distress we have occasionally heard that there were thousands of sewing-women in the city of New York, and other large cities, in a suffering condition; and some having children on the borders of starvation,—by reason of the low prices paid for their labor, and a deficiency of work. If large numbers of them would go into smaller cities, and into the country and country villages, and do housework, or any other work, proper for females to do, that they could get, they could all find comfortable homes, and get fair wages; the labor market for sewing-women in the large cities would be relieved; and those that remained there would get more employment, and better pay.

The remedy now sought, by a large class of talented women, for low wages and all the wrongs and evils females are subject to, is female suffrage. They overlook the fact that the prices of labor are governed by custom and the laws of trade, and not by statute laws; that they are regulated by demand and supply, and cannot be prescribed by statute, without doing mischief instead of good; and that there is no connection between the elective suffrage, and the prices of labor. The English reform bill of 1867 extends the right of suffrage to nearly all the laboring men of the kingdom; but it has had no sensible effect upon the prices of labor. The only effect it can ever have upon the welfare of the laborer, will be an indirect one, upon legislation—to lessen and equalize the burdens of taxation, remove the oppressive powers and privileges of the aristocracy and the clergy, and promote good government. We have no such evils to correct, and if we had, do not believe we could correct them by female suffrage. The unfortunate condition of many females as well as men in this country, and particularly of sewing-women in the large cities, is not owing to the government, nor to the law; but to the nature of things—to the state of society, to the sentiments and prejudices of women—to their aversion to do housework, and many other kinds of labor which they might do—and to their improvidence, in not saving more of their wages, to accumulate something for a future day.

If those engaged in the woman's rights movement, would lend their efforts to change public opinion in relation to female employments—to collect and disseminate information among females, as to the demand for and prices of female labor in different cities and sections of the country, and in different employments—to remove the prejudices of their sex against household labor—to enlighten females as to the importance to their future welfare, of saving as much as possible of their earnings, and depositing them on interest in savings-banks, or investing them in national, State, city, or other bonds and good securities, drawing interest, to accumulate something for a future day—those eloquent women would render an invaluable service to their country, as well as to their sex. They would do what cannot be effected by the ballot, by legislation, nor by the government. They would aid in correcting evils, which have not been produced by the workings and errors of the government; but by the workings and errors of society. Hence the remedy must be social, and not political.

CHAPTER V.

THE EXPANSION OF THE POPULATION OF THE UNITED STATES; THE ACQUISITION OF TERRITORY; THE INCREASE OF STATES AND OF POWER, OF INDUSTRY AND OF WEALTH; AND THE POPULAR IDEA OF THE MANIFEST DESTINY OF THE UNITED STATES.

SEC. 1.—*Expansion and increase of the population of the United States.*

THE population of the United Colonies, at the time of the Declaration of Independence in 1776, was less than three millions.

As reported by the census of 1790, it was as follows:

Whites........................	3,172,464
Free colored persons..............	59,466
African slaves....................	697,897
Total..................	3,929,827

Exclusive of about 100,000 Indians.

By the census of 1800 it was......	5,305,937
" " 1820 "	9,638,191
" " 1840 "	17,069,453
" " 1850 "	23,191,576
" " 1860 whites......	26,973,843
" " " free colored.	487,970
" " " slaves......	3,953,760
Total in 1860............	31,415,573

Exclusive of about 300,000 Indians.

The increase by immigration,

From 1790 to Sept. 30th, 1819, was about...	220,000
From Oct. 1st, 1819 to Dec. 31st, 1860.....	5,062,414
Increase by purchase of Louisiana, about....	32,000
" " of Florida, about.......	18,000
" acquisition of Texas, California, and New Mexico, about...............	160,000
Increase by excess of births over deaths.....	21,993,332
Total increase in 70 years...........	27,485,746

This is the greatest and most rapid increase of population which ever occurred in the history of the world; and yet the natural increase in the British North American Provinces, has been about the same; but the increase from immigration has been there, much less. The natural decennial increase of the white population of the United States from 1790 to 1810, was over 33⅓ per cent.; from 1810 to 1820, was nearly 32; from 1820 to 1830, over 31; from 1830 to 1840, about 28; and from 1840 to 1850, it was nearly 25 per cent.; while from 1850 to 1860, it dwindled to less than 23 per cent.

The diminution in the ratio of increase has been caused by greater density of population, more luxurious and expensive living, and later marriages. The diminution of decennial increase in 40 years, from 1820 to 1860, was about 9 per cent.—equal to 2¼ per cent. decline each ten years; we may reasonably expect it will continue, from the same causes, to diminish at the rate of about 2 per cent. each ten years, until it gets down to the ratio of Northern Europe—that is, about 1 per cent. annually, near the middle of the next century: and after that, the ratio of decline may not exceed 1 per cent. in ten years.

Notwithstanding many manumissions, the decennial increase of the slaves of the United States from 1810 to 1830 was nearly 30 per cent., and from 1840 to 1850, nearly 28 per cent.; and including manumissions and fugitives, it was over 24 per cent. from 1850 to 1860—while the natural increase of the free colored people, from 1850 to 1860, was less than 8 per cent. This is a curious fact—indicating that free colored men are not much inclined to marry early, and incur the burthens of raising a family, and that they raise but few children—many dying from want of proper attention, medical attendance, and the comforts of life—while the children of slave mothers, being better provided for, are more generally raised.

Great numbers of the colored population of the South, and particularly of the women and children, died from want, during the war; which so reduced their numbers, that the whole in the United States, probably will not exceed 4,000,000 at the census of 1870; and the increase heretofore, of the free colored population indicates that we need not expect their decennial increase hereafter, to exceed 6 or 8 per cent. But notwithstanding the decline of the ratio of natural increase of our population, both white and colored—under our benign system of receiving and treating immigrants, we may reasonably expect the immigration from Europe and Asia will continue to increase, and to fill more and more the avenues of common labor; and thus keep the aggregate decennial increase of our population up to a high, though gradually declining ratio, until the natural resources of our country shall have been fully developed, and its industry shall have been arrested, by a deficiency of fuel and timber.

Food and materials for clothing can be cultivated by industry and science, much easier, quicker, and more abundantly, than fuel and timber; and hence the exhaustion of the latter will arrest the increase of our industry and population, long before the utmost capacity of the country to produce the former, shall have been reached. The better and more comfortable style of living which obtains in this country than in Asia, will never admit of such a density of population as they have in China.

Considering the great extent, and the diversified and vast natural resources of our country; the active industry and enterprise of our people, and the extensive system of railroads and other improvements made by them; the laws which govern the natural increase of population; the over-populated countries of the Old World and the large streams of emigration to this, I should estimate the probable future population of the present United States and territories, as follows:

In the year	1870	at over..........	39,000,000
"	1880	" about.........	51,000,000
"	1890	" "	65,000,000
"	1900	" "	80,000,000
"	1950	" "	160,000,000
"	2050	" "	320,000,000
"	2100	" "	400,000,000

Many persons, estimating from the past ratio of increase, without understanding the laws of population and the decline of the ratio of increase as population becomes more dense, have estimated our future increase as much more rapid, than I have. I have given the elements of increase. Let the reader judge and estimate for himself. It will require a more careful preservation of wood and timber, than has ever yet obtained in this country; and also a vast system of irrigation in all the interior and southern portions of our country, from the Missouri river to the western limits of California, and thence south to the Republic of Mexico;—and the extensive planting and successful growing of wood and timber in vast districts of country where it does not grow spontaneously, to furnish fields of industry, and the means of support, for such immense numbers of people, as I have stated in my estimates.

It will tax to the utmost degree, the energies of our people, and their institutions and civilization, and the capacities of our schools,—to Americanize and assimilate such vast streams of foreign emigrants and their children, together with our African and Indian population; and prevent our country from finally sinking into anarchy and ruin. Our system of representation and elections must be reformed, or our government and institutions cannot endure such a strain.

SEC. 2.—*The area of the United States in* 1783, *and the acquisition of territory since.*

The area of the United States by the treaty of peace of 1783, and the subsequent acquisitions of territory—including the Lakes, Gulfs, and Bays, over which the government exercises jurisdiction, and the southern half of the chain of Lakes forming the northern boundary, may be stated in round numbers as follows:—

	Sq. Miles.
The thirteen original States, adding Maine and Vermont, about........................	400,000
Kentucky, Tennessee, Alabama, and Mississippi..................................	180,000
The five States north of the Ohio and east of the Mississippi, including the Lakes and the part of Minnesota east of the Mississippi river..................................	270,000
Total from 1783 to 1803.........	850,000

	Sq. Miles.
of which the land comprised about..........	800,000
and the Lakes, Gulfs and Bays about........	50,000
Added in 1803 by the purchase of Louisiana, extending from the Mississippi river to the Pacific Ocean..........................	1,235,000
Florida, purchased in 1819, over............	59,000
Texas proper, lying east of the Nueces river, annexed in 1845, about....................	200,000
Acquired from Mexico in 1847 and subsequently, Western Texas, New Mexico, California, and the intermediate country, about.......	700,000
Alaska, purchased of Russia in 1867.........	580,000
Total since 1867................	3,624,000

being nearly equal to the whole of Europe.

SEC. 3.—*The power to acquire and govern additional territory, and the admission of new States.*

For some years after the organization of the federal government, it was regarded by many as a question, whether the government had power to acquire additional territory; and whether the acquisition of Louisiana by purchase in 1803, was not a violation of the Constitution of the United States. The great importance to the people of the United States, of the navigation and control of the Mississippi river to its mouth, and the whole country drained by that noble river and its tributaries, induced the purchase of Louisiana. The peace and general good of the country also induced our government to purchase Florida. The public good thus induced a liberal, practical, and common-sense construction of the Constitution —that the power to declare and wage war, hold diplomatic intercourse with foreign nations, make treaties, and regulate foreign commerce, implied power to make conquests, and to acquire territory by conquest or treaty; and when so acquired, to govern it, according to the express provision of the Constitution in relation to the government of territories. For more than fifty years, the States, and the people of all political parties, have acquiesced in that construction, as correct: and there is no reason to doubt its soundness.

Prior to the dicta of Chief Justice Taney, in the Dred Scott case, (which the nation has repudiated,) the most of the provisions of the Constitution, and the limitations to the powers of the federal government prescribed therein, were understood not to apply to the Territories; and hence Congress, soon after the organization of the government, fixed the tenure of office of the territorial judges, at four years; and it has not been changed for more than three-fourths of a century—though the Constitution prescribes that "*the judges, both of the Supreme and inferior Courts, shall hold their offices during good behavior.*" The action of Congress thus gave a practical construction to the Constitution of the United States—affirming their power over the Territories, as unlimited by the provisions of the Constitution, which prescribe and limit their powers within the States.

The limitations to the powers of the federal government prescribed by the Constitution of the United States, were intended to limit its powers within the States—not beyond them; to secure the absolute and unlimited sovereignty of the States, in all municipal, police, and local governmental matters, within their respective limits; and do not apply to the powers of the government beyond the limits of the States. Hence its powers beyond the limits of the States, to wage war, acquire and govern territory, regulate foreign commerce and navigation, and to incorporate companies to navigate the ocean, carry on foreign commerce, and to acquire, colonize, and govern distant islands and territories, are as ample and unlimited as those of the governments of the Netherlands and Great Britain.

At the time of the Declaration of Independence, and also at the time of framing the Articles of Confederation, it was hoped and very generally expected, that the Provinces of Canada and Nova Scotia would join the Union; and the hope that those Provinces would be eventually annexed, still continued, when the Constitution of the United States was formed. Hence the language of the Constitution in relation to the admission of new States was made broad and general—that "*New States may be admitted by Congress into this Union;*" and there is no restriction, limiting the new States that might be admitted to such as might be formed out of the territory ceded by Great Britain by the treaty of 1783, and then belonging to the United States.

By refusing to admit Senators and Representatives from the seceding States, holding and subjecting them to the military power of the federal government, and providing, by the acts known as the reconstruction acts, for the formation of new constitutions, and the organization of new State governments therein, the 39th and 40th Congresses of the United States treated them as *de facto* (practically and in fact) out of the Union—as conquered provinces or territories—to be governed as other territories are.

Including the seceding States not yet re-admitted, but under military rule as Territories, the original States and the territory ceded to the United States by Great Britain by the treaty of 1783, now form twenty-five States; and the Territories acquired since, now (1869) form twelve States and nine Territories, besides the Indian Territory, west of Arkansas.

Great benefits, and no great evils, have resulted from the extension of territory, and the multiplication of States; but it should be remembered that the territories acquired were all new, having very few inhabitants, and large natural resources inviting settlers and colonists from our country. The Louisiana territory, at the time we acquired it, had a population of French and Spanish descent, about 32,000; Florida, 18,000; Texas, 20,000, of Mexican origin; California, 50,000, and New Mexico, 60,000. In the present State of Louisiana, French manners and customs, and French law, have had, and still have, a great influence; and in many districts French customs and the French language still maintain the ascendency. A similar state of things exists in New Mexico; but all the other new States and Territories, acquired since 1783, have been mostly settled by Anglo-Americans, who carried with them the English language, Anglo-American customs and institutions, attachments and sympathies, Anglo-American law, and generally the Protestant religion; so that nearly all the States west of the Mississippi river, are as thoroughly American, and as strongly attached to the Union, as the States east of that river are. There have been but very few members of Congress of either House from the States west of the Mississippi river, who were not born east of that river, or of Anglo-American parentage; and hence the Senators and Representatives from those States have not introduced any foreign and discordant elements into Congress, and have not been a source of discord in our government.

So long as the jurisdiction and powers of the federal government are confined to national and inter-State objects and purposes, it will not be seriously embarrassed by a multiplication of contiguous States, having many interests in common; always provided, that the people generally speak the English language—are sincerely attached to the Union and the government, and to our Anglo-American institutions—and that the most of them are educated and assimilated to a large extent to our people, in manners and customs.

A few of the northern States of Mexico, lying mostly north of the 27th degree of latitude, and having each but a very small population, might be annexed to our country without detriment to it; because they could be settled and improved by our people and thoroughly Americanized—as much so, at least, as Texas or Louisiana; but such is not the case with the remaining twenty-one States, lying in a hot climate, having a mixed population of about 8,000,000, speaking a foreign language, and mostly uneducated, ignorant, and superstitious, and without any attachments to our Union, government, or institutions. To Americanize them, and assimilate them to our people, would be impossible. To admit such a people, living in a tropical climate, into this Union, with over forty of their members in the United States Senate, and Representatives in the other House of Congress according to their numbers, would introduce into our government and country elements of discord; which would necessarily demoralize our politics and government, and eventually involve the country in civil war, and destroy the Union.

There would be the same objection to the acquisition of Cuba and Porto Rico, and admitting them into the Union as States, allowing them to participate in the election of President and Vice-President of the United States, and admitting their Senators and Representatives into Congress. The only difference would be, that two such States would be less dangerous to the Union than twenty.

There is no such objection to the voluntary admission of the British North American Provinces; for the reason that the people of those Provinces are mostly of the same races and origin as those of the United States; speak the same language; have, to a large extent, the same history; are accustomed to institutions, laws and usages, and to a system of representative government very similar to ours; and have the same habits of industry, and the same energy, stability of character, and regard for law and order, as the people of the United States. Their geographical situation is such, and the character of the people so nearly assimilated to ours, that they would bring no new discordant elements into the Union; and their commercial, industrial, educational, religious and social, as well as political intercourse with our people, would soon become extensive and intimate. But no such state of things could ever exist between the people of the United States and those of Mexico, or Cuba.

SEC. 4.—*Increase of industry and commerce, wealth, and power.*

The industry of a people must depend,

1st. Upon the climate, the extent, and natural resources of the country they inhabit.

2d. Upon their advance in civilization, and the mechanical instruments they have to labor with.

3d. Upon facilities for internal and domestic commerce, and also for foreign commerce.

4th. Upon the character of the government and its policy, the administration of justice for the protection of person and property, and the system of taxation.

A dense population creates markets for the products of industry, which cannot exist in a sparsely peopled country. The denser the population, the greater the facilities for trade and commerce, and the mutual interchange of the products of industry, the more trade and commerce will react upon industry, give it encouragement and stimulus, diversify it, and increase its products—if the resources of the country be sufficient to give full employment to the people. The resources of our country have been ample, and superabundant; but spread over so large an extent of territory, as to induce our people to scatter so much, as to impede commercial intercourse, and industry also, and increase the cost of products; and at the same time lessen the value of nearly all products, at the places of growth or production.

By means of the steam-engine and other mechanical inventions, made since the middle of the eighteenth century, Great Britain now supports more than three times as many inhabitants as it did then; and with much greater comfort. Their coal and iron were of but little value to the inhabitants, until after the invention of the steam-engine, and machinery for rolling iron. Since those inventions, the importance of coal and iron has been increased by every new invention and improvement, but more by railroads and locomotives, and by steam navigation, than by all others. The large agricultural resources, and the immense mineral resources concentrated in so small a country, together with the density of the population, and numerous good harbors, all contributing to give facilities to a diversified industry, and to both foreign and domestic commerce, have given to the industry of the people of Great Britain great advantages over that of the scattered population of the United States. British manufacturers have also had the advantages over the Americans, in priority of time, in the establishment of their factories and workshops; in training their workmen, to enable them to acquire skill; in a superabundance of laborers and capital; and in the low prices of labor, and low rates of interest.

American industry has been constantly brought into competition with the great manufacturing establishments of Great Britain, France, and Germany, under all the disadvantages referred to; and if it had not been for the incidental aid arising from the duties levied upon imported foreign products for the support of the federal government, any considerable growth of American manufactures would have been impossible; and we must have remained, like our Canadian neighbors, mostly an agricultural people—dependent upon Europe for the most of our clothing, iron, and hardware—with but little industry, energy, and wealth, compared with what we now have; and with vastly less population—for with less industry and wealth, we should have had fewer canals and railroads, less employment for labor, and fewer attractions to induce emigration from the Old World.

The freedom and workings of our political and religious institutions, freedom of domestic commerce, the press, and the common-school education of the whole people of the North, together with the higher institutions of learning for the professional classes, have given to our northern and northwestern people, as a whole, more activity of mind, and more diversified mental and physical activities and intelligence, than any other people on the earth; and put them in the front rank of modern civilization. The printing-press and the post-office, steam navigation and railroads, locomotives and the electric telegraph, diffuse information so rapidly, that mechanical inventions and discoveries in science made in Europe are known and put into practice in this country, almost as soon as in the country where they originate. Though some branches of our manufactures have been at times greatly depressed, by reason of the adverse circumstances referred to; and the finer and more delicate grades of manufactures have not been established among us, yet for mechanical industry and all the more common grades of manufactures, which are made with machinery, and the manufacture of tools and implements of industry, our people have shown themselves quite equal to any people of Europe; and the superior mental activities and freedom of our people, have put them ahead of all other people, in the number, variety, and importance of their mechanical inventions, made since 1789.

Nearly all the great inventions of Great Britain were made prior to the organization of our present federal government, in 1789. Since that time the processes of spinning and weaving, and rolling iron by machinery, have been improved; the processes and instrumentalities for the manufacture and use of coal illuminating gas, for lighting buildings and streets, and the locomotive also, have been invented in England; some other minor original inventions have also been made; and many improvements upon former inventions have been effected in that island, though but few of a novel character.

The mechanical inventions and improvements made in the United States since 1789, exceed (I think) in number, those of all the rest of the world; many of which have been, and are of great value to the human family—including the cotton-gin; the steamboat; the process of cutting nails; the electric telegraph; planing machines, and various machines and instruments for working wood, iron, and other metals; improved printing-presses; mowing and reaping machines; ploughs, cultivators, drills, and other agricultural tools; revolving five and six shooting pistols; revolving turrets for heavy guns in gunboats; and sewing-machines to aid in making clothing. By means of modern inventions and improvements, agricultural industry, as well as most other industries in the

United States, are at this day, at least twice as effective as they were at the close of the eighteenth century.

For some years, many branches of mechanical and manufacturing industry in our country, were depressed by oppressive internal revenue taxes; but the removal of such taxes to the amount of about fifty millions of dollars, has greatly relieved them.

Duties have been imposed upon many imported articles, for the double purpose of raising revenue to support the government, and also to give incidental aid to competing domestic industry; but great mistakes have been made by Congress in their tariff acts, in not discriminating properly between imported manufactures, and raw materials imported, to be used here in manufacturing. To give incidental aid to American manufacturing industry, by means of duties imposed upon imported foreign products, such duties should be imposed only upon imported manufactures, and not upon materials to be used here, and worked up into American manufactures;—nor upon machinery and the mere tools and instruments of industry. Heavy duties imposed upon foreign wools and dyestuffs, balance and neutralize, to a large extent, the duties levied upon imported woollen goods; and tend to cripple the woollen manufactures of our country. So with ship-building. The heavy duties imposed upon many of the materials used here, have nearly destroyed the business; and the utter prohibition of registry to foreign-built vessels, prevents their purchase by American navigators and shipping merchants, and has thrown nearly all the passenger business, and the largest part of the transportation between the United States and foreign countries, into foreign ships. All the lines of steamships running between the United States and Great Britain, France, and Germany, which carry our mails, are owned in those countries. None of them are owned by American citizens.

Heavy duties should be levied upon imported manufactures and luxuries of all kinds; and low duties, or no duties at all, upon breadstuffs, provisions of all kinds, fuel, materials to be used in manufacturing, and the tools and instruments of domestic industry. When the condition of the country (as it does now) requires taxes for revenue purposes, to be levied upon all classes of imports, comparatively small and low duties should be put upon food and fuel, materials to be used in manufacturing, and the tools and instruments of industry and practical business. Ships and vessels are the tools and instruments, with which the great and important employment of navigation is carried on. Iron ships are coming into very general use. They can be built cheaper on the Clyde, in Scotland, than in any other country. The iron ships for the British Government, for France and Germany, and also for England, are mostly built on the Clyde. There is no good reason why American citizens should not be allowed to purchase abroad, and import iron ships, upon the payment of a moderate duty of ten or fifteen per cent., and to have them registered and used as American vessels. To prohibit them from doing so, is *carrying the doctrines of protection to such absurd lengths, as to defeat their general purposes, of promoting domestic industry.*

Notwithstanding the enormous taxation which is imposed upon our people, our inflated currency, and the many disadvantages under which many branches of manufacturing industry are laboring, nearly all branches of American industry are in a reasonably prosperous condition, *with the exception of ship-building, navigation, and the manufacture of woollen goods.*

To transport the products of industry and carry on interior commerce, we have over 4,000 miles of navigable canals, over 2,500 miles of navigable lakes and bays, nearly 10,000 miles of river navigation, and over 40,000 miles of railway. These extensive improvements and instrumentalities, and the large amount of business done on them, attest the magnitude of our industry and interior commerce. The making of such immense and costly improvements, attests also the enterprise of our people, the magnitude of their industry, and the increase of our national wealth and power.

Statements and estimates, founded upon the census reports, of the values produced in the United States, during the undermentioned years, ending June, stated in millions of dollars and fractions.

	1840.	1850.	1860.
Mining, making iron, castings, salt, &c.	$26.65		
Manufactures and mechanic arts.	196.68	$464	
Flouring and saw mills, and oil mills	23.58		$854
The forest, except fuel	14.76	25	
The fisheries	10.33	11	
Agriculture and fuel, exclusive of mineral coal	580	800	1,250
Commerce and navigation, transportation and banking, &c.	188	300	526
Total	$1,040	$1,600	$2,630
Amount to each person	$60.87	$69	$83,63

The foregoing table includes only commercial values, inherent in material and tangible products, which are the subjects of sale and delivery. It does not include the rent, or use of dwelling-houses, furniture, household labor, teaching, or labors in the legal, medical, or military profession, the ministry, or in any public service.

The productive industry of the people of the United States for the year 1869, valued in like manner in gold, would probably amount to $4,000,000,000, or over $100 to each person. Prior to the year 1800, it did not exceed

$50 to each person. The following table shows the value of the domestic products exported from the United States at different periods, and the increase thereof.

Statement in millions of dollars and fractions thereof, of the aggregate value of cotton and of all domestic products (exclusive of coin and bullion) exported from the United States, during the under mentionedfiscal years.

Years.	Cotton.	Other Products.	Total of Domestic Products.
1790.......	·04	19·62	19·66
1810.......	15·1	27·26	42·36
1820.......	22·3	29·38	51·68
1830.......	29·67	28·85	58·52
1840.......	63·86	47·80	111·66
1850.......	71·98	62·92	134·9
1855.......	88·14	104·61	192·75
1860.......	191·8	124·44	316·24
1865.......	5·72	248·76	254·48
1866.......	*281·38	186·66	468·04
1867.......	202·91	182·81	385·72
1868.......	152·78	217·66	370·44

The values for the year 1865 and since, are stated in currency; from which about one-fourth part should be deducted to reduce the amount to the value of coin.

Though our industry and exports have been large, and increasing rapidly; our extravagance, imports, and consumption, have increased still more rapidly than either. Our imports of foreign products have exceeded our exports, and the excess has been constantly increasing; draining us of nearly all the gold and silver which our mines produce, and involving us more and more in debt to the manufacturing nations of Europe.

* 650,572,829 lbs., valued at an average of 43 cents.

SEC. 5.—*The Destiny of the United States.*

The increase of the American Union from 13 to 37 States; the territory thereof, from about 850,000 to over 3,600,000 square miles; and of the population, from less than four millions, to nearly forty millions, in about eighty years, has impressed our people very generally, with an exalted idea of the future destiny and power of the United States. Many think that all North America and the West India Islands also, will be eventually annexed to the United States, and that it is the manifest destiny of our country to rule the continent.

If we can reform our system of elections and representation, and thereby make our government a government of the whole people, instead of a government of the leaders of the dominant party; moderate the intensity and violence of party spirit, and revive a spirit of patriotism among the people; and arrest the downward course of corruption in our national and State governments, and the thirst for dominion and new States, there can be no doubt of our future progress, power, and glory as a nation. But if we continue the present system of party domination, and scramble for office, and downward course of prodigality and corruption, which have been increasing upon us since the acquisition of Texas, our destiny as a nation is uncertain. That we shall continue to increase in numbers and industry, commerce and wealth, and also in national power, for half a century or more to come, seems certain; but if we continue to reach after more territory, and grasp after the States of Mexico, the West India Islands, and the Provinces of British America, and acquire them one after another, and incorporate them into the Union as States, with equal political rights and an equal representation with the original States, in both houses of Congress, our national interests will become so numerous and incongruous; our population so heterogeneous; the national character and sentiments, religious views and aspirations of the people of different sections so discordant; the bonds of union so weak; corruption and profligacy so rank and bold; and sectional ambition so rampant—that the American Congress will become a discordant and turbulent mob, and it will be impossible to reconcile the jarring elements, and prevent the flames of insurrection and civil war from bursting forth; which may rage and devastate large sections of country, and eventually result in the division of the national territory and the people thereof, into several different nations, according to their affinities of race and origin, religion and language.

Those who suppose that the whole of North America and the West India Islands, and the various populations thereof, of different races and origin—speaking different languages, professing different religious creeds and opinions, and accustomed to different institutions, laws, and usages, can all be permanently united under one federal, representative, republican government, with equal rights and powers—overlook, or sadly misunderstand the facts of history. To assimilate them, and form a national character for the whole, would be impossible. Climatic influences, if nothing else, would prevent such a result. The people of the torrid and temperate zones, and high latitudes, can never live in harmony, on terms of equality, under one and the same republican government. Our history shows, that the descendants of the Cavaliers in the Southern States, and the descendants of the Puritans in the Northern States, could not assimilate, so as to form a homogeneous national character; though both have had the same origin and national history, speak the same language, and profess substantially the same religion. Climatic influences prevent the assimilation.

If the peoples of two small and contiguous countries, or parts of the same country, (like Holland and Belgium,) having the same origin, and no radical differences except language and religion, and such as have been produced by differences of language, religion, and government, cannot live together under one government, and that a limited monarchy, it is vain to think that the people of the present United States, the Mexicans, Cubans, Canadians, and the Negroes of St. Domingo and Hayti, can all live together in harmony, on terms of political equality, under one and the same representative, republican government. I may say to our ambitious partisan politicians, Ahoy! there are breakers ahead.

Great Britain has long governed from an hundred to an hundred and fifty millions of people in Hindostan, by and under the colonial system; but finds it very difficult to govern less than five millions of Catholics in Ireland, with a representation in the British Parliament, elected by the subjected people. If the inhabitants of British India were as well represented in the British Parliament as Ireland is, according to their numbers, the British Empire and government would soon crumble to pieces; and several governments and independent nations would emerge from the ruins. The West India Islands and the States of Mexico can never be admitted into this Union upon an equal footing with the present States, without endangering the stability of the Union and federal government, and eventually destroying them. If they should ever come under our federal government, they can be governed with safety to the Union, only on the territorial or colonial system; or we must exercise over them very limited powers, in the form of a protectorate.

CHAPTER VI.

THE REVENUES AND TAXATION, DEBTS AND FINANCES OF THE UNITED STATES—COIN AND SPECIE PAYMENTS—CURRENCY AND BANKING.

SEC. 1.—*Revenues and taxes, debts and finances of the United States.*

REVENUES of the United States for the fiscal years ending June 30th.

	1868.	1869.
From Customs	$164,464,600	$180,048,427
Internal Revenue.........	191,087,589	158,356,461
Lands....................	1,348,715	4,020,344
Direct Taxes.............	1,788,146	765,685
Post Office and other sources	46,949,033	27,752,830
Total, exclusive of loans..	$405,638,083	$370,943,747

EXPENDITURES OF FISCAL YEAR 1869.

Interest, &c., on the public debt.......	$130,994,242 80
Pensions and Indians................	35,519,544 84
Civil Service.......................	56,474,061 53
War Department	78,501,990 61
Navy Department....................	20,000,757 97
Total	$321,490,597 75
Surplus to apply on debt.............	$49,453,149 46

On the 1st day of December, 1869, there were outstanding United States bonds, issued to the Pacific railroads, payable thirty years from date, with six per cent. currency interest, amounting to $62,625,320. The Railroad Companies being required and expected to pay those bonds and the interest thereon, they are not regarded as a debt of the government.

Statement of the debt of the United States on the 1st day of December, 1869, exclusive of the Pacific Railroad bonds:

DEBT BEARING INTEREST IN COIN.	
Five per cent. bonds..................	$221,589,300
Six per cent. bonds....................	1,886,348,700
DEBT BEARING INTEREST IN CURRENCY.	
Three per. cent certificates............	$47,195,000
Navy Pension fund, three per cent......	14,000,000
Debt on which interest has ceased......	4,292,026
Treasury notes bearing no interest......	356,113,258
Fractional currency..................	38,885,565
Certificates of gold deposited...........	36,862,940
Interest accrued.......................	42,947,893
Total..........................	$2,648,234,682
Amount in the Treasury—coin........	$105,969,949
Amount in the Treasury—currency.....	11,802,766
Sinking Fund, and United States bonds and interest......................	76,902,232
Amount to be deducted.............	$194,674,947
Balance of debt......................	$2,453,559,735
1865, Sept 1st.—Balance of debt.......	2,757,689,571
Paid off in four and one-fourth years....	$304,129,836

The revenues and expenditures of the federal government, all derived from taxes, customs, and postages, except from one to four millions annually, received for lands sold, were as follows, for the fiscal years ending June 30th:

Years.	Revenues.	Expenditures.
1866	$558,032,620	$520,750,940
1867	490,634,010	346,729,120
1868	405,638,083	377,340,285
1869	370,943,747	321,490,598

The expenditures include the annual interest paid upon the public debt; the surplus revenues being applied to reduce the principal of the debt. Such enormous revenues collected in time of peace, from a people impoverished by war, attest the extravagance and prodigality of the government, and the oppressive taxes imposed upon the people. So large revenues were never before collected from any people, in proportion to their numbers, in time of peace.

The dominant party seems to have had an unnecessary anxiety to pay off the national debt rapidly, and in a few years; and, for fear the interest of it would oppress the next generation of people, the present generation has been oppressed and almost crushed with taxation, to pay not only the interest, but on an average over seventy millions of dollars annually, of the principal. Our State and city governments do not pursue such a policy. They contract large debts for public purposes and improvements; are content to pay the interest only; and leave to the next generation, who will be more numerous, and enjoy the advantages of the expenditures, to pay the interest in like manner. Great Britain and other countries of Europe have pursued such a policy, for more than a century past.

Statement of the amount of the funded and unfunded debt of the United Kingdom of Great Britain and Ireland, at the undermentioned periods :—

		Debt in pounds sterling.	Decrease.
1817	February 1st......	£840,850,491	
1838	January 5th......	792,306,442	£48,544,049
1855	March 31st.......	775,215,519	17,090,923
1860	" "	802,190,300*	
1865	" "	786,510,795	15,679,505
1867	" "	777,497,804	9,012,991

Since 1860, large amounts of the public debt have been converted into terminable annuities; no less than five millions sterling were so converted in 1864; and the estimated capital of such annuities was thus increased from 1860 to 1867, nearly six and a half millions sterling —so that the real decrease of the public debt of Great Britain, in seven years of peace, from 1860 to 1867, was only £18,230,000—about ninety millions of dollars; while the public debt of the United States has been decreased by payments, in four and one-fourth years, more than three hundred and four millions of dollars. The policy of England is, to impose no heavier taxes and burthens on the people than are necessary to pay the current expenses of the government, and the interest on the national debt; and leave their successors to bear equal burthens with themselves.

Sec. 2.—*Income tax.*

The first act of Congress to impose a tax on the incomes of individuals and corporations, was approved July 1st, 1862. As amended March 3d, 1865, the law exempts

* The debt was increased by the Crimean war with Russia.

from such tax, $600 of income, and also the rent actually paid for a dwelling-house for the family, or the rental of the dwelling owned and occupied for a residence, ordinary repairs thereof, and all national, State, county, and municipal taxes paid, and losses in business, incurred during the year; and imposes a tax of five per cent. on the excess of incomes over $600 and under $5,000, and a tax of ten per cent. on the excess of taxable incomes over $5,000. It also imposed a tax of five per cent. on the dividends, and net surplus profits of banking, canal, insurance, railroad, and turnpike companies; and a like tax on the interest paid by such companies upon their bonds —which virtually represent so much invested in such companies; the bonds being substitutes for stock, and the interest thereon for dividends.

The Act of March, 1867, under which the tax upon incomes of the calendar year 1866, or fiscal year 1867, and subsequent years were levied, exempts from tax, rents and taxes as before, and $1,000 income; and imposes a uniform tax of five per cent. upon all incomes over $1,000, and also upon the dividends, surplus profits, and interest on the bonds of corporations.

Statement of the number of persons charged with income taxes, and the aggregate amounts collected, during the undermentioned fiscal years, ending June 30th:

	1866.	1867.	1868.
No. of persons taxed..........	460,170	259,385	240,000
U. S. officers and employés...	$3,717,395	$1,029,992	$1,043,561
Other persons, 5 per cent......	26,046,760	31,492,694	32,027,611
do do 10 per cent.....	34,501,122	25,547,946	
Bank dividends and surplus profits........................	4,240,663	3,774,975	3,624,775
Canal companies' dividends, &c.	203,234	195,382	215,280
Insurance companies.........	783,882	563,474	605,490

	1866.	1867.	1868.
Railroad dividends, &c........	$3,461,769	$3,379,262	$3,889,430
Turnpike Co., dividends, &c..	27,333	30,703	49,551
Total on incomes............	$72,982,158	$66,014,428	$41,455,698
Deduct half of 10 per cent. tax	17,250,561	12,773,973	
	$55,731,597	$53,240,455	

For fiscal year 1869, reported at..................$34,791,856

If all the income taxes were collected the same fiscal year they were levied, and the incomes were all honestly and truly returned, and the number of persons charged with income taxes were reported, those taxes would show with accuracy, the amount of net incomes during the previous calendar year, of that class of persons; but it seems that nearly half the amount levied is collected the following year after the levy—so that though no ten per cent. tax was levied in the year 1867, more than 25 million dollars of that class of taxes were collected in 1867, which were levied the previous year; and by means of the change of time for levying income taxes from May to March, made by the statute of 1867, the ten per cent. tax reduced to a uniform tax of five per cent., and the exemption increased from $600 to $1000, more tax was collected than was levied, during the fiscal year 1867. The Commissioner of Internal Revenue should report, for the information of the public as well as the Secretary of the Treasury and Congress, the amount of income taxes levied each year, in each district, and the number of persons taxed, as well as the amount collected. Such information would be of great value.

Business was better and profits larger during the calendar years 1865 and 1866, than they have been since; and the Commissioner's reports indicate that, reckoned at the uniform rate of five per cent. they would amount for the fiscal year

1866,	with	the $600	exemption,	to about	56	millions.
1867,	"	" $1000	"	"	48	"
1868,	"	" $1000	"	"	42	"
1869,	"	" $1000	"	"	36	"

The stocks and bonds of the banking, railroad, canal, insurance, and other companies that pay income taxes, are nearly all owned by the same persons that are taxed in the income accounts; and the dividends, surplus profits, and interest, may be reckoned as a part of their incomes.

Statements and estimates from the Commissioner's reports, of the number of each class of persons assessed with an income tax in the fiscal year 1867,—including the stockholders and bondholders of corporations, charged with income taxes; the range of amounts and the average amount assessed to each class; and a calculation of the actual amount assessed.

Amounts from		Running to	Average amount paid.	No. of persons.	Amounts assessed.
		$20	$10	68,000	$680,000
$20	to	50	30	48,000	1,440,000
50	to	100	60	32,000	1,920,000
100	to	500	200	58,000	11,600,000
Over $500 each			600	54,000	32,400,000
Total				260,000	$48,040,000

The rate of the tax being uniformly 5 per cent., the taxable income is calculated from the amount of the tax, and the amount of incomes exempted must be calculated from the number of persons, and estimates of the rents and rentals of their dwellings, and of the value of products consumed, mostly by farmers, which are not included in their accounts of income. The exemptions for rents,

&c., over and above the $1,000, of the two lowest classes of tax-payers, may be fairly estimated at $300 each; of the next class at $500 each, for rents; of the 4th class at $1,000 each, for rents; and of the 5th class, for the rental of their residences, many of them of a palatial character —valued from $20,000 to $200,000 or more, at $2,000.

Statement, based upon the foregoing estimates of rentals of dwellings, and other exemptions, of the average and aggregate net incomes of each class,—including the value of the rental of the dwelling-houses and premises occupied by their families:—

Classes.	Average.	Persons.	Aggregate.
1st class	$1,500	68,000	$102,000,000
2d do	1,900	48,000	91,200,000
3d do	2,700	32,000	86,400,000
4th do	6,000	58,000	348,000,000
5th do	15,000	54,000	810,000,000
		260,000	$1,437,600,000
Add for persons not included		10,000	
Add $4\frac{2}{3}$ per cent. for omissions and under-statements			62,400,000
Total incomes of about 270,000 families			$1,500,000,000

The 270,000 persons who were assessed with income taxes in 1867—including the 10,000 other persons omitted, were generally heads of families, and with their families reckoned at an average of $5\frac{1}{2}$ to the family, they numbered about 1,485,000 persons; or one twenty-fifth part of the whole population of the United States.

The 200,000 additional persons, or families, who were assessed with an income tax in 1866, under the $600 exemption, and omitted in 1867, under the $1,000 exemption, had incomes from over $600 to $1,000 each—over and above the rental of their dwellings and gardens, and the farm products consumed by farmers; which would swell their net incomes to an average of about $1,000 each, over and above taxes. Of the 6,480,000 remaining families, nearly one-third of them probably had incomes averaging $800 each; one-third of them $600 each; and the remaining third, or about 2,100,000 families, comprising more than nine-tenths of the colored population, had incomes from labor only, varying from $250 to $500, and averaging about $400 each.

RECAPITULATION AND RESULTS—INCOMES.

270,000 families, mostly charged income tax					$1,500,000,000
200,000	"	having $1,000	income	each	200,000,000
2,080,000	"	"	800	"	1,664,000,000
2,100,000	"	"	600	"	1,260,000,000
2,100,000	"	"	400	"	840,000,000
6,750,000 families having net income, of over and above taxes, except duties on imports, during the calendar year 1866.					$5,464,000,000
U. States taxes, over and above duties,					314,000,000
State, county, city, township, school, and road taxes, estimated from returns of census of 1860 at					140,000,000
Total incomes (currency values)					$5,918,000,000

The incomes from unproductive as well as productive labor, and from property also, are included—embracing merchandising, official and professional services, teaching, printing and publishing, household work for pay, and the rental of all the dwelling-houses in the United States.

Out of that gross sum, the duties on imports were paid —amounting in gold to $176,417,000—equal in currency to $235,000,000
To which add other national taxes 314,000,000
State, county, city, and other local taxes 140,000,000

Total taxes for the year.................. $689,000,000
equal to over 11½ per cent. of all the earnings and incomes of the people of the United States. No other people were ever so borne down with taxation, in time of peace!

Such are the taxes and incomes, and the great disparity in the incomes of the people of the United States. The figures show that one twenty-fifth part, or four per cent. of the people, have and enjoy over 27 per cent. of the aggregate net amount of incomes over taxes of the whole population of the United States; and yet we have public men, and editors also, who are opposed to a renewal and a continuance of the income tax; and others who advocate a reduction of the amount thereof; who are in favor of retaining nearly all other taxes as they are, for the present, and for some time to come. It would be well for them to consider the facts here presented.

Income taxes take only a small portion of the surplus, of those that have a surplus; which is not needed for the comforts of the family, except in very few cases. They do not burthen industry, business, nor the poor; but simply take a part of what would otherwise, as a general rule, be needlessly expended, or added to the accumulations of the wealthy and the middle classes.

Heads of families, whose annual incomes are less than $1,000, cannot accumulate much; and very few of them can live comfortably and accumulate anything; and hence we may fairly estimate, that three-fourths of the amount of all the accumulations of property in the United States, are made by the classes that pay an income tax. To relieve these classes from the income tax, and retain other taxes to support the government and pay the interest on the national debt, would only enable the wealthy and the successful business classes, to accumulate forty or fifty millions of dollars more property annually, without relieving industry, or the laboring classes, in the least.

The laboring classes, as consumers of tea and coffee, sugar and molasses, spices and fruits, salt and rice, drugs and medicines, and other necessaries imported, pay at least half as much tax per capita, as the wealthy do; and it is impossible to reach the wealthy classes, to any considerable extent, by federal taxation, except by either an income tax, or a direct tax on real and personal property. Direct taxes are often very oppressive to small property holders, who have small incomes. The income tax is a modern substitute for a direct tax; and with proper exemptions, it is more equitable and less burthensome—for it does not touch dead property, which yields no income, and does not burthen poor families, who have only a house and lot, or a little farm, and a small amount of other property, with an income from all sources, less than $1,000—over and above taxes. Without an income tax, the wealthy men, who have large incomes, would not pay to the federal government one-tenth part as much tax in proportion to their incomes, as the laboring classes do.

The exemptions in the income tax law might be improved; but as a system of taxation it is sound, and eminently just and wise. There seems to be no propriety in allowing very large sums for house rents, nor in allowing a single person or two persons, the same amount of exemptions as to a family of eight or ten. Why not allow about three hundred dollars for one person, six hundred for two, and one hundred dollars for each additional person in a family—with a sum not exceeding $200 for the rental of a house?

SEC. 3.—*Duties on imports.*

Statement of the aggregate amounts of duties paid upon each of the following classes of articles, imported into the United States during the fiscal year ending June 30, 1868, compiled from the report of the Bureau of Statistics:—

Duties upon	Amounts.
Chemicals, drugs, and dyes	$4,085,228
Hemp, gunny cloth and bags, and hemp carpeting	2,422,471
Chocolate and cocoa	61,336
Coffee	10,657,845
Tea	9,414,664
Fruits	2,588,946
Ginger	74,822
Pepper, cloves, and other spices	1,950,455
Gums	629,844
Hides and skins	977,325
India rubber—raw	196,911
Pig-iron	1,011,110
Linseed, olive, and other oils	549,687
Sugars, sugar candy, molasses, and melada	34,858,066
Boards, plank, and scantling, timber, staves, firewood, lath, and other lumber	1,317,598
Coal	492,557
Wool	1,645,448
Salt	1,136,225
Rice	1,146,286
Total on the above articles	$75,216,824
Duties on other articles	$89,247,776

The duties upon the articles and classes of articles specified in the foregoing table, are excessively high, unnecessarily burthensome to consumers, prejudicial to American industry, and especially injurious to the laboring classes. As a general rule, duties should be levied for purposes of revenue only, upon raw materials to be used in manufacturing or as a means of industry, and upon all agricultural and raw products other than luxuries, which do not come into competition with domestic industry; and high duties should never be imposed upon such articles, unless the exigencies of the country imperatively demand it.

Experience has shown that the farmer derives no substantial advantages from the duties imposed upon wool, and particularly upon coarse and common wools; nor upon hides and skins imported into the United States—though such duties are very prejudicial to the manufacture of woollen goods, and of leather, boots and shoes, and burthensome to the consumers of such products. Nor do the heavy duties imposed upon sugar and molasses, salt and rice, lumber and hemp, coal and pig-iron, promote domestic industry and the general interests of the country, in a degree commensurate with the burthens thereby imposed upon the consumers of such articles; and great injuries to other branches of industry, arise from the duties on lumber and hemp, and on wood, coal, and pig-iron.

As to the other articles named, some of them are used in the arts and in manufacturing, and none of them come into competition with domestic products; and therefore the duties should be levied for purposes of revenue only; and should be as low as the exigencies of the Treasury will permit. Perhaps half the present duties should be taken off from sugar and molasses, salt and rice, and pig-iron; that the duties upon other articles named should be reduced—some to one-third, and some to one-fourth the present rates; and that the duties on drugs and dye-stuffs and on lumber, should be reduced still lower. If fifty or sixty millions of taxes on these articles were taken off, it would be a great relief to people of all classes as consumers, and greatly promote many branches of American industry.

Heavy duties on lumber from Canada and other British provinces, raise the prices to consumers of domestic as well as foreign lumber, lessen importations, and encourage the cutting of timber rapidly in our own forests.

Our railroads, canals, and navigable waters, furnish such facilities for transporting and distributing sawed lumber and timber, that nearly all the pine fit for sawing, now growing near navigable or floatable waters, will be cut off during the next twenty years.

We have immense prairies and plains, with very little wood and timber near them; and it should be the policy of the government to preserve, not to destroy the wood and timber, and especially the good sawing timber of the country. Looking to the future good of our country, sound policy would dictate that very small duties should be imposed upon lumber, wood, and timber, imported or brought into the United States; and that such importations should be encouraged—to save our timber as long as it may be practicable to do so. It would be much better policy for the State governments to exempt wood and timbered lands from taxation, and as a substitute, to impose an equivalent amount of taxes upon cord-wood, saw-logs, or sawed lumber and timber, when taken from the land,—and thereby encourage the preservation of wood and timber, rather than to encourage their rapid destruction by heavy duties upon such imports. Our railroads consume immense quantities of fuel; and wood and timber are diminishing rapidly, in every section which is supplied with them. In three-fourths of Europe, Asia, and Northern Africa, it is more difficult for the people to procure fuel than food; and such is the case now in more than half of the States of this Union.

On account of the great importance of railroads, the extremely large demand for railroad iron—much beyond the capacity of the American iron mills to supply, it would seem that the duties on railroad iron should be reduced. They amounted during the fiscal year 1868, to $2,196,142.

The dogmas of free-trade and the doctrines of ultra and indiscriminate protection of all branches of domestic industry alike, are in many respects diametrically opposed to each other; and there is between them a wide domain, for free-trade in some articles, and the imposition of large duties upon others, to raise revenue—whereby incidental aid, and what is called protection, will be afforded to American industry. The protectionists embrace numerous classes, many of whom carry the doctrines of protection to such extremes as to favor the indiscriminate protection of all branches of American industry; and think it good policy to impose large duties upon imported wool, as well as woollen goods; upon raw hides and skins, as well as leather boots and shoes; upon coal, wood, and pig-iron, as well as bar-iron and hardware; upon sawed lumber, timber, and hemp, as well as upon manufactures of wood and hemp; and to prohibit absolutely, the purchase of foreign-built vessels by American citizens, and the registry thereof, as American vessels.

Indiscriminate duties upon raw products used in manufacturing, as well as upon manufactured articles, which require skill and science, and also the concentration of capital, skilled labor and machinery, to produce, serve to neutralize and balance each other, so far as any benefits to American manufacturing industry are concerned. Duties upon raw materials to be manufactured aid the foreign manufacturer, by increasing the cost of American manufactures which come into competition with imported goods; and thereby discriminate against, and tend to depress American industry. England, France, and other manufacturing countries of Europe, have learned a wiser policy. They generally impose no duties, and very low duties if any, upon raw materials to be used in manufacturing—that their manufacturers may make goods at as little cost as is practicable, to enable them to sell at such prices as to be able to undersell their neighbors, and compete successfully in foreign markets.

SEC. 4.—*Financial, industrial, and commercial condition, at different periods.*

The foreign debt of the people and government of the United States, in 1830, was only about 100 millions of dollars; but we then had but few miles of railroad, and but few canals and other internal improvements, compared with what we have now, and very little capital employed in either manufacturing or mining industry. Now (January, 1870), we may estimate the cost of our railroads, rolling stock and buildings, at nearly 2,000 millions of dollars, and they will soon be worth, in the aggregate, as much as they cost.

The capital invested and employed in mechanical, manufacturing, and mining industry in the United States in 1830, did not exceed 200 millions of dollars; in 1840, it was, as appears by the report of the census, 296 millions of dollars; in 1850, it was over 525 millions of dollars; in 1860, it had increased to nearly 1,010 millions of dollars; and it may be fairly estimated now, at 1,600 millions of dollars; while our foreign debt has swollen to thirteen or fourteen hundred millions of dollars.

The debts of the States were constantly increasing, from the commencement of the Erie canal, in 1817, until the end of the rebellion, in 1865. In 1830 they were about 40 millions of dollars; over 198 millions in 1840; over 250 millions in 1860; about 348 millions in December, 1865; and 323 millions of dollars in December, 1868. Nearly all the State debts, contracted prior to the commencement of the rebellion in 1861, were for making canals, improving the navigation of rivers, and building railroads, or aiding incorporated companies to build them; and half or more of the State bonds were sold in Europe, to procure the means of making such improvements. The most of our foreign debt arose from such sources.

The canals and river improvements in the United States, had cost in 1830, about 40 millions of dollars; 100 millions in 1840, and over 160 millions in 1860. The amount invested in railroads, depots, and other railroad buildings and bridges, and in rolling stock, was, in 1830, about two millions of dollars; in 1840, about 130 millions; in 1860 it was reported at $1,151,558,000; December, 1867, $1,655,483,000; December, 1868, $1,869,525,000; and in January, 1870, it may be fairly estimated at 2,000 millions of dollars.

With the exception of the large amounts expended during the rebellion, the moneys borrowed by the States were very generally well and profitably expended. In most of the States, the State debts represent property to their full amount; and so far from the people being poorer, or burthened by reason of the contraction of such debts, they are actually wealthier—for the improvements made with the monies borrowed, have been very generally productive, and pay the interest on the loans. They not only facilitate business and promote industry, but they have actually increased the value of property, often from two to five times as much as their cost.

Our city debts have also become large. In 1840, the debts of thirteen of the then largest cities in the Union, exceeded twenty-five millions of dollars. Since that time they have been constantly increasing, and probably at this time (January, 1870) they amount to from 100 to 150 millions of dollars. A large portion of them was contracted for water works and market houses, railroads, and other productive improvements, and now represents productive property, the income of which pays the interest on their cost; but large amounts of the city debts were contracted for public buildings, school-houses, sewers, bridges, parks, &c., which produce no income—though they are useful and valuable. Nearly all the city debts represent valuable property. The debts for school-houses and educational purposes have increased taxation more than those of any other class.

The debts of railroad corporations, and other incorporated companies, are also very large. They represent a portion of the capital invested in such improvements and business—the stock of the companies representing only a part of the capital so invested.

So far as our national, state, city, county, and corporate bonds are held by our own citizens, our country and citizens in the aggregate are none the poorer on account of them—though the interest on the national bonds, and on some of the other bonds also, render it necessary to impose taxes upon the property and industry of the whole people, for the benefit of the few who hold them; but so far as they are held abroad, they not only oppress the industry of the country, and impoverish it to pay the interest, but they also embarrass the commercial relations of the country, and drain it of specie.

It is very generally estimated that nearly 1,000 millions of dollars of our national bonds are held abroad, mostly in Europe, together with 200 or 300 millions of State, city, and corporate bonds and stocks, besides a mercantile debt against our country of 100 millions, or more—making an aggregate of 1,300 millions, or more; on all of which, except a portion of our mercantile debt, interest must be paid—amounting, in gold, to from 75 to 80 millions of dollars, annually. The effects of such a drain must be obvious to every reflecting mind.

Statement, showing the outlines of the financial condition of the United States:

	In 1840.	December, 1869.
Population	17 millions.	39 millions.
National debt	$5⅛ do.	$2,453⅓ do.
State debts	198 do.	323 do.
City debts	25 do.	over 100 do.
Foreign debt of the country	230 do.	1,300 do.
PRODUCTIVE INVESTMENTS.		
In canals and river improvements	100 do.	165 do.
In railroads and bridges	130 do.	2,000 do.
In mechanical, manufacturing, and mining industry	296 do.	1,600 do.

The canals and river improvements, railroads and bridges, and investments in mechanical, manufacturing, and mining industry, costing, in 1840, only about 526 millions of dollars, and in December, 1869, about 3,765 millions, constitute our principal instruments and agents of industry, and interior commerce. They also constitute our principal assets, which must be set against our national, State, and corporate debts, and especially our foreign debts; and taken in that view, they are indices of the great progress we have made, during the last thirty years, in industry and interior commerce, and show that the financial condition of the country, with its immense war debt, was vastly better in 1869 than it was in 1840.

The productive industry and aggregate incomes of the people of the United States, valued in gold, were nearly four times as much in 1869 as in 1840.

I have heretofore carefully estimated,* from the census of 1840, the productive industry of the United States for the preceding year, at................ $1,021½ millions.

The Internal Revenue reports indicate, that in 1869 it amounted to about.... $3,800 millions.

The total incomes of the whole people, from unproductive as well as productive industry and business, including the rental of dwelling-houses, in 1840, amounted to about................ $1,250 millions.

And in 1869, they probably were (in gold) $4,600 millions.

And in currency, nearly.............. $6,000 millions.

By reason of railroad facilities, the growth of cities, and the much larger proportion of the people being employed in mechanical, manufacturing, and mining industry—whereby the markets for breadstuffs and provisions have been increased, agricultural products, at the places of growth, have increased, perhaps twice as much in gold values, as in quantities.

Average annual amounts of the exports and imports of the United States (exclusive of coin and bullion), during the under-mentioned periods of five fiscal years each—stated in millions of dollars:—

	Exports.	Imports.
5 years, ending in 1827,	$75 millions.	$78⅔ millions.
5 do. do. 1832,	71⅜ do.	80⅜ do.

* See my Essays on the Progress of Nations, vol. I., pp. 461, 462.

5 years, ending in	1837,	$108⅛	millions.	$130⅔	millions.
5 do.	do. 1842,	110½	do.	114	do.
4¾ do.	do. 1847,	118	do.	94⅜	do.
5 do.	do. 1852,	155¾	do.	176⅓	do.
5 do.	do. 1857,	246⅞	do.	295⅝	do.
5 do.	do. 1862,	293	do.	288⅝	do.
5 do.	do. 1867,	321¼	do.	324½	do.

This table shows not only the great and regular increase of the foreign commerce, and particularly of the exports of the United States; but also presents evidence of the increase of the national industry.

Coin and Bullion.	Exported.	Imported.
In 25 years, to 1847....	$143⅓ millions..	$234.44 millions.
Excess of imports,...............		91.1 do.
In 20 years, to 1867,...	$974¾ millions..	223½ do.
Excess exported,..	751¼ do.	

Nothing but the gold fields of California has enabled the commerce and industry of the country to sustain such a drain of specie. The production of gold has had a wonderful influence upon our commerce, and has greatly stimulated our industry. It has also stimulated the avarice and ambition, pride and extravagance of the American people.

The loyal States prospered during the war—notwithstanding the enormous weight of taxation, and the heavy drain of men from the industrial and business classes. The industry of the seceding States was entirely crushed; but it has been rapidly reviving since the close of the war. With the exception of the shipping and ship-building interests, the manufacture of woollen goods, and some minor industries, the industrial interests and business of the whole United States are in a reasonably prosperous condition; and yet, owing to our immense foreign indebtedness, much larger (and perhaps three or four times as large as any other nation ever had), our inflated paper currency, and inflated prices of labor, as well as of nearly all property and products—the mania for more railroads, and the prodigious amount of capital absorbed annually by the construction of new roads—and the general extravagance of the people, as well as of the government, our country is in a critical condition; and the most of our business men and capitalists are apprehensive of a coming crash—of a sudden fall in prices and in the value of property, and a great depression in industry and business.

What is most needed by the people, is to be relieved as much as possible from the burthens of taxation—to have the tariff laws properly adjusted to the condition and industrial interests of the country, and the currency slowly contracted, or kept steady, and not allowed to expand. To be relieved from the public debt and the burthens of taxation to pay the interest, is impossible, without dishonor; but to impose taxes to pay off the debt rapidly, is needlessly oppressive and cruel.

SEC. 5.—*Evils of a depreciated currency.*

A redundant or superabundant currency is always, and necessarily depreciated, in its purchasing capacity. A depreciated currency tends to increase the prices of all the products of industry, the cost of living, the prices of labor, and the prices of rents and all kinds of property—to raise them all above the standards of the commercial world—to derange the business relations and industry of a country, and the relations of debtor and creditor—and to raise the prices of products so high as to check and lessen exports, and invite an increased amount of imports; and thereby create an unfavorable balance of trade, and embarrass the foreign commercial relations of the country.

While the process of inflation is going on, it tends to make some suddenly rich, and to foster pride and extravagance. Our country has been laboring so many years under the influence of a depreciated currency, that its evils have been fully developed, and are very generally recognized; and I may safely say, that they are now very greatly exaggerated, by a large class of persons, who are inclined to attribute to the currency, evils which are incident to and produced by an immense public debt, the prodigal expenditures of the federal government, and the enormous taxation imposed upon the people to pay the interest on the debt, and support the government.

The system of carrying on the war, paying off the army and the public creditors generally, with treasury notes, was so easy, the first effects were so good and so apparent, and the evil effects mostly so distant and slowly developed, that the people as well as the government were very generally lulled into a false security, and did not realize, until after the war closed, that the redundant paper currency increased the cost of the war and the public debt, five or six hundred millions of dollars; and perhaps more. It levied a sort of forced loan upon the people, which enabled the debtor class to pay their debts in a depreciated currency, and to take advantage of their creditors, to the amount of several hundred millions of dollars.

These evils have been perpetrated and are past, and there is no remedy for them. There can be no remedy for past public evils. They have been endured by the creditor, and there is no remedy for him; the government can have no remedy for its losses, without dishonor; and those classes that have suffered from it by reason of the enhanced cost of living, can have no remedy for the evils which have been imposed upon them. The people have now accommodated themselves to two currencies—one of gold, used by importers to pay for foreign goods and the duties imposed upon them, and one of paper, used in all other transactions; for the importer, after paying the cost of his goods and the duties upon them in gold, calculates their cost in currency, and regulates his sales by their cost in currency. The cost of labor and of all the products of the country, and the price of labor and products are adapted to each other upon the currency standard; the banks and the currency have performed their functions admirably well, with great regularity, and with as little fluctuation in prices as has occurred in any country during the last four years. During all that period the principal evils the people have suffered, have arisen from enormous, and in many instances crushing taxation; which has hung like an incubus upon the laborer, the capitalist, and the business man—depressed the business and the industry of the country, and lessened the comforts of the masses of the people.

There has been of late a great clamor for the resumption of specie payments—as if that could cure the principal evils under which our country is laboring. The hopes and expectations upon which that clamor is based, are as delusive as those of the administration were, when they were issuing hundreds of millions of treasury notes; which answered a temporary purpose in carrying on the war, but, being carried to excess, produced enormous evils in their effects. To return suddenly to specie payments, when our currency is equal to about eighteen dollars to each person in the United States, would oppress the debtor classes of the community, and derange again the business and industry of the country more injuriously and disastrously, than the original inflation, and soon end in failure.

SEC. 6.—*Standard of value, and causes of depreciation of value.*

It is said that gold and silver are standards of value, recognized as such throughout the commercial world; and the only standards of value that are so recognized. That is very true; but though the best and only standards of value we have, they are very far from perfect and uniform standards. A portion of their value is artificial —arising from the practice of coining, and from the laws of civilized nations, making them a tender for debts. Like everything else, their value, when measured by labor, or the products of labor, has fluctuated very much in different countries, and gradually declined, ever since the discovery of America, and the opening of the rich mines of Mexico and Peru. Though labor and the common products of labor fluctuate more quickly and frequently than the precious metals, yet taking long periods of time in any country of Europe into consideration, the price of a day's labor, of a bushel of wheat, or of a pound of iron or copper, has changed less than that of either gold or silver.

Prior to the discovery of America an ounce of gold or silver would generally purchase in Europe about three times as much wheat and provisions or other products of labor, as it would in 1850; and the relative value and purchasing power of those metals have depreciated not less than twenty per cent. since the discovery of the gold mines of California and Australia—so that £1 sterling in gold at this day possesses no more purchasing power in England, France, or Germany, than sixteen shillings sterling in gold did, twenty years ago.

The value of gold, like everything else, depends upon the relation between the demand and the supply; and the supply has increased so rapidly during the last twenty years, and become so much in excess of the real wants of the commercial world, that it has depreciated in value to such an extent as to require one and one-fourth ounces of gold to buy as much grain or other products, as one ounce would pay for in 1850.

Paper money becomes depreciated by redundancy—by an excessive supply beyond the wants of a healthy commerce—by the same causes which depreciate the value of gold, the value of labor, and all the products of labor; and when it becomes redundant, it ministers to and stimulates unhealthy speculations in stocks, and property of various kinds. It may also become depreciated by a want of security for and confidence in its redemption and payment. But such is not the case with our present currency—furnished by the federal government and the national banks—all resting upon the credit and power of the government, and the resources and wealth of the country—receivable for taxes and nearly all dues to the government, and much of it made by law a legal tender for debts between private persons.

It is undeniable that our paper currency is all depreciated, for three dollars in gold have been sold for four dollars or more in paper, the most of the time since the war closed. The law having made the most of it a legal tender for most purposes, the principal cause of its depreciation is redundancy—the excessive amount of it which has been issued. The amount of treasury notes, fractional currency, and bank-notes in circulation and deposited in the banks, amounts to nearly seven hundred millions of dollars; or about eighteen dollars to each person. No other country ever had such an excessive circulation of paper money, which did not very soon become nearly worthless. The average circulation in Great Britain and Ireland, during the last fifty years, (including coin and bank-notes) has been about ten dollars to each person; and in France it has been still less.

SEC. 7.—*Specie payments.*

It is supposed by some that specie payments possess a miraculous power to prevent as well as to cure an inflation of the currency—to raise the value of an inflated and depreciated paper currency, and to maintain it at the par value of gold. The experience we have had in the United States ought to dispel and extinguish all such fallacious opinions. For many years previous to May, 1837, our banks regularly paid coin for their notes when presented, with the exception of a few that failed. And yet, the expansion of the circulation commenced in the fall of 1834, continued to increase during the years 1835 to 1836, and until about the first of January, 1837, when it attained its maximum; and including the coin in use, it was equal to about eleven dollars to each person. The fact was, money became excessive in amount—greater than the wants of the country required; and as the paper money was convertible at will into coin, *both paper and coin were depreciated in value.* This was made evident by the general rise of the prices of property and products. The inflation of the currency and its excessive amount, stimulated a spirit of speculation into a perfect furor of excitement; and the result was a great revulsion, a panic, and a general suspension of specie payments by all the banks, in May, 1837, numerous failures and almost a suspension of business for many months, throughout the country. All this occurred when our country was free from any national debt, or any cause of disturbance or embarrassment, except what arose from a redundant currency, the speculations stimulated by an excessive amount of money, and the anxiety to invest advantageously; and from excessive imports of foreign goods.

Having largely reduced their circulation, the sound banks resumed specie payments again in 1838; but the circulation was still so large, and the imports of goods and the exports of specie so large in 1839, that the banks were compelled to suspend again in October, 1839; and they were not able to resume specie payments again until 1842—when the whole money in circulation, both coin and bank-notes, had been reduced to about five dollars to each person. From that time until 1850 the circulating medium of our country was gradually increased from five dollars to about seven and a half dollars to each person; and after the discovery of the gold fields of California, the paper money and coin in circulation continued to increase, until they amounted in 1857 to over nine dollars to each person—when another panic, revulsion, and suspension of specie payments by the banks occurred, which spread embarrassment and bankruptcy far and wide.

All these things have occurred in time of peace—in Europe as well as in our own country—when we were free from a national debt or any unusual cause of embarrassment, and when our taxation was light compared with what it is now. They occurred also, when all the banks in the United States in good credit were paying coin for their notes when presented; when bank-notes were convertible into coin at the will of the holder. These facts show that *specie payments have no power to prevent an inflation of paper money, and the disastrous consequences which necessarily follow such inflation.* The history of banking, and of inflations, revulsions and suspensions of specie payments in England, have been of a very similar character. The most commercial and industrial nations of Europe have generally had only from eight to ten dollars circulating money to each inhabitant; and whenever we have had more than eight dollars to each person in the United States, it has always stimulated speculation, produced an inflation of prices, and led to a suspension of specie payments, and to a great revulsion. Nothing but the legalized suspension of specie payments has saved our country for years past, from a more severe revulsion than even that of 1837; for our burthens of taxation are three times as heavy as they were then.

Our experience shows that *a mixed currency of paper money and coin, the former convertible into the latter at the will of the holder, serves to delude the people and lull them into a false security and belief that all is safe*—while an expansion may be going on and increasing, before the excess becomes so great as to be much noticed; but when it becomes so great as to become very palpable to bankers and capitalists, it soon leads to efforts at contraction, to a stringent money market, embarrassment, panic, and revulsion, and often to wide-spread bankruptcy and ruin. *Some other and more effectual remedy than specie payments merely must be sought, to limit the amount of paper money, and the aggregate circulating medium of the country.*

Even if specie payments were an effectual panacea under favorable circumstances, and when the currency is not inflated, I do not believe it possible to resume and maintain them, until the aggregate amount of paper money shall have been reduced to about eight dollars to each person, so that with the addition of the coin that will be in use, the whole circulating money of the country will not exceed ten dollars. So long as the foreign debt of our people and country amounts to 1,200 or 1,400 million dollars, and requires 70 to 80 millions annually in gold to be exported to pay the interest, and the balance of trade is also against us, it must be very difficult to maintain specie payments until our circulating medium is reduced in amount below that of either Great Britain or France; whose national debts are due to their own people, and not to foreigners. With so large a foreign debt, drawing coin annually to pay the interest, and a balance of trade against us constantly calling for coin, if specie payments were resumed, how long would it take to drain so much specie from our banks as to alarm them, induce a curtailment of discounts and issues, a stringency in the money market, a panic, and a severe revulsion?

SEC. 8.—*Reduction of the currency.*

The late Secretary of the Treasury, in his annual report in December, 1868, said "*Our debased currency must be retired, or raised to the par of specie*, or cease to be lawful money, before substantial progress can be made with other reforms." The second alternative of the Secretary's proposition, *to raise the currency to par with the present value of specie*, without retiring a large portion of it, is an impossibility.

It should be remembered as a well-known law of trade, that the volume of money in circulation in proportion to the annual products and business of a country, determines its purchasing power, and the prices of labor, and of property and the products of labor, offered in the market; and that coin as well as paper money depreciates in value, when it becomes excessive in amount. It may be affirmed as a truth, that whenever there is a mixed currency excessive in amount, consisting of coin and paper money, and the law compels the issuers of the paper to redeem it in coin, the natural tendency and effect is, to degrade the value and the purchasing power of the coin to the standard of the paper, and to equalize the commercial values of the two. This truth is illustrated by our high prices in 1836, when we had a mixed currency of coin and convertible bank-notes. Such is the necessary effect, until the aggregate currency is reduced, by retiring a portion of the paper, or exporting a part of the coin.

As prices depend upon the volume of the currency, it is impossible to reduce the prices of products and labor, and the expenses of living, to a proper standard, without first reducing the volume of the currency. If we had a circulation of 700 millions exclusively coin, the prices of products and labor would be and remain the same as they are now—until the amount of the circulation should be reduced by exportation; but the evil would tend to correct itself, and it would not be long before the amount would be reduced by exportation to the proper standard. Hence there is no danger of having prices inflated very long by an exclusively metallic currency. But a mixed currency and compulsory specie payments by the banks, furnish no safeguard against inflation—as our experience in 1836 and 1856 plainly shows; and hence a resumption of specie payments, before the volume of the currency has been reduced to its proper amount, would be of no sort of consequence, except to increase the exportation of specie, and bring on a revulsion.

If it were possible to resume specie payments while we have in circulation 700 million dollars of paper money, and to put all that volume of treasury and bank-notes on a par with coin, the necessary effect would be, not to raise the purchasing power of paper money, but to depreciate the purchasing power of gold to the present depreciated standard of paper money; and property, products, and labor, whether paid for in paper or gold, would remain at the same prices as they are now—so palpably above the prices in other countries as to lessen our exports, discourage and lessen domestic production (as was the case in 1836), and invite still larger imports, until our supply of gold to pay with became exhausted, and the banks and the Treasury were again relieved from the pressure upon them, by a general suspension of specie payments.

The inexorable laws of trade are such that it is impossible to reduce prices and the expenses of living and of production in this country to a proper standard, without first reducing the volume of the currency. And with a very large foreign debt drawing interest in coin, with a considerable balance of trade against the country, it will be impossible to resume and maintain specie payments, until the volume of money is so reduced, as to reduce the prices of provisions and agricultural products generally, below the prices in other countries—so as to admit of an increase of exports, and a more favorable balance of trade.

Looking at our present foreign debt, and the circumstances and condition of the country now, and in 1837 and 1857, and the causes of the terrible revulsions of those years—resulting mostly from a redundant mixed currency, and enormous extensions of the credit system, stimulated by an excess of paper money, it does not seem probable that we can resume and maintain specie payments, until the aggregate amount of our currency shall have been reduced below ten dollars to each person. Considering the increase of our population, if the currency could be reduced 30 or 40 millions a year for five years in succession, we might perhaps successfully resume specie payments at the end of that period.

The laws of trade are fixed in the nature of things and of man. They are inexorable, and cannot be controlled by statutes of Congress, by public opinion, nor by any human device. Man must conform to them, or suffer the consequences of violating them. There is no escape from the penalty, when the laws of nature are violated.

SEC. 9.—*Preparations for specie payments.*

Let us suppose that Congress provide by statute for the resumption of specie payments by the government and the banks, in July, 1870, or at some later period; some preparation must be made, both by the government and the banks, to meet such an event. The government should provide at least 150 millions of dollars of coin, and the banks 100 millions, over and above the amounts now on hand. How can that be done?

During the three years ending June 30th, 1868, the coin and bullion exported from the United States amounted to $240,696,731, and the imports were only $46,473,495; excess of exports over imports $194,223,236, equal annually to $64,741,078, and absorbing all the products of our mines. In fact, nearly all the products of our mines, during the last twenty years, have been exported, to pay interest and the balance of trade against us. How can the government and the banks accumulate the coin necessary to provide for a return to specie payments? Can either procure coin in any mode, except by sending United States bonds and other American stocks and bonds to Europe for sale, and importing their proceeds in gold? In that way we should increase our foreign debt nearly 300 millions, to procure 250 millions in coin, and should render our condition as a people and a nation, worse than it is now.

As a part of their preparation, the banks would lessen their discounts, and gradually draw in and lessen their circulation; and while the process was going on, capitalists, and perhaps mostly foreign capitalists, would be hoarding our treasury notes and bank-notes, ready to draw and export the specie when the time for resumption should come. During that period, the amount of money in actual circulation would be decreasing; the money market would become more and more stringent; the debtor and business classes of the community would find it more and more difficult to meet their engagements; the future would look more and more uncertain; all of which would deter capitalists from loaning freely, and deter business men from entering into new engagements and new enterprises; and the seeds to produce a panic would be gradually accumulating.

When the period for resumption had come, the flood of paper that would probably be thrown upon the Treasury and the banks for redemption, would reduce the circulation very rapidly—until as in 1839, we should find the bottom of our troubles, in the necessity of suspending again, with a circulation reduced to 300 or 400 millions of dollars.

SEC. 10.—*What is the remedy?*

It appears to me that a gradual reduction of the amount of treasury notes, is the only remedy that is practicable, safe, and certain. If, to avoid the disturbance of business and industry that would necessarily follow a sudden contraction of the currency, which would precede and attend an early resumption of specie payments, the government should withdraw and fund for several years in succession, 30 or 40 millions annually, the difficulty could be tided over without any great national shock. But to resume at an early day and maintain specie payments without a reduction of the currency, would be an impossibility.

It is said, however, that a gradual reduction of the currency, by withdrawing and funding treasury notes, has been tried, and proved a failure. I know it has been partially tried and a clamor raised against it; because it pinched some classes, and tended to check speculation. But it was tried under a very unequal and unfair distribution of the currency; and it may be remarked, that it will be impossible in any mode, to get down to a sound currency, *without producing some hardships and suffering in the process.*

As the creditor class suffered while the inflation was going on, it is inevitable that the debtor class must suffer some, during the process of returning to a sound currency; and hence the importance of modifying and lessening the evil, by extending it over a period of some years —and giving all classes an opportunity to calculate its consequences in advance, and of regulating their business and making new contracts in reference to them. The business and debtor classes must necessarily suffer some, upon contracts previously made, from a reduction of the currency; but what cannot be avoided must be endured. The advantages to the country will greatly overbalance all the evils it can produce. It would check speculations in gold and railroad stocks, real estate and mining shares; which would be a glorious result, and an unmixed blessing to the country.

Let us now look at the unequal distribution of banking capital and bank-notes. On the 30th of September, 1868, the circulation of the banks of the six New England

States was............................	$104,549,234
and of the State of New York...........	68,853,726
and of all the other States and Territories only............................	126,403,605
Total of the United States......	$299,806,565

New England, with less than ten per cent. of the population, has over 34 per cent. of the banking capital and circulation of the United States; New York, with less than 12½ per cent. of the population, has over 22 per cent. of the banking capital and circulation; while all the other States, with over 77 per cent. of the population, have less than 44 per cent. of the banking capital and circulation of the country. *Is that equal justice to the people of the South, and the West?* Massachusetts has over 80 millions banking capital, and her banks have over 57 millions of dollars of notes in circulation. With less than two-thirds as many inhabitants as Illinois, Massachusetts has more than six times as much banking capital and circulation. Massachusetts has obtained the lion's share, and seems inclined to hold on to it. She is always provident, and looks out for her own interest.

Having but little banking capital, the circulation of the Western and Southern States is mostly treasury notes; and hence the withdrawal of treasury notes immediately and very sensibly affects the people of those States—but does not affect New England—which has an immense circulation of bank-notes—equal to more than thirty dollars to each person. Equalize the banking capital as near as may be, and the circulation of bank-notes, and the West can then stand a gradual reduction of treasury notes, without very great inconvenience.

By equalizing the banking capital and currency, I do not mean to give each State the same amount in proportion to its population; but in proportion to its business wants. States like Massachusetts, Rhode Island, and New York, extensively engaged in manufactures as well as commerce, require from two to three times as much banking capital, and circulating medium, in proportion to their population, as States do whose people are mostly devoted to agriculture; but they do not require from six to ten or twelve times as much, as they have now.

To equalize the currency, it is not necessary to equalize the banking capital of the country,—nor to reduce the banking capital of Massachusetts, Rhode Island, and New York; but let Congress authorize the creation of banks with 100 millions or more capital in the Western and Southern States, properly distributed; —limit the aggregate circulation of all the banks to 300 millions, as they are now limited; distribute that circulation properly, according to the business wants of the several States—allowing the banks in some of the States to issue from 80 to 90 cents on the dollar of capital, and restricting those in other States to 30 or 40 cents on the dollar capital, according to the excess of their capital—and requiring those having an excess to reduce their circulation to the prescribed limit. As it is the business of a bank to loan capital and deposits, as well as to loan its own notes, the banks of commercial cities usually have much less circulation in proportion to their capital, than country banks have; and hence such limitation to the issues of the banks of New England and New York as I have suggested, could not be productive of any great evil or injustice.

Sec. 11.—*Our new system of banking.*

Our present system of banking is, in some of its features, entirely new—being unknown in any other country, and very different from all the systems heretofore known in this country. It is based upon the national credit much more fully and completely than the Bank of England is—legal-tender treasury notes being the reserve held by the banks, instead of coin, with which to redeem their notes—and over 340 millions of dollars of United States bonds being deposited as security for the redemption of their notes.

The system is new. It is, or was at first, only an experiment; but it has now been in operation more than six years, *and a more successful financial experiment was never tried* in the history of the world. As the legal tender notes with which the banks are required to redeem their issues, are receivable for taxes and all dues to the Government (except duties on imports), and are a legal tender for private debts, they have answered the purposes of money for all domestic uses; and the notes issued by the banks have been equally useful. During the dark and critical periods of the war, when it was doubtful if the Confederate government could be overturned and the Union restored, and whether the federal government could ever meet all its pecuniary liabilities—treasury notes, and with them the notes of our national banks, were all depreciated, by reason of the doubtful credit of the government; but they were depreciated still more by the excessive amount of treasury and bank-notes put into circulation. Since the great rebellion was put down, in April, 1865, the redundancy of the currency has been the only cause of its depreciation; but that is an evil which can be provided against, and is not inherent in our new banking system.

Though the currency has been depreciated, it has been depreciated alike in all parts of the United States; and during the last five years the exchanges and business of the country, and the distribution of its products, have been carried on with the aid of the national banks, with greater uniformity and facility, than ever before, in the history of our country. Treasury notes, bank-notes, and high duties upon imports, carried us safely through the most gigantic war ever known in the history of the world; and they did so without any financial revulsion. The same causes have stimulated industry and enterprise to such an extent, that our country (with the exception of the rebel States), has been as prosperous during the last five years, as during any period of five years since the organization of the federal government. *Extravagance and prodigality, excessive taxation and speculations in stocks and gold, have been the principal obstacles to both individual and national prosperity.* We have enjoyed as a people and a nation, the highest degree of prosperity, when compared with several periods in our history, of profound peace—when the industry, business, and property of the whole country, were terribly depressed. Those gloomy periods were from 1784 to 1790, from 1818 to 1824, from May, 1837, to 1843, and for two years, commencing in September, 1857. The reader should study the history of those periods, and inquire into the causes which produced so great, so general, and so prolonged embarrassment and depression in our country.

Our new banking system, with all its virtues, is based upon new light in relation to the powers of the federal government, and *upon new constructions of the Constitution put by Congress*, and not yet passed upon by the Supreme Court of the United States. The redemption of the issues of the banks is based upon legal-tender treasury notes. But whatever ground there may be for holding the issue of legal tender notes a violation of the Constitution—so far as they apply to debts contracted before the passage of the act authorizing them—there can be no injustice, and I think no good ground to question the power of Congress to apply them to contracts made subsequently. Without such power, the notes would have been of little value; they would have given the government very little aid in carrying on the war to restore the Union; and the war would have been a failure.

Again, in passing the banking act in February, 1863, the federal government exercised a power which had been exercised by the States for three-fourths of a century—some of the time concurrently, but for the last 27 years exclusively. The banking law is based upon the theory that the practice in England and in this country prior to 1787, made bank-notes, as well as coin, money—that the provisions of the Constitution giving Congress power to coin money and regulate the value thereof, and prohibiting the States from coining money, issuing bills of credit, or making anything but gold and silver coin a legal tender for debts, taken in connection with the power conferred on Congress to regulate commerce among the States, *included by implication, and conferred, power, to regulate and control the issue of bank-notes, as money, and the medium of commerce.*

There is great force in the reasoning which supports that theory; for if the States can charter banks, and authorize them to issue an unlimited amount of paper money, the constitutional provision inhibiting the States from emitting bills of credit is thereby practically evaded; and that provision inhibiting them from making anything but gold and silver coin a legal tender for debts, becomes almost a nullity.

If this new construction of the Constitution be sustained by the Supreme Court of the United States—as the welfare of the country requires it should be, then our new banking system, resting on the credit of the government, is based upon a good and durable foundation; but if the Supreme Court should overturn that construction, and declare the National Banking Act unconstitutional, and all the acts and contracts of the banks without authority of law and invalid, the most wide-spread embarrassment and ruin would occur, which ever afflicted our country. Such an unsound and mischievous decision, upon much less plausible grounds, was made by the Supreme Court of Michigan, many years since—declaring the general banking law of Michigan contrary to the constitution of the State, and all the acts and contracts of the banks organized under it, and the bonds and mortgages they had given as security, invalid and void. Our new banking system is not, and will not be free from danger, until the validity of the act shall have been passed upon by the Supreme Court of the United States.

If the validity of the banking law and the policy of the Government in relation to the currency be sustained, giving to Congress full power to regulate and control banks of issue, and paper money of all descriptions, then, with some amendments, a proper equalization of banking capital and issues, and a wise limitation of the aggregate amount of paper money, we shall have, not only the best banking system, but the cheapest and most convenient, and in some respects the best currency in the world. We should soon have a mixed currency, partly coin, but mostly paper; and when the paper becomes reduced to its proper amount, the difference in value between coin and bank-notes will fluctuate from nothing to only one or two per cent. Under our new system, our banks cannot be disturbed and driven into suspension or bankruptcy, by an adverse balance of trade, and large exports of specie.

Sec. 12.—*The test of depreciation, or non-depreciation.*

Gold has been sold for paper money for several years past, at a large premium—the amount of premiums varying from time to time—being affected, first, by the good or doubtful credit of the government, and secondly, by the amount of paper money in circulation. *The premium paid for gold measures the depreciation of the paper.* The sales of gold under our financial and banking systems, measure with precision the depreciation of our paper money; and they would continue to do so, if the quantity of paper money should be reduced to one-half its present amount.

Whenever the treasury and bank-notes in circulation shall have been so much reduced in amount, that the holders of coin voluntarily exchange it for bank-notes at par, or for a small premium of one per cent. or less, *that fact itself will furnish conclusive evidence that the paper money is not depreciated; and that it is not redundant, nor in excess.* But if specie payments be resumed, the compulsory payment by the banks, of gold for their notes, will furnish no test whatever, that the amount of circulation is not redundant and depreciated,—as was the case in 1836 and 1857, when the banks redeemed their notes in coin. Under the old banking system, with compulsory specie payments, we had *alternate expansions and contractions, as incidents of the system*—first expansions, until wild and visionary speculations, with large exports of specie, caused a panic; which soon resulted in excessive contraction, and wide-spread embarrassment and bankruptcy. Under the new system, with a wise limitation by law of the amount of bank issues, the currency can be kept steady and nearly uniform in amount, without expansion or sudden contractions, and the business and industry of the country would soon be in harmonious relations with it, and with each other.

If my reasoning be correct, we have found *a practical and certain test, by which it is easy to determine when paper money is in excess, and how much it is depreciated,* if any; and as Congress has assumed and exercises the entire control of the currency of the whole country, including paper money as well as coin, all that is necessary is to reduce the circulation gradually, from year to year, until the excess shall have been withdrawn, and the balance remaining in use shall have risen to par, or nearly par with coin; to note the amount retained in circulation in proportion to the population of the United States, and *the problem of the amount of circulation needed, will have been solved.* Congress can then regulate and limit the amount of paper money to be issued, from time to time, in accordance with the increase of our population and the wants of the country, with almost unerring certainty.

We should then have the cheapest and most convenient, and in some respects the best currency ever known in the world. The best for general use, and *for security against inflations and contractions—enormous extensions of the credit system and excessive speculations—panics, hoarding, and severe revulsions.* It is true, we should have two currencies—coin and paper money—coin for change and for foreign commerce, and bank-notes and some treasury notes for general use. But the difference between the value of the latter and the former would be so small, that it could not derange nor disturb either the industry or the business of the country.

SEC. 13.—*Deceptive as well as evil influences of a redundant paper currency.*

Paper money is deceptive and delusive in its influence upon business, and upon public opinion. Gold and silver being extensively used in the arts and for matters of ornament, have great intrinsic value in the estimation of civilized nations. They are, therefore, in universal demand for purposes of exchange and commerce, and are often concealed, hoarded, and kept for future use. Paper money having no intrinsic value, can be used only for commercial purposes, as a medium of exchange, in the country where it is issued. It cannot be sent abroad to pay foreign debts, and there is no inclination to hoard it. Every person having paper money is anxious to use it, to make it productive—either by loaning it on interest, or by buying stocks or personal or real property of some kind, from which he expects to get an income, or make a profit. An increase of money or currency increases the number of anxious buyers, without increasing the amount of property to be sold. By increasing the demand for many kinds of property, without increasing the supply, the tendency is to increase prices, and to make many suddenly rich by the increase of prices. The constant increase of prices for weeks and months in succession, and the prospect of a continued rise, makes many persons anxious to buy; and as this speculative movement goes on, all kinds of property and labor also are more or less raised in price, and continue to rise with the increase of the volume of currency, until a perfect fever of speculation is excited in many kinds of property, and a panic eventually ensues, which checks it. All such advances of prices and speculative movements render a larger amount of money necessary to carry on the business of the country; and as prices advance, the issue of more and more paper money is required to supply the demand. *The issue itself, by enhancing prices and stimulating speculation, instead of satisfying, tends to increase the demand for it, and to create a demand for still greater issues;* and thus the matter goes on, until a panic and a financial crisis occurs, and the people come to their senses. As more money is constantly demanded, and seems to be needed by business men and speculators, *the public are deceived by appearances*, and are incapable of understanding that there is an excess in circulation already. They do not understand the fact that *the demand itself is artificial, and is mostly created by the enhanced prices and the spirit of speculation caused by an excessive and redundant paper currency.* By inflating prices generally, including the prices of labor, and increasing the cost of production, a redundant currency tends to raise products so high as to invite large imports from abroad, and to lessen exports, by raising the prices of domestic products so much above those of other nations, that they cannot be exported with profit. It tends to neutralize the influence upon domestic industry of duties on foreign products—to supplant domestic by foreign manufactures, and to undermine and paralyze the manufacturing and mining industry of a country. *Such are the necessary tendencies, the deceptive influences, and the delusive effects, of an excessive paper currency.* The increase in the prices of property deceives great numbers of persons with the idea that they are getting rich, when they are, in fact, only marking up the supposed value of their property. Others deceive themselves by making money on paper, by uncertain credits. *The whole tendency of a redundant currency is to deceive and mislead, to create false conceptions of wealth*, to encourage a spirit of speculation, extravagance, and prodigality, and to discourage industry and attention to business. In any correct view which can be taken of the subject, it operates as an impediment to the progress of a nation.

If this reasoning be correct, how important it is to prevent any increase of paper money, either by the Government or by the banks.

SEC. 14.—*Free banking, with a circulation practically unlimited.*

Some of our politicians and newspapers are discussing the subject of free banking—of allowing the establishment, under general laws of Congress, of as many banks, with as much capital, as the people of each State and community may desire—with an aggregate amount of issues limited only by the demands of the people for currency. In its operation, such a system would furnish a currency practically unlimited in amount.

There is no necessity of limiting the amount of capital that may be employed in banking in any city, State, or community. As capital is loaned, and kept on hand in banks, for the purpose of being loaned, the government may very properly allow the amount of banking capital to be regulated by the business wants of each community—by the principles of demand and supply; but the amount of bills and notes to be issued in a State or country, to circulate as money, cannot be regulated by such means, and should be limited by law—to prevent excessive issues, and the evil effects of a redundant currency. There can be no good objection to the gradual increase of the banking capital of the United States to five, six, or eight hundred millions of dollars, as the owners of surplus capital may see fit to employ it in that mode, provided the amount of issues of bank-notes in each State be so limited by law, that the aggregate amount in the United States shall not be increased.

As avarice has no limit, and the speculative spirit and desire to get money to use, to make a profit by its use, is very general in our country, there is practically no limit to the demand for the gradual expansion and increase of the currency. The depreciation thereof and the increase of prices commence and go on *pari passu* with the increase of the volume of the currency. The increase itself, by its own natural operation and influence upon the prices of products, property, and labor, creates an additional demand for currency—so that the increased demand for, and use of currency, go hand in hand with the increased supply—whereby the public mind is deluded and misled.

Banking and currency form several instructive, and in some respects disastrous chapters in American history; not the least disastrous of which has been the history of free banking under State laws. The disasters of the past should not be forgotten, nor overlooked; but kept in mind as a warning to the future. If the circulation of national banks were ever so well secured, and limited in amount to seventy-five cents on the dollar of capital, the aggregate amount of circulation in the United States would be practically unlimited, if there were no limit to the establishment of new banks and to the addition of banking capital, with the enjoyment of equal privileges by all the banks to issue notes.

When Michigan was first admitted into the Union as a State, her active and speculative, but comparatively inexperienced population, and juvenile Governor, conceived the brilliant idea of teaching the world a new and free system of banking. The Legislature of the State passed a general banking law in March, 1837, and an amended act in November of the same year.

During the years 1837 and 1838, forty-nine banking associations were organized under the statutes, went into operation, contracted debts to the amount of over a million of dollars, and all but two or three failed during the year 1838; and all those which continued in business after January, A.D. 1839, failed soon afterwards. The

Legislature, in 1839, repealed the acts by which they were organized, and passed an act for winding them up in Chancery, and collecting up and distributing their assets by means of receivers. Prior to 1838, the Legislative Council of the Territory, and Legislature of the State, chartered sixteen banks, with two branches, which went into operation with a nominal capital of over seven millions of dollars; all of which, but one, finally failed, and swindled the public in the aggregate, probably twice as much as the banks organized under the General Banking Acts, known as "WILD CAT BANKS." The population of Michigan was then less than 180,000; almost exclusively agricultural and speculative; imported almost everything they used or consumed, including not only manufactures, but much of the provisions they lived on; exported nothing but a few furs and some few fish; had nothing to sell or dispose of but *wild lands and bank-notes, and had no legitimate* use for more than one bank. The State alone lost nearly half a million of dollars by one of the chartered banks in which the State funds were deposited. Receivers were likewise appointed for the greater part of the broken down chartered banks, but some of them were so utterly worthless, that no creditor ever deemed it worth while to incur the costs of proceedings to get receivers appointed for them. About three-quarters of those banks were chartered, and the General Banking Acts passed, when the cry and clamor throughout the Union was strong against *corporations* and the power of *associated wealth*, as dangerous to the liberties of the people; and numerous charters were granted, and the General Banking Acts passed, to give poverty, inexperience, and popular ambition, an opportunity to associate for banking purposes, to counterpoise the associations of wealth, and neutralize their dangerous effects.

The Supreme Court of the State finally declared the general banking laws unconstitutional and void, and all the notes issued, and contracts made by them, void also; and by a series of decisions nullified the obligations of the banks, and of the directors and stockholders thereof, and the securities given by them, and left their creditors without remedy. They were unsound decisions, based upon fallacies and false assumptions, and supported by sophistical reasoning. They show that the Courts can do almost anything in Michigan, as well as in the City of New York.

Such has been the experience—the sad experience of Michigan upon the subject of banking. The experiment of free banking has been tried in New York, Indiana, Illinois, and Wisconsin; and the system utterly failed in the three last named States; though being better secured and regulated by law, and the circumstances more favorable, the failures of the banks were not so sudden, nor were the disasters so great and ruinous in those States, as they were in Michigan. The ultimate success of the present national system of banking will probably depend more upon the limitation of the aggregate issues of the banks, than upon all other regulations and causes.

NOTICES

OF

"ESSAYS ON THE PROGRESS OF NATIONS,"

WRITTEN BY THE SAME AUTHOR,

AND PUBLISHED BY

CHARLES SCRIBNER & CO., NEW YORK.

NOTICES OF THE FIRST VOLUME OR SERIES.

From the Evangelical Observer.

"Many original views and reflections will be found in it. Its leading topics are indicated by the title, "*On the Progress of Nations.*" The object of the writer is to trace the influence of the great laws of nature on the condition, transactions, and welfare of individuals and nations, likewise of education and of government, both civil and ecclesiastical, and of agriculture, commerce, the mechanic arts, and other vocational pursuits."

From the New York Tribune.

"It is a most valuable contribution to the Literature of Political Economy, and will be duly appreciated, we doubt not, by numerous classes of inquirers into whose hands it may fall. If it could be perused by every voter throughout the United States, it would add much to the stock of knowledge, and produce a most salutary effect in enlightening the public mind on many subjects now imperfectly understood.

"It is a most truthful and instructive work, which should find a place in our village and school libraries, and be studied by every fireside.

"Mr. Seaman's work will be readily understood by any one, and no one can read it without acquiring broader and juster views of National Policy, and a wise Public Economy."

From the Commercial Advertiser, of Buffalo.

"It is in truth a work of great research, honest and convincing in its expressions of opinion, and admirably calculated, by its array of incontrovertible facts, to dispel the many erroneous and mischievous notions of mere theorizing political economists. We warmly commend it to public favor, as a book of great interest and utility."

From a Letter of Hon. Millard Fillmore.

"It brings within the reach of every man a vast store of useful information as to the progress of agriculture and the arts among mankind, which can be found nowhere else in so condensed and cheap a form. Your sound views of political economy are sustained by statistical details, which serve at once to illustrate the subject, and carry conviction to the mind."

From a Letter of Hon. Ross Wilkins, of Detroit.

"Every topic discussed is of public importance, and the sources from which you have derived your facts and data, accurate and authentic. I think I can safely say, you have rendered a great service to the country."

From a Letter of Rev. Geo. Duffield, D.D., late of Detroit.

"I account it a valuable publication, which cannot fail to be of great utility to the general reader, as well as to statesmen, editors, professional and public men; and hope that its extensive circulation among our legislators, and those who are and ought to be studious in political economy, will secure to it a measure of usefulness equal to its value."

From the New York Evangelist.

"The discussions of this volume pertain to some of the gravest and most important of human inquiries; and the conclusions of a candid and thoughtful mind are both interesting and valuable. There are positions taken which will not command universal assent; yet none can fail to derive instruction from his reasonings, and from the numerous facts and statistics by which his arguments are illustrated. The style is perspicuous, and the whole management of the argument candid, clear, and able."

From the American Review.

"We cheerfully express our opinion of the great value of Mr. Seaman's book, entitled "*Essays on the Progress of Nations.*" *It has high merits in a political and philosophical point of view. The author evidently views the Tariff and kindred subjects from a position higher than that from which they are ordinarily contemplated.* The reader will find, on the examination of this work, that these are not questions merely of temporary prices, or market fluctuations, but that they have a permanent bearing on the highest well-being of the nation. The author demonstrates that the encouragement of a national industry, in its various branches, is far more than a mere nominal matter of cheap buying (although even here its advantages are in the end more clearly shown), but that it is more intimately connected with the moral welfare and highest prosperity of a country."

From the Christian Examiner and Religious Miscellany.

"Mr. Seaman has more than fulfilled the promise of his title-page. Besides twelve essays upon the topics which he professes to treat, he has given us five preliminary chapters that are chiefly devoted to the moral bearings of his subject. In these chapters he discusses the laws of nature, with their operations upon the condition of individuals and of nations; then, industry and exercise; then, the course of civilization, from the life of the herdsman to that of the modern manufacturer; and finally, the influence of governments, civil and ecclesiastical, upon the operations of industry. In these preliminary essays a healthy moral sentiment is manifested."

From a Letter of the Hon. Walter Forward, late of Pittsburg, Pa.

"The truth is, it is a most valuable acquisition to the country.

"The '*Progress of Nations*' is a work for farmers and mechanics to read. I trust they will read it, and acquaint themselves more familiarly with the true grounds of our American Policy."

NOTICES OF THE SECOND SERIES.

From the New York World.

"ESSAYS ON THE PROGRESS OF NATIONS IN CIVILIZATION, PRODUCTIVE INDUSTRY, WEALTH, AND POPULATION. Illustrated by Statistics of Mining, Agriculture, Manufactures, Commerce, Banking, Internal Improvements, Emigration, and Population.

"The first volume of these essays was issued some years since, and in this, the second, we have chapters on the elements and agents of the progress of nations; on impediments thereto; on law, organization, education, and religion; on the difference in races of men; on Mohammedan countries; Mongolian countries; on Asia, Australia, Africa, etc.; on Africa and Africans; on Oceanica; the West Indies; Catholic America; the United States; British North America; and Europe. Chapter twenty-five, on the differences in the races of men, and chapter thirty-three, on the United States, are of special interest, and exhibit marks of exceeding industry and care.

"The entire volume is replete with useful information. The author's views on the influence of climate, on intellect and character, as set forth in pages 478–481, are of considerable moment, as also his statements in connection with a subject of such present importance as paper money."

From the New York Observer.

"These are no mere discursive discussions of theories, but a copious collection of facts and statistics, illustrating valuable thoughts and pregnant suggestions. So well arranged and concisely presented is the mass of material, that the volume will be always valued as a book of reference. * * * The influence of Christianity and its institutions is recognized as among the main elements of true progress."

From the New York Times.

"Mr. Seaman reviews the progress of human affairs from the earliest ages, and sums up its results, pointing out at the same time those natural adaptations and aids, which necessarily led to the civilization we have inherited or accomplished. His essays, comprehending all the motions and means of artificial society, are very suggestive, presenting those general views and conclusions which are received by our chief social writers and political economists, but which must be always, more or less, the subjects of controversy. The chief merits, however, of this large and well printed octavo, are in the historic summaries of the various nations, and their statistics of population, natural products, and social progress. * * * All Mr. Seaman's commentaries on the progress or condition of the various nations, will be found interesting; and his comparison of the Hindoos with our own especial people, the Chinese, is rather attractive just now."

From the North American Review.

"The title of this work accurately describes it, and understates, rather than overstates, its extraordinary fulness of detail and information. We must admire the rare patience and industry which were employed in gathering, sorting, and adjusting this mass of facts about nations, ancient and modern, large and small, civilized and savage, Christian and heathen, Caucasian and Mongolian, in continents and islands, in every clime, from the tropics to the poles.

"Mr. Seaman has, nevertheless, a higher end than merely to catalogue facts. While he is no theorist, *he has the spirit of a philosopher, and means to show the causes of the national rise and decline, which he chronicles in so many ways.* He holds tenaciously to certain general ideas, and is no believer in the doctrine that history is only a succession of events, and is summed up in mere 'annals.' In some particulars he agrees with Dr. Draper and Mr. Buckle, especially in *the influence of climate*, which is with him the most important factor in the product of national prosperity and national character. No civilization of any high order shall come in the torrid or the frigid zone.

"Ethnological questions of the highest importance are frequently started. Where did the tribes of Oceanica originate? How came the Indians in North America? Mr. Seaman does not commit himself to the theories of Darwin and similar thinkers, yet he is not a blind believer in Biblical cosmology.

"On the question of 'Reconstruction' Mr. Seaman's views are in harmony with those of the moderate party. He approves substantially of the thirteenth and fourteenth amendments to the Constitution. He does not think that the South ought to have votes for the negroes whom they disfranchise; yet, as he believes that education and intelligence should be conditions of citizenship (or rather of the elective franchise), he would not give votes to ignorant negroes.

"We should be glad to notice more of Mr. Seaman's mature opinions on a variety of topics, but must refer our readers to his well-filled volume."

From the Philadelphia Press.

"This is a most important work, combining political economy with history, geography, and statistics—the latter being brought down to the present year. It is philosophical, too, without allowing the subject to sink into the obscurity of metaphysics. Whoever wants to learn the present condition of any country, can do it from this book."

From the Presbyterian, of Philadelphia.

"The book is certainly a great repository of facts, of importance to every student of the history of nations. We do not know of any volume in which so much that is of interest to every man is condensed, as this one of Mr. Seaman's."

From the Chicago Tribune.

"It is a hand-book of facts and suggestions, which every student of human affairs should have. *The questions of social and political philosophy, which come up at every step, Mr. S. discusses briefly and judiciously*, leaving them as much as possible to the decision of statistics. He has attempted to show the influence of climate and circumstances upon the character and destinies of peoples, and has handled this part of his subject with judgment and learning. * * * *The work is indispensable to scholars, writers, teachers, and whoever wishes to study to any purpose the tendencies and prospects of the human race.*"

From the Chicago Journal.

"It is, in its way, a complete cyclopædia. The author has evidently bestowed immense labor upon it, and possessed rare fitness for the task he has accomplished with so much thoroughness. The sections that we have read are peculiarly satisfactory."

From the Age, of Philadelphia.

"The author exhibits constantly the spirit of an earnest seeker after truth. * * * He seeks out the most reliable sources of information; and with a full knowledge of the critical condition of our country, while avoiding extreme theories not tested by experience, he is careful to eschew anything partaking of a partisan spirit, or tending to promote mere partisan ends. Lessons are taught in these pages to which we, as a nation, will do well to take heed, lest, through our neglect, we are forced to learn them in the school of bitter experience."

www.ingramcontent.com/pod-product-compliance
Lightning Source LLC
LaVergne TN
LVHW010211110826
845151LV00004B/1051

* 9 7 8 1 4 2 5 5 2 8 6 6 9 *